SPIRITUALITY AND WELL-BEING

By the same author

— Social Behaviour of Children
— Violence and Religion Cross Cultural Opinions and Consequences
— Contemporary Social Science Research

About the Author

Ralph Tanner has a B.Sc. and Diploma in Social Anthropology from Oxford University and a D. Phil in Law from Stokholm University. He has done fieldwork in Thailand, the Philippines, Guyana, Zambia, Zimbabwe, Tanzania, Uganda and Kenya as well as in Britain and Eire. He was Chairman of the East African Institute of Social Research and Lecturer in Comparative Religion in the University of London. He has published books on Murder in Uganda. Witchcraft killings and religions and successful change and a cross cultural study of the Roman Catholic Mass. He has co-authored books on the social ecology of religion and the environment. He has written numerous articles on the social aspects of religious change, translation and language use in religion, as well as on behavioural theories in the *Journal of Modern African Studies,* Africa, *Journal of the Social Sciences, Nordic Journal of African Studies, Antropos, Studia Missionalia* and others. He is currently working on a study of Probability and Chance.

SPIRITUALITY AND WELL-BEING

R.E.S. Tanner

CONCEPT PUBLISHING COMPANY, NEW DELHI-110059

ISBN-13: 978-81-8069-611-4 **ISBN-10: 81-8069-611-1**

First Published 2009

Published and Printed by

Concept Since 1974

Concept Publishing Company
Regd. Office:
A/15-16, Commercial Block, Mohan Garden
New Delhi-110059 (India)
Phones : 25351460, 25351794, *Fax* : 091-11-25357109
Email : publishing@conceptpub.com,
website: www.conceptpub.com

Editorial Office:
H-13, Bali Nagar, New Delhi-110 015, India.

Cataloging in Publication Data--*Courtesy:* D.K. Agencies (P) Ltd. <docinfo@dkagencies.com>

Tanner, R. E. S. (Ralph E. S.), 1921-
Spirituality and well being / R.E.S. Tanner.
p. cm.
Includes bibliographical references (p.).
Includes index.
ISBN 13: 9788180696114 ISBN 10: 8180696111

1. Well-being--Religious aspects. 2. Health--Religious aspects. 3. Spiritual life--Cross-cultural studies. I. Title.

DDC 204.4 22

Dedication

Father J. Mahoney, S.J.

Preface

It has been a feature of the social sciences alomost from its foundation, that it has rarely given public religion and private spirituality any comprehensive place in its studies of human behaviour. There are always been the factor that most researchers have had a secular framework of thought. This resulted in these aspects of human behaviour receiving little attention which might have related to any general sense of well-being and in a general sense paralleling other abstract matters of importance in art, music and literature.

The pervasive feeling in many social science areas of research that religion and spirituality were intellectual delusions bound to decline with education and rationality in public affairs may apply to some degree in Western developments in relation to public religion rather than to private spirituality.

Globally it would seem that not only in society but also politics and economics religion has become increasingly important by whatever approaches are used in assessments. The social sciences have either sidelined this importance particularly in psychology but have tended to concentrate on deviant and destructive forms of religious and spiritual behaviour, perhaps because these forms may be easier to research and to get academic and agency support.

It would seem that research about the persistent connection between these ideas and practices and well-being however defined is a social science necessity. The personal feelings of well-being correlating to the holding of abstract ideas as much as social and addictive practices in beginning to be widely recognised in the West as much as it has always recognised in the East.

This author's considerable research experience has repeatedly shown that public religious activity claims but that there is in all contemporary societies as much in Japan, China and India as in the United States and Russia a pervasive almost commonplace practice of private self-created and maintained forms of spirituality contributing to well-being.

This study aims to show that at all levels of cross-cultural thinking and practice private spirituality as distinct from public religious behaviour contributes to personal well-being either as a parallel system to orthodox faiths or as personally created systems continue to make an important contribution to well-being.

Acknowledgements

Working on a subject which appears to have few connections with current social science research and publications outside the western world particularly, it is necessary to read widely beyond conventional boundaries in the hope of finding related information and ideas.

The understandings leading to this study depended on the provision of books and photocopies by the Librarian of Trinity College, the University of Oxford, the Librarian of the Institute of Social Anthropology, The University of Oxford. More particularly the Librarians of the Hampshire County Libraries and the British Library, London who provided a seemingly endless stream of books and photocopies. I am most grateful for such help over the years without whose help this and other works could not have been produced.

Contents

1 Introduction

This is a study of three interrelated ill-defined ideas, spirituality, well-being and health about which there is little information overarching societies and cultures. What are the basic problems in trying to find correlations between these three important themes in contemporary societies. All three are linked to personal self-assessments of which only health may have some pragmatically accessible bases. Since there are always some assumptions of normality in all societies, attempts at assessment tend to concentrate on what is culturally defined as abnormal.

It is not only that much of the data is produced in English but the relationship of spirituality, well-being and health has usually been studied both in the context of Western societies and by Western or Westernised researchers, but in ways that contrast its individuality to more organised religious ideas and practices.

In this Western context it seems likely that those within the orbit of religion will also have systematic and unsystematic ideas and practices in forms running parallel to their more official religious commitments. These forms of individual and private spirituality will be contrasted to and often in opposition to their avowed publicly practised religion. There will also be these other forms of spirituality carried out within the recesses of the individual mind. So it may be that in Western societies there are many spirituality practices which are independent of known organised religions be they cults, sects or large institutionalised faiths. It may have the form of a pyramid in which religions form the apex and spirituality in its individualities form the broad bases of faith and practice.

In the East, Africa and Latin America it seems that religious practices are numerically far more numerous than in Western societies and that in the absence of creeds, definitions and institutional control, individuality and its spiritualities as conceived of by Western analysts, are much more a part of known religions. It is difficult to divide spirituality from religion in ways that can be attempted with Western practices.

So we start any enquiry into spirituality and well-being with a primary division in both Western thinking and known practices between forms of spirituality which are certainly if not predominantly part of religion and which can to some extent be examined separately. In addition there are quantities of practices classifiable as spirituality which have no relationship to known religions which have been called 'Sheilaisms' because of their exclusive individualities (Bellah *et al.*,1985), named after an American woman who stated that she was religious but in her own personal way.

There has been much published research in the Western world on the social and psychological aspects of spirituality and religion. Much of this careful work has concentrated on the abnormal rather than the normal with the implication that much of this behaviour should be seen as aberrations rather than part of a necessary need for humanity.

The situation for the Eastern faiths for which there are massive amounts of historical supportive literature, is rather the reverse with much theological and philosophical research but in comparison to the West, fewer studies of less elitist understandings and practices. This is in part due to a general shortage of fundings and the fact that their political leaders have a secular approach to the use of public money. However, it may also be due to the fact that spirituality and religion are closer together in Eastern faiths because there has been little centralising institutionalism of these faiths and no accompanying dominance of creedal definitions. If that is the case then individual Chinese, Indians and Japanese since they are theologically unsupervised, may have their forms of spirituality within their undefined religions and find there the fulfilment of both individual and communal needs.

The distinctions between Eastern and Western forms of

spirituality and religion is shown in their respective religious art in which for example any Hindu picture of their Gods and Goddesses is so overloaded with symbols and vibrant contrasting colours that individuals can draw from them whatever they consciously or unconsciously want. A typical picture of Vishnu makes no attempt to relate the God to human realities. His skin is dull mauve and he has four arms each holding a different symbol and he is lying in the sea on the coils of a multi-headed crowned cobra, and a green string coming from his navel leading to a lotus floating in the air on which another four-armed figure is sitting. Most noticeably there is no writing in the picture. A large religious poster purchased in Shanghai depicts nineteen distinct Gods, Goddesses or Bodhisattvas supported by masses of symbols and again without any explanatory writing.

In contrast modern Christian popular art in Western societies is pallid and to a large extent non-existent, while in Judaism and Islam religious art is confined to beautiful calligraphy, a delight to the balanced eye but probably unreadable by those who possess these printings. If we are looking for precise depictions of popular Eastern conceptions of religion and its spirituality, it would be impossible to find them in the multiple combinations of symbols in their popular religious art from which individuals draw their personally satisfying interpretations.

In attempting to analyse spirituality and well-being there is another cruder distinction between Eastern and Western understandings. The extent to which non-Western popular understandings are based on very much larger populations than Western ones. More attention should be paid as far as the data permits to the spiritualities and conceptions of well-being of Africans, Asians and Latin Americans in their billions.

The aim of this study is to distinguish between the Western religions of the book—Christianity, Islam and Judaism—with their linear conceptions of divine authority and carefully prepared definitions with the Eastern religions with their diffuse origins, understandings and their disinterest in definitions.

Then to attempt to assess these fundamental differences in

relation to health which in the context of bio-medicine will be the work of outsiders according to the standards of their training and understandings of evidence which would be acceptable to their professional colleagues. These may will be clear enough in relation to the primary reasons for such conclusions. But before this stage is reached and any possible correlations established, there are the lengthy processes by which the spiritual ideas and practices of individuals as well as their concepts of well-being are filtered through their own unconscious psychological make-up and the more conscious continuing processes of socialisation through which they are kept in touch with their own situations. Traditional ideas are holistic while bio-medicine is divisive.

We take spirituality to be the highly complex relation-ship with a particular religious entity elaborated in classical theological texts and related to particular schools of belief and practice, but to all forms of relationship to the non-pragmatic world. All activities which are related to the 'other world' at whatever level of intellectual and social elaboration. Consequently this is very much a bottom-up approach rather than one which is top-down and elitist.

This then is a study in generalities not in order to attract the attention of a more general reader but because the areas of religious practices relating to spirituality, health and well-being cannot be forced into categories restricted by definitions. Too much of human behaviour can only be categorized by its extremes. The far larger grey area in-between fluctuates in size and significance as those involved come under varying social pressures and varying personal priorities. There is also a basic tendency for the social sciences to attempt to quantify humans behaviour without accepting the transitory and individual nature of all human behaviour. This makes statistics an inadequate approach for the study of these three ill-defined but commonplace themes.

A Restricted Scenario

Outside theological and philosophical concerns there is not much interest in what effects religious and spiritual ideas and practices have on society except when something goes wrong and its extremism attracts attention as with Islamic suicide bombers. Parallel to this there has been increasing interest in their connection with improving health and what religion and spirituality may be able to do to improve the lives of sufferers from ill-health and misfortune.

So we have plenty of data on religious behaviour which disturbs the normalities of social life such as the mass suicides in Jonestown, Guyana, the body piercing in the worship of the Hindu deity Murugan in Malaysia, the Holy Spirit Mobile Force in Uganda kidnapping children and their rituals providing protection against bullets and Muslim suicide bombers who believe that in so doing they gain immediate entrance into Paradise.

In the matter of religion and health there is adequate data on the Jehovah's Witnesses', refusal to accept blood transfusions indeed far more information than the frequency of such occasions would justify except as a medical curiosity. In other matters data are widely spaced and concentrated and largely confined to the Western world with the majority of references relating to psychology. The bibliography provided by the United States Library of Medicine has eleven thousand references connecting health and religion, 269 connecting spirituality and well-being, 1532 connecting it with health and 653 with medicine. No doubt there are many more which can be found in combinations of these words. This coverage is not in proportion to populations and even more their coverage is heavily related to the major hospitals and in experimental work with university students research is often related to convenience.

There is a growing quantity of scientific and social science studies connecting religion rather than spiritual practices in relation to the reduction of distress. In such work there is on the one hand a significant amount of hard data from the scientific recording of physical states. The other side of the equation shows that religion and spiritual activities are inevitably outside scientific assessment and the possibilities of definitions. It does indeed often appear somewhat pointless to attempt the evaluation of religious activities according to scientific standards when the transcendent whether in poetry, pilgrimage or prayer is outside the rational possibilities of such attempted pragmatics.

So in contemporary terms there are several thousand studies carried out within Western societies in which religion is correlated to some aspects of health as well as a growing number of studies from Eastern cultures. Of the positive connections between health and so-called tribal or traditional religions very little is known. What is practised is not seen as sufficiently stabilised to justify the attention of researchers except in the more general sense of that behaviour being assumed to contribute to ill-health. The white coats of physicians do not associate happily with the varied and potentially septic costumes of traditional practitioners.

While religion has an institutional flavour to its activities and thus is seen as justifying some scientific attention, spirituality could be described as a scientific illusion and only having personal relevance and understanding; Its practices are so varied and individual as to make comparisons difficult. Well-being is even more of a problem because to define it in terms of the absence of negative factors would probably miss the whole point of such feelings. So when it comes to relating spirituality with well-being which may or may not have any correlations much less connections with health. The amount of data is severely limited and again largely confined to the Western world with its more ostentatious and pluralistic individualism. Furthermore we have to come to accept the fact that neither spirituality nor well-being have any stability in terms of social science objectives.

The Predominance of Bio-medical Data

The social sciences in trying to understand and explain human behaviour about which they have achieved comparatively little as contributions to the more efficient administration and betterment of mankind, seem to have found themselves largely stuck with attempts to quantify aspects of this infinite variety. Such a conclusion is based on the fact that by the time that research has been published, the social and demographic environment on which it was based as moved on into history. What has been researched with such great care has always been washed away by the tide of passing time. However it would seem obvious that other than qualitative work which provide informed opinions rather than proof about whatever has been observed, their only source of reliable data which might connect spirituality and well-being will be what is available from bio-medical sources.

It is likely that there are few if any aspects of human behaviour about which there are not some appropriately connected bio-medical data in which the conclusions are scientifically acceptable for a generation of scientists. The American computerised medical bibliography PubMed on being asked for references connecting the words 'spirituality', 'well-being' and 'health' produced over twelve thousand references published in the last twenty years in English. Even allowing for some duplication and a limited number of translated works from other languages, this is a stupefying total which would be far exceeded if it included works in other major Western languages let alone those published in Asian ones.

It is logical therefore to start any enquiry into spirituality and well-being which may have but not necessarily will have any exclusive connection with health with the bio-medical rather than psychological and social data available (Reynolds and Tanner, 1995), as we can start there with some assumptions of hardness. At the same time it is prudent to remember that a substantial amount of this data in medical journals is not scientifically validatable. It quantifies and pairs hard laboratory information with the results from questionnaires, self-reporting and interviews in which there are numerous unquantifiable variables paralleling the methodological shortcomings of the social sciences in their attempts to quantify behaviour.

An overlap certainly between hard data which can be confirmed by other scientists using the same material and investigative techniques and variable information. This may be correct but for which there are no ways that other scientists can reach the same conclusions when the information is based on so many personal variables and the passage of time. So we often find bio-medical research mixing hard data with information which cannot have the same substance. This is not to state categorically that what is concluded is necessarily wrong but that it is substantially weaker than the other half which has been produced in verifiable statistical form. It is a false assumption perhaps made worse by the decimal point and elaborate statistical verifications using the same set of unverifiable facts to prove its own reliability. Whether it is classifiable as such or not, social science information is almost invariably qualitative despite the fact that much of the data is produced in quantifiable form as if it had some identifiable on-going permanency. So this study of spirituality and well-being must start with the vast amount of bio-medical data which is available.

The Nature of Spirituality

Spirituality is a broader term than religion (Sulmasy, 1999) and has been defined as the name given to an individual's or group's relationship with the transcendent and their search for its meaning. While people mostly express their spirituality in religious practices, with definitions which are often tautological, most consciously or unconsciously would express their spirituality in much wider terms.Their relationship with nature, their expression of sexual affection, their love of music and art, even their philosophical beliefs and of course their family (Astrow *et al.*, 2001). This seems to be a definition that covers any liking which is not based on pragmatics and would cover commitment to a political ideology, the subjective experience of gambling, the liking for Bollywood stars and indeed any pleasurable activity from which there are no predominantly material gains. This is too wide an approach however valid it may be, to be tied to the narrower specifics of well-being and health.

So we take it to be any attempted or subjectively successful relationship with any transcendent entity. A god, goddesses, nature spirits, saints, bodhisattvas, ancestors and the ghosts of the unborn.

Charismatic persons and those who become possessed by spiritual entities and who gain spirituality from looking at the sacred. We will attempt to see to what extent these forms of spirituality contribute or hinder well-being and to their correlations with health.

The Nature of Health

Health or its absence is defined by medical examination or clinical tests and it seems unlikely that individuals can be defined as healthy because they have not been defined as ill. There are many social factors to consider in assessing well-being and health; these are both not only variable but ill-defined. Health statistics may be reliable enough for some comparisons and evaluations to be made but this is tenuous. The spread of available medicine is uneven in even the most politically and economically developed states. There are whole social areas in which ill-health is only known in relation to certain mass diseases. Very little is known of degenerative ones where there are neither the staff nor the money to cope with such inevitabilities. Most elderly persons have more than one degenerative disease but it would seem that most have a sense of well-being.

So the existence of a disease or indeed its absence is established by the rare high quality health services but elsewhere much data are provided by the special interests of individual doctors who are looking for particular ailments. For large populations in many developing countries such bio-medical services are thin on the ground and are limited in their effects by the costs of medicines and poorly paid and corrupt personnel. There is always the problem of correct diagnoses and the position is complicated by the fact that individuals may be suffering from multiple health handicaps. Whether the diagnoses are correct can only be satisfied by post-mortem examinations and laboratory confirmations. This is statistically only more or less comprehensively available in some Western societies and patchily elsewhere.

We are mesmerised by the statistics which are available and pass over the fact that the majority of deaths in underdeveloped and developing countries are not medically known and are attributed in quite specific terms to karmic inevitability, malevolent ancestors and ghosts, the witchcraft of neighbours and evil spirits. For the understandings of those involved, this is more useful knowledge than a medical diagnoses which explains nothing and cannot be related to currently available quasi-traditional processes. Scientific diagnosis's have limited social uses and scientifically understandable deaths have still to be explained in social and religious terms.

Even the most reliable of health statistics remain static facts and tell us little about their epidemiology and how these might be related to socio-religious factors and nothing at all as to how their incidence on an individual basis might relate to well-being. An elderly person with five degenerative conditions for which she is taking medicines might well consider herself well enough to do all that she wants to do.

At least with health statistics there are some reasonably satisfactory definitions of what is happening to individuals and even more reliable when there are outbreaks or epidemics of special diseases such as Legionnaires disease, Ebola fever and of course AIDS, all of which receive substantial scientific attention. Health information in the form of statistics are relatively stable facts which apart from evaluative difficulties relate to the relatively small area in which spirituality, religion and well-being can be correlated with some significance. This connection is never hard to find with the devout behaving or not behaving in ways dictated by their religions whether over diet, alcohol, smoking as with the Seventh day Adventists or marrying close relatives such as the Amish and Kenyan Swahili. There are millions who go to Mecca on the Hajj or the even larger numbers to go to the Hindu *Kumbh Mela* on the Ganges. Recently Dr. Abdul Katme head of the Islamic Medical Association in Britain has stated (*Sunday Times*, 28 January 2007) that Muslims should not be vaccinated against measles, mumps, polio, diphtheria and rubella as the vaccines contained ingredients unlawful for Muslims to take; he argued that leading their lives according to the requirements of Islam would be enough to ward off illnesses and diseases. So much of the data connecting religious practices with ill-health is retroactive and the conclusion is worked out backwards; of course the pilgrims who rush into the Ganges on the occasion of the *Kumbh Mela* get infected by the water. The water there and in their villages or during the journey there is undeniably secular and is just as likely to infect them.

Since spirituality must affect both mental and physical processes, we have to consider in what ways this may aid or hinder human survival as biological units contributing to the survival of the species. This would be a very long-term and detached approach which would be unlikely to be a factor in almost all people's thinking except for those who think in terms of family survival.

Then there are negative issues to consider when behaviour based on spirituality leads to economic distress and social ignominy. So data relating health to well-being has to be seen in the contexts of social relationships which might be advantageous, neutral or hostile. It is personal in how it is viewed by those involved and not just according to the understandings of outsider researchers. A senior Christian clergyman who had been decorated for bravery in a recent war on being asked why he had behaved in this way replied 'it seemed to be the right thing to do at the time', but one can presuppose that retrospectively he put his behaviour into a more elaborate moral context.

It is in these contexts that manifest and latent functions are important and who is evaluating? If an enduring item of spirituality does not fulfil manifest functions as might be the case with a practice that helps the younger members but not the older ones of a society, then it may still be fulfilling latent ones. If such a practice is dysfunctional for some parts of a society, its persistence implies that it must have positive functions for meeting the needs of other parts (Merton, 1957).

It does seem unlikely that any practices of spirituality can ever have across the board positive or indeed negative influences on a population. Hinduism provides spiritual foundations for male dominance and the consequences may be against the health interests of women as opposed to men. They eat last and when daughters are ill medical attention is delayed in comparison to sons. Just as in Muslim societies where male dominance has been offset by women developing their own spirituality practices in shrines and religious teaching centres in Iran. Zar possession cults in the Sudan are beyond the control of men despite the fact that such behaviour is against the tents of Islamic orthodoxy.

The Nature of Well-being

Well-being has to be seen as an entirely personal feeling which the individual may have at one moment and not at the next. It is a fluctuating state and while it may have group aspects from time-to-time in the euphoria following a political or military victory or cessation of violence, it is a very individual feeling and largely an ephemeral one which comes and goes with environmental, physiological and psychological change. A dialectical conscious and unconscious process between the individual and their surroundings. The definition of well-being in English is said to be 'the state of being or doing well in life, a happy, healthy or prosperous condition'. This involves an understanding of 'good', an abstract noun which must include all kinds and degrees in whatever commands itself to feeling, taste, reason and translatable in a corresponding variety of ways.

In the East African Swahili language well-being is defined as 'hali njema', the state, condition or circumstances which are good, 'usitawi', a flourishing condition, healthy development, full activity, success, 'afya', good health, sound condition and 'raha' , rest, repose, peace, bliss and comfort. So if the research project involved the use of Swahili, the natal language of East African coastal peoples combining Bantu and Arabic roots and the national language of Tanzania, the choice of words used in the question would dictate the answers. Those questioned would not ask what the words used meant but would reply according to the key words; 'afya' health and 'raha' bliss do not mean the same thing.

If we should concentrate on the word for health then there is the difficulty over what sort of health we are referring to. Ability or incapacity to do something physically or mentally and this would depend on how the individual assesses their own role. The Yao chief Mataka in Tanzania who had been half paralysed by poliomyelitis ruled his chiefdom effectively by force of character so many in similar conditions might have come to terms with their incapacities and feel themselves to be in states of well-being. A Sukuma diviner possessed by an ancestor spirit who might will be defined by a Western trained psychologist as schizophrenic, would be seen by his clients and assess himself as in a state of prestigious well-being.

Well-being has been extensively researched by Western social scientists and there must be several hundred studies on this topic published in the last three decades which all suffer from methodological shortcomings. Perhaps like all social science works these studies have been too narrow in scope or too wide to produce anything definite because they have been studies of particular universes which limit their applicability except for the satisfactions which they give to the researchers themselves. Most of these studies have been of Western samples so we know very little about the well-being of individuals in societies which are not well provided with efficient welfare schemes. Much depends upon the effectiveness of the care provided by extended families and the widespread use of complementary and alternative medicine to cope with physical and psychological misfortunes.

Of course well-being can be correlated to pragmatic effects such as the immediate effects of sudden unemployment, accidents or illnesses as well as the longer term adjustment to these same factors. Social scientists would prefer that their assessments of well-being should have some quantifiable factors which might allow for their tabulation in support of their conclusions. Income is often introduced into such studies but its relationship to well-being seems to relate more to comparisons within a community rather than to its individual meanings. We shall see that these quantifiable approaches are largely unreliable and fail in their scientific aspirations.

The first difficulty is that well-being itself cannot be defined and that it depends on how an individual may feel at the time that they are asked or complete a questionnaire. A commuter in Mumbai getting home easily or having to stand in the train for hours may override his or her happiness in their homes and children or that it is a lovely day. The number of factors which might affect well-being are innumerable and beyond quantification except by processes of deliberately limiting those that will be considered. For example one of the drawbacks to the question 'how are you' is usually asked when someone is known to have something wrong with them or alternatively is part of the general process of greeting which has no more than ritual significance.

Research in which a stranger asks questions about their well-being has no parallel in ordinary social life apart from semantic and translation difficulties. It might indeed be an innovation in many societies when a person who has been defined by their relatives or feel themselves to be in trouble goes to a stranger for treatment. So the problem of well-being is that it is not a commonplace consideration for most people; they assume or are assumed to be well because they are not socially incapacitated.

If we take Maslow's hierarchy of needs, it might be that well-being is classified in different ways at different times. Photographs of British naval officers on warships during the battle for Crete in World War Two has them all smiling and as the author remarks perhaps they are smiling just because they are still alive. So any assessment of well-being is made more difficult by its periodic and personal nature. Individuals might well fluctuate in and out of a state of accepted well-being because of situations which will always be to a very large extent beyond their control.

Winston Churchill's remark that 'a day was a long time in

politics' so we can assume that in a day of the ordinary person in Banaras, Beijing or Bali whether industrialist, shift worker or farmer will fluctuate in and out of a variety of states of mind. The office workers in Mumbai Monday is not likely to be associated with any sense of well-being which might come into their feelings about mid-day on Friday. The Sukuma farmer in Tanzania knows that rain will always be irregular so that he will feel elated after a shower on his fields, miserable when there is a thunderstorm near to harvesting his crops, and in despair when wild pigs dig up his family's famine reserve of cassava. Researchers do not easily cover the periodicity of well-being when they rarely know much about the private lives of those who are being questioned except for the few long-term informants and in most cases will know just their bare demographic details. Since a question about well-being in the sense of being asked a very personal question requiring a thoughtful and considered reply, is not something that is common in anyone's life. How can it be answered with any accuracy when it cannot be closely defined in the first place.

So we must conclude that whether individuals consider themselves to be in a state of well-being is very much a day-to-day assessment in which what the researcher's question gets as an answer is likely to be a matter of coincidence with what they are trying to find out. Any wider understandings beyond these coincidences would probably depend on what the researchers may already known about these people individually rather as just one person answering out of a required sample.

Whatever aspects of well-being are approached we are faced with an enormous number of variables acting on the individual simultaneously. This is the problem which Parallel Distributive Processing methods endeavour to solve; this suggests that the human mind works much quicker than a computer and though thinking might be analytically linear, to all intents and purposes decisions are instantaneous. It would seem that with so many variables any attempts to quantify what constitutes well-being is doomed to be no more than personal attempts to advance understandings which may never in this way go beyond its methodological failings. This should not be interpreted as a criticism of the social sciences but drawing attention to its limitations when there are no effective foundations on which to build statistically supported verifiable conclusions.

What are some of the factors which would have to be involved in any assessments of quantifying well-being. Physiological factors which have been inherited or acquired, physiological changes from cyclical or circadian rhythms, inherited or acquired mental abilities in the ability to cope, psychological make-up in its individualisms and group aspects, cultural understandings of what life should be, regularity or irregularity of daily experiences and the availability of material and spiritual resources to offset misfortune. It does seem that to attempt to assess well-being according to the requirements of science is to tie much effort into questionable results.

How then are we to approach the possibility of correlations between the practices of spirituality and any sustained or indeed temporary experiences of well-being. Perhaps there is a graded approach such as the cultural expectations which we have; it is God's will when we should die or it is in our *karma*. Then there is what we say we do when we are in difficulties or what we do to insure well-being and finally there is what we actually do according to the observations of social scientists. So first we must look at the seeming failure of social science to quantify much that relates to spirituality and well-being and to seek out the methodological alternatives.

The Field of Enquiry into Spirituality and Health

The scientific enquiry into the realities of any such connections between spirituality, health and well-being is not whether such connections exist since quite obviously the human mind consciously or unconsciously will make such correlations. Since mind and body are connected and one will affect the other, research is more concerned with the possibility making water-tight connections. Much data are dominated by Western small scale studies based on western paradigms which are always compromised not so much by methodological criticisms as by particular environmental circumstances which are always receding in time; their results are historical rather than contemporary. What we are looking into is the sub-strata in human living which keeps in existence a need for forms of spirituality. In the Western world these would appear to be preoccupied with the cracks left over from the unfulfilled hopes of pragmatism. In other cultures their understandings of spirituality would appear to have retained their precedence and to be largely independent of pragmatism.

Pragmatism in most of the world is subsumed to an assumption that the spirit world in some form or another exists. Since this cannot be defined or confined to any particular physiological or psychological manifestations, it would not seem sensible to try and assess this side of our question by scientific methods. We have to start from the statement that if something is believed to be true, then it is real in its consequences.

So on one side of the question there are spiritual powers and influences which have been constantly assumed to exist. The powers of God, Gods, ancestors, spirits, *karma*, luck or whatever and people acting on this reality, which is not assumed but known to exist. Acting on this men and women have consistently used up varying amounts of time, energy and resources to have these powers on their side rather than potentially against them.

The difficulty is that there are no boundaries to these assumptions and we cannot know with any certainty when they come into play in the lives of individuals and groups. When we consider health we are on firmer but still imprecise grounds in that is largely that in the absence of any physiologically or psychologically diagnosed conditions, people are considered to be healthy. It is possible to relate this quite clearly to some spirituality practices such as the accumulation of micro-organisms in the moisture on the surface of Christian icons and Buddhist statues from the serial touching of believers. But this is a likely correlation not a causal sequence as we do not know what else these people may have touched.

In any study of spirituality and well-being there are the problems of attribution since we need to know what are the results of practices in the minds of believers. Many people meditate but we know that the effects of these practices as far as we can observe them are indistinguishable from dozing which may be what is going on despite the practice being labelled meditation. We know that the numbers of authenticated miracles is extremely small but yet there are many thousands in all faiths who believe that their misfortunes have been reduced as a result of their requests to these spiritual powers. We also know that a high proportion of illnesses are cured without any medical intervention or go into remission which sufferers are likely to see as divine intervention.

We are always left with a very small proportion of human activities which can be linked tightly enough with spiritual practices to constitute proof according to the scientific requirements of outsiders. Much ingenuity has gone into creating double blind tests connecting prayer with biologically verifiable consequences in which the prayers and the prayed for do not know each other or indeed that they are being prayed for at all. The results are not so much statistically small but of little significance which is surely out of all proportion to the enormous quantities of prayers performed which those involved consider to have had valuable effects. In the sense of cost-benefit evaluations which the innumerable prayers carry out for themselves it may be that such tests are irrelevant.

For most people in all cultures their involvement in spirituality is likely to be a very small proportion of their daily lives in terms of used up time. For others it may involve no more than few moments of reflection before critical events. Each of the Japanese aircraft carriers had a Shinto shrine and each of the pilots about to take off for their attack on Pearl Harbour bowed to the altar beforehand. The Spanish bull-fighter before entering the arena and the dangers from the enraged bull prayed before the Roman Catholic shrine there.

In so far as we can link the practices of spirituality to health we can expect to find small amounts of primary data for which there may be some close correlations and a large quantity of secondary data from which we may be able to draw conclusions. There are probably in line with the patterns of thought with which the social scientists approached the topic in the first place. There are subtle distinctions between pilgrims in search of spiritual returns and the adventure of visiting strange and exciting places shared with thousands of others whether on the Hajj, Lourdes, Banaras or the *Kumbh Mela*.

The same difficulties over not so much assessing as assuming correlations under set-piece situations would apply to attendance at the Roman Catholic Mass ceremony and Friday communal prayers for Muslims. There are minimal variations in these two ceremonies except for the numbers attending and seasonal changes. We cannot assume without proof that the people are there for even predominantly religious reasons. Muslims have been seen to answer their mobile phones during prayers in the principal mosque in Old Delhi (Stubbs, 2007) as was the case in the Jade Buddha Temple in Shanghai.

It would be reasonable to assume that those who participate in regular spiritually related ceremonies get a sense of well-being from just being there and possibly this is augmented by deeper participations. Even in relatively closed environments we cannot be assured of any correlations with health. Western Christians often embrace each other as a sign of peace but Indians do not do so as touching strangers does not feature in their body language agenda. Does this mean that the British Roman Catholics are more likely to catch infections from their fellow believers and Indians less so. This would be difficult to prove apart from the fact that we would have to investigate cultural patterns of cleanliness in which it might show that Westerners are dirtier in their personal habits than Easterners. Holy water can always be a source of infection for

Christians and Hindus (Losito, 1946) and devout Muslims have been shown to have higher rates of internal parasites from pre-prayer washing in infected water (Farooq and Mallah, 1966). So we see that evidence may become firmer by excluding data and that even with the firmest of sources there will always be the uncertainties of attribution.

Then we come to well-being and its relationship to spirituality. Much is often made of the practices of spirituality being in some ways related to a failure of intelligence and self-reliance. This is waiting to be reduced if not eliminated by education and political authoritarianism whether in communist China, Russia or indeed Shia Iran or Sunni Saudi Arabia. Nevertheless it seems clear enough that in the absence of any ability to define spirituality and thus construct its meanings and functions, that almost all if not all humans have some elements of an indefinable spirituality in their understandings if not their behaviour. Leaving aside whatever elements may or may not be due to fear and mental illness we must surely assume that whatever their functions may be, they are felt to contribute to well-being. But we have to admit that well-being is as indefinable as spirituality and that it may be an entirely personal assessment of a state of mind which may or may not have any assessable connection with their physical conditions according to medical evaluations.

Analyses Miss the Experience of the Sacred

It seems clear that the relationship of the practices of spirituality to well-being may be caught on the need for binary classifications whereas it may be more likely that what occurs are transitory and accidental relationships. It may be more likely to be a binary relationship of inexactness and any exactnesses are the creation of the researchers wanting orderliness to be created out of the scientific discomfort with disorder. There are vague themes which come together and change in response to personal difficulties and satisfactions and environmental stresses which come into prominence and fade. At the most we may find that there is a fluctuating consistency resting in the individual mind and its supporting culture, but neither have borders in any classificatory sense.

Of course the word 'analysis' can include the theological and philosophical examination of the processes of spirituality. In both fields this involves examining highly abstract systems of thinking for which there is a limited pragmatic basis or perhaps more specifically produces results which those who have transcendental experience are likely to comment that this is not what had happened to them. For most people an analysis of spirituality involves the breaking down of very personal events whether prayer or performance into what these outsiders think are their component parts. So social scientists take an action which has been identified by them as a form of spirituality and break it down to what they consider to be its constituent elements (Eliade, 1963: xiii) of physiology, psychology, sociology, economics, linguistics, art or any other specialisation. The appreciation of a good meal would not rest on knowing the ingredients and the method of cooking.

But this form of understanding splits as if in fact the majority of people in practising their form of spirituality were in the main motivated by material considerations of cost, status and a known return to good health on previous occasions, then breaking the experience to its social science elements is perfectly correct. This is even if at the same time we reach conclusions about the dubious morality of their actions by accepting the dismissal of spirituality along the lines pronounced by Marx and Freud (Green, C., 1990; Wallwork, 1990). If on the other hand spirituality does involve the transcendent as is the conclusion of those who have such experiences, then the analyses of social scientists miss the point which is the experience of the sacred. It would be prudent for social scientists to remember that the English writer Pope wrote 'for fools rush in where angels fear to tread' (Pope, 1711) and the Irish poet wrote even more poignantly 'I have spread my dreams under your feet. Tread softly because you tread on my dreams' (Yeats, 1969).

This then is not a study in which finite connections are made between spirituality, well-being and health from which conclusions pragmatically link events and spiritual ideas and practices. No such conclusions can be reached even within a single allegedly homogeneous society because of two insuperable factors. Firstly, neither spirituality nor well-being can be defined and secondly, no society is homogeneous in any dominating sense. The innumerable variations in individuality and the constantly varying environments in which individuals develop and practice their particular forms of spirituality.

Even if we confine to our considerations to the United States where most of the research into spirituality has been carried out, we have no supra-individual conclusions of any exactitude and certainly few which cover the processes of social change in the environments of participants. In terms of population numbers any such conclusions than those reached about Asian religions and spiritual ideas and behaviour which have few links to the Western ideological dominance of individualism, would have limited value.

We have also to shed the dominance of theological thinking which may have equally limited influences on the practices and ideas of spirituality for the majority who have little concern with what intellectuals have written and indeed could be said to be ignorant of their conclusions. If we can confine ourselves for the moment to Roman Catholicism the official philosophy of the Church was never much more than an intellectual game played with zest and rancour and small regard for fair play by theologians for theologians. The spectators, whether Catholic or Protestant, might applaud or boo; but the children of the Enlightenment, the precursors of our present secular society, were already saying with Voltaire 'Oh, those fat volumes of theology – of course I never open them, nor does anyone else' (Voltaire, 1994; Candide: xxv). For them as for most of us, theology which once had the imprudence to call itself 'queen of the sciences' had become the plaything of desiccated mandarins (Zaehner, 1970: 280).

If this is a fair comment on contemporary Christian theology how much truer it will be of the venerated theological writings of Taoism, Hinduism and Buddhism written in arcane dialects and unread by the millions at whom they are directed. These writings provide some parameters for belief and practice, no more than vague delimitations for spirituality practised by specialists. Hindus generally may have heard of the *Bhagavad Gita* but it seems unlikely that more than a few will have done so out of the seventy millions who went to the last *Kumbh Mela* on the Ganges, but many more will have seen the *Mahabharata* Hindu epic in all its many episodes on television.

Knowledge in its scientific sense may be confined to the highly trained intellectuals but in its narrow application and its almost caste-like assumptions. The others do not have any capacity to attain this knowledge or to understand it 'Formerly when religion was strong and science weak, men mistook magic for medicine; now when science is strong and religion weak, men mistake medicine for magic' (Szasz, 1973). Any knowledge about the correlations of spirituality to well-being and health is almost inevitably spelt out in a specialised linguistic code which excludes those about whom these specialists have written from understanding what has been concluded about their own behaviour and understandings. Knowledge about spirituality or indeed any social activity which can only be known at best from its external expression, is never an abstract finite quality.

The knowledge of human understandings and practices cannot be detached from its social environment without losing its essential adaptive quality. It is in most senses a personal possession which is from time-to-time verified by sharing. Extracting certain parts of human understandings and calling it knowledge with a special defined validity so that 'imagines or stating that you have knowledge of all too easily justifies not enquiring too carefully or critically lest it upset the illusion. The greater the claim to global dominion, the more such knowledge is likely to ignore what people are actually doing' (Hobart, 1995). This means that in any study of spirituality we should pay closer attention to what 'ordinary' people say and do as average Buddhists, Christians, Hindus, Muslims and traditionalists in their partial conformity to their Great (religious) Traditions (Redfield, 1956). It is the Little (spiritual) Traditions which illustrate the day-to-day spirituality. This has so much constant and unplanned variability that knowledge must surely remain with those who have their own individual conceptions and understandings which do not fit into the detached consistencies of outsider analyses.

In support of this approach we have to accept that the social scientists continual attempt to be detached and the assumption that they have significantly achieved this status, is a well meant delusion and the result of this inevitability are significant handicaps to a more human understanding of spirituality. It is inconceivable that the presence of anthropologists in the societies they are studying or the ways in which their field notes are turned into publications can be dismissed as irrelevancies or of minimal significance or that the continued vigilance required in our composition of concepts in field notes as not a central rather than incidental element in any future theorizing (Parkin, 1995).

2 Quantitative Approaches to Spirituality and Well-being

What data is available which is reliable enough to be used in connecting spirituality to well-being and health? Certainly there is a mass of published data relating to these topics but in terms of reliability according to scientific standards, there may be very little.

Social scientists often hope to be able to research religious behaviour and to produce viable scientific results which will have approved professional acceptability. Too often these produce 'tables summarising research in terms of patterns of significant differences (which) are little more than complex causally uninterpretable outcomes of statistical proved functions' and 'the excessive reliance on significance testing is partly responsible, being a poor way of doing science' (Meene, 1978).

We must surely approach the data produced by social scientists as failing to fit into the requirements of science but this should not be just scepticism but founded on the numerous difficulties in attempting to confine human behaviour to narrow categorisations which would produce finite data. Scepticism is only a short-term approach quite justified if their results could be the last word on those particular aspects of the topic but in practice are little more than contributions on the fringes of possible accuracy. What does one make of comprehensive surveys of contemporary Japanese religious beliefs which vary between concluding that they are secularist and other similar comprehensive surveys which show so much religious belief that the conclusions can be reached that a substantial proportion of the population believe in more than one God (Klass, 1996). What are the methodological issues which may cumulatively detract from the scientific but not necessarily the social science value of data. There are numerous limitations to the quantifying of behaviour.

The Individuality of Everyone

It must be basic to any understanding of human behaviour that each individual is a biological and psychological isolate and even more so from the individuality of their social experiences. In any understanding of the meaning and practices of spirituality the only accurate and appropriate descriptive adjective must be 'each' rather than 'all' people in any particular category which has been applied to them. In this context we should remember the lengthy study of the ethical ideas of a single elderly non-literate Navajo American Indian (Ladd, 1957).

Individual differences are difficult to work out when the units of measurement are economic but much more so when these units are without agreed definitions; hard science has internationally agreed units of measurement but in the social sciences there are none. How indeed could there be when the units of spirituality are wrapt in theological and philosophical arguments and often extend to violent confrontations. Social scientists would agree that their own individualities are not and cannot be duplicated but yet put the behaviour of others into categories which repeatedly imply just such duplications. They almost instinctively group behaviour while probably accepting that the practices of individuals in their spiritualities are always different in how they are constructed and how they are utilised.

While it is obvious that the spiritualities of religious leaders such as that of the Ayotollah Khomeini, Krishnamurti and Mother Teresa are certainly individual. There is a reluctance to accept that everyone's ideas are individual to some extent, not only cultivators in Bengal and the Yangtse valley but also those who are intellectually handicapped. Children with Down's Syndrome can certainly appreciate religious ceremonies in their own ways of understanding. Break these groupings down into individual behaviour and very complex patterns emerge of great personal significance to those involved.

We can only assume that a group of Buddhists, Christians and Hindus who state that they are meditating and appear to be doing just that according to their religious obligations and definitions, are in fact conforming to the same ill-defined requirements. We have no evidence at all not so much that they are meditating or not but they are conforming to a single pattern of spirituality. It is not just that they may be dozing or thinking about their business problems which can occur in the silences of Quaker meetings.

It is possible to be clinically accurate about some biological conditions such as the rare recessive gene diseases among the Old Order Amish (McKusick, 1973) but not about its surrounding mental and social factors by which those involved cope individually with these serious abnormalities. Social scientists probably accept this overall individuality but move away from its inevitability because it is so much harder to deal with both theoretically and in terms of the cost of any methodology to individualise their work in this way and to accept the limitations which it would impose of their generalising conclusions.

The Inappropriateness of Breaking Down Unitary Activities

Individuals at whatever level of intellectual development rarely if ever breakdown their behaviour into the parts which social science tends to do. When thinking of their religion they do not divide their feelings into how often they attend, how much they pay in donations and certainly not how much of orthodox thinking they know. Those who appeal to God, the Virgin Mary, the Goddess of Mercy in China or to the spirits in the family household shrines in Japan experience what they are doing as a single all embracing activity.

An additional built-in weakness of attempting to make into facts essentially personal behaviour and thinking patterns whether they are scaled or not, is that no one except possibly a very small number of logicians give out their thoughts in terms of agreement with one point of view to the conscious exclusion of others. It is just not the way that people function except possibly specific choices when an individual has to decide to do this or that in a materialistic environment.

It would seem to be an almost insoluble problem for the social scientist to confront people with questions or opinions about which they have never given any detached thought. In semi-formal situations which are likely to be to some extent confrontational and to expect them to express different shades of agreement or disagreement. This is even more likely to be difficult when both parties are operating within different linguistic and social codes. Moreover when their degree of literacy is confined to the sports and television pages of the popular large print newspapers, there are going to be difficulties in coping with questionnaires.

We can surely assume that everyone in whatever cultural or intellectual environments they live, thinks that their own understandings are consistent. We can similarly assume that in most of the logic necessary for survival, there have always been choices and that in general they have made the right ones for survival. To reach this level of environmental survival there is no reason to suppose that individuals cannot believe in matters which are logically in opposition to each other. Ideas and beliefs change their meanings with very little more than a nudge from changed circumstances. Individuals are more or less unconsciously adaptive.

When social scientists attend a religious ceremony and analyse what they have seen or heard from participants, they usually break down their data into what they assess as its constituent parts. A typical example of this approach would be a tabulation of the regression on the independent and control variables, standardised regression coefficients which list religious saliences, church attendances, orthodoxy, other-worldly orientation, religious comfort beliefs and perceived health correlated to four demographic characteristics—education, age, marital status and race (Petersen and Roy, 1985). When one looks at the pages of tables in other studies (Poloma and Pendleton, 1991) we can state that whatever forms of religious behaviour they are attempting to analyse, they have totally avoided the essential element in any religious experience. It is always personal and unitary and coincidental aspects are often obtained by excluding the details of personal differences.

Perhaps even common-sense should suggest that a Jew praying at the Wailing Wall in Jerusalem or a Nepalese putting another stone on an existing pile of stones at a pass in the Himalayas cannot be better understood in their terms than by breaking down their activity into several categories. Categories which indeed are far from clear either to those acting in this way or in their social science definitions within which they are analysed. The fact that by this process they are taking these religious actions out of the context in which they were performed.

It is not that these social scientists have tried to analyse religious behaviour in a methodologically sound manner presumably to the satisfaction of their professional colleagues, but that the whole approach is misconceived. The individuals who are praying in whatever form and under whatever religious ideas are examples of personal ego-centred concentrations. In the first example leaving aside the obvious point that there are no assured means of finding out the truth of answers obtained from some three hundred people whose names were randomly obtained from a telephone directory. It is usually accepted that their answers were provided in good faith and even that is an unverified assumption, so it cannot mean that they are necessarily accurate in any scientific sense. Individuals just do not breakdown their understandings of their own and indeed other people's religious activities by the same bureaucratic methods with which they would approach a bank manager in asking for a loan. An individual's experience of their own lives is always a unitary one.

Another problem in such bureaucratic approaches to the complexities of religious behaviour is the putting of replies into scales in reference to the subject of the question. People are not often questioned for their opinions and they can be asked to assess their relationship to God or whoever on a scale of one to seven which certainly requires a high standard of literacy. It is not much easier for the researchers to do the same with the answers which they have received. Even when the questions such as 'I often wonder what life is all about' get replies and these are graded on a scale of one to five by the researcher (Yinger, 1977). How an individual reaches conclusions enough to make such statements remain undisclosed. The social and psychological environment is unknown and the meaning of the question remains undefined. While there may be confirmation of these views in their generalities from subsequent interviews and questionnaires, there is no means of knowing the inevitably different frames of mind or social backgrounds from which the answers came.

Apart from the fact that answers put into a scale on one day, might produce different answers on the following day as the respondents may have become happier or more miserable since then and indeed have had disagreements with their local priest, imam or sadhu. A textbook on the measuring of religiousness (Hill and Hood, 1999) lists no less than 121 different scales in English almost entirely from American sources. One can only wonder at the persistence with which the social sciences have tried to rigidly these personal experiences, practices and understandings of religion. The consistent feature of the results of this scaling of data is the need for statistical rectitude rather than any recognition of the intrinsic variability of religion as much as any other personal experiences.

We can assume that there is a connection between psychological distress and the practices of religion. People's assessment of their own health status as 'good,' 'fair' and 'poor' is reasonable even if there is no definition of what these categories entail and their connection with medically defined realities. However then to go further and give very precise multiple regression coefficients for these perceived health status is probably going further than the data justifiy (Tessler and Mechanic, 1978).

Other surveys go much further in producing numerically

expressed results. One such study reaches a series of such conclusions that perceptions of the divine as a rule are correlated negatively with global happiness, while the perception of the divine in remedial terms is related positively to life satisfaction (Pollner, 1989:99). Such conclusions are valuable as hypotheses and may be assumed to have relevance by which people use their religious ideas expressed in hard numbers for a whole series of indefinable categories is perhaps misusing two methods of understanding which do not fit together.

Another example would be the numerically expressed connection between religious devotion and religion as a moral guide with the hostility and suspiciousness of those responding to enquiries about whether black Americans who are religious are nicer than the less religious people (Ellison, 1994). The conclusions may be valuable but not when a whole series of indefinable characteristics are related to three places of decimals. A discussion of such correlations has muted value when it is linked to such inevitable inaccuracies. There are very large numbers of published research which link indefinable categories in numerical terms suggesting the status of such correlations is scientific.

Some pieces of research bring together most of the objections that can be made on methodological grounds for examining religious behaviour and ideas in ways that attempt to copy those of the exact hard sciences. A study of Pakistani Muslims religions orientations and experience in relation to Eid-ul-Azha, the festival terminating the pilgrimage month which has some parallels in the Christian excitement over Easter (Khan and Watson, 2004). The questionnaire written in Urdu was administered by psychology students from Karachi University to members of their own families during this festive season. It was made as brief as possible because families would be busy at this time, and their answers to these three fixed questions were assessed on the scales of 0 to 9. The intrinsic one 'my whole approach to life is based on my religion', the extrinsic one was what religion offers me most is comfort in times of trouble and sorrow and finally, the extrinsic social orientation question was 'I go to the activities associated with my religion because I enjoy seeing people I know there'. These are all leading questions which would not be allowed in American, British or Indian courts and in fact they were devised by American social scientists in relation to their own research work (Gorsuch and McPherson, 1989). Since these matters were chosen by outsiders we have no means of knowing whether the respondents would have produced them as important matters in this context. The respondents were then asked to identify their responsibilities in which five different items were asked of each sex to be answered 'yes', 'no' or 'partially'. Finally, they were asked to respond to ten positive and ten negative words used in other research work (Watson *et al.*, 1988) graded on a scale of 0 to 5. Finally, they responded to self-esteem questions such as, 'I feel that I am a person of worth at least on an equal basis with others.' Have social scientists questioned the realities in which such questions and evaluations are asked and made ? It is just not how people think and much less how they express themselves. It is the imposition of categories forcing what people say into numerical categories which have no relevance to their own understanding of spirituality. There is another aspect to such enquiries which has to be considered which is that there is no other data available on this matter. Such hard work should be assessed as an initial contribution towards understanding the unknown to which subsequent researchers can add data.

Direct questioning is probably a very Western way of eliciting information and one moreover which is connected with official outsiders usually associated with interference. It is based on the needs of the researchers rather than any pre-research consideration for the feelings of the researched. It seems unlikely that anyone being questioned in such direct ways whether subsistence farmers in China or Maputo or the urban people in Bengal or Banaras without developing some hostility to these cultural outsiders. If the questions had been open ended it might will have resulted in a variety of answers and without the artificial grading of the answers. An open ended question given to a sample of 5000 Tanzanians 'what is wrong with the Church today' produced answers which were placed under over three hundred different headings (Tanner and Morgan, 1976).

Since the majority of the world's religion believers are not monotheistic and even those who are may will be polytheistic in practice with their beliefs in spirits, saints and bodhisattvas, it would seem that such questions may have limited relevance to personal practices. It seems more likely that people play along with such invasions of their privacies in the same way that they may reply to questions about their preferences for some marketable product.

So in order to assess the functions or understandings of religious behaviour, social scientists as outsiders break it down into sections which is not a process which they even apply to themselves. Apart from any ethical issues in splitting up intensely personal practices, it is methodologically wrong in turning unitary acts into a variety of subdivisions which those people have never thought themselves to be a necessary part of that experience. If a religious experience is a unitary one whether attending the evening Mass at Lourdes or bathing in the Ganges at the correct astrological time at the *Kumbh Mela*, then it cannot be split up into any constituent parts without losing the emotional reality of any such experience. We should accept that not only do people experience their own understandings in unitary terms but that what they experience is likely to have more than one dimension within this unity. 'Understanding individual religiosity (and individual desecularization, for that matter) as a multidimensional phenomenon leads to the possibility of it taking many forms and switching between different forms (Kazemipur and Rezani, 2003).

However, it has long been suggested that there are five possible dimensions of religiousness; experiential, ritualistic, ideological, intellectual and cognitive and that 'being religious in one dimension does not necessarily imply religiosity on other dimensions' (Glock and Stark, 1965:22). So we are left with this possibility of five simultaneously active dimensions but surely role play comes into this. Individuals may have more than these five which might apply more convincingly in traditional societies which at least theoretically are relatively homogeneous. However in contemporary societies where there are more and well separated roles individuals may have different and none the less genuine religious ideas and practices for different reasons in a social business or religious group, in the presence of their children or in that of the in-laws (Young and Ikeuchi, 1997; Bibby *et al.*, 1973), but there is still the fact that these individuals do not think that they are acting dimensionally but as a single unit of behaviour and thinking.

The way forward to a better understanding of religious experience and practice would surely belong the lines of Parallel Distributive Processing. It is accepted that the mind as the central unit in processing multiple variables processes the information that it receives at speeds faster than any computer and reaches decisions almost instantaneously. Its results cannot be seen in lineal or categorical divisions. So the methodo-logy for examining the relationship of religious behaviour to human well-being suffers from a fundamental misunderstanding of the nature of human emotion. The individuals who fall in love, appreciate art, nature, poetry, fall ill and have a relationship with the divine however defined, feel that what has happened to them is a unitary experience. It seems very doubtful that anyone other than an extremely detached emotionally dead person would workout in a list their reasons for such appreciations. Even more unlikely that such a list would convince a reader of their emotional significance.

Since spirituality and religious behaviour generally are multidimensional, we are left with the alternatives of seeing it as a single unitary experience although tied to the personal and social factors of the moment. The alternative is to try and subdivide the phenomena into different factors and different characteristics and consequences. This may be a valid method of analysis when individual motivations and understandings are not important, except that those who see that religious behaviour is being studied are unlikely to see their own experiences in this way.

As many as twenty-one factors have been identified in one study (King and Hunt, 1975) and even more when the questions are open ended (Tanner and Morgan, 1976) and provide innumerable answers. Even if we examine religious behaviour in relation to stress, we find that it can have various functions which an individual might will experience at the same time. It can serve as a means of expressing emotional disturbance, as a haven from stress, as a means of gaining social acceptance and confrontation or as a means of growth fulfilment (Spilka and Werme, 1971). There is little in religious behaviour which would suggest that it can be examined as a series of alternative ways of behaving.

There is an almost trivialising element in many of these itemised enquiries into the nature of religious behaviour which may be momentous enough for the individual such as dipping their fingers into holy water before entering a church or putting a flower down before a statue of Kali but such behaviour is not likely to be subject of much personal reflection about what they are doing and why? It must be rare indeed for the pilgrim to Lourdes, Banaras or Mecca to say to themselves that they are there because they believe in this, that or the other. It is and was a total experience and on reflection of great importance which analytical enquiries might appear to trivialise.

The understandings of the religious behaviour and the values obtained from this way of looking at their lives, should lead us to give equal weight to the feelings of the peasant and the philosopher as individuals. How can anything of value and understanding emerge from a sample of three thousand students (Bohrnstedt *et al.*, 1968) or two thousand Roman Catholic adolescents (Smith, G.B. *et al.*, 1979). This is surely trivialising the religious understandings of these people when we remember that the study of the moral ideas of a single elderly Navajo American-Indian took-up four hundred pages (Ladd, 1957). The complexities of religious emotion in anyone regardless of their intellectual and social status requires individual and unitary attention must surely be recognised.

The Nature of Truth Obtained from Single Informants

Without getting into philosophical discussions about the nature of truth, we can assume that there is information which researchers believe to be true and are used to compose formal conclusions. There are enormous leaps of faith in any such assumed continuities. Firstly, let us consider the passing of information from an insider to an outsider; how can an outsider successfully evaluate the 'truth' of what has been passed over an objective divide. Even within a culture it is extremely difficult to reach any substantiated conclusions as we know to be the case within legal systems dedicated in a criminal trial to an objective binary conclusion about guilt. In hard science it is possible to isolate facts in some sort of linear calculation but in social behaviour it is not possible to isolate any particular piece of behaviour without the individual's behaviour being linked to a whole series of similarly connected undefined and indefinable facts. The informant may state that he has attended a religious service and that at the primary level may be true, he was there but in what sense did he attend.

It may be possible after quite a long period of acculturation into a particular and usually small community to know whether the information passed on by an informant fits into a social whole but what is the role of that man or woman in those circumstances. Unless this standard of understanding is reached, there is very little reason not to suspect, not so much the accuracy but the undefined but expected partiality of what these informants have said unless it is tied into facts obtained from other sources. Much that is said is tied into the informant's own spirituality and social needs and he or she may consider that the spirits may be listening. Why indeed should informants share the needs and objectives of an outsider who is somewhat arbitrarily enquiring about something as indefinable and private as spiritual practices.

It would be unusual indeed for any individual in any culture to talk to a stranger interested in their private thinking and practices related to the spirit world for reasons which are at the best of times obscure and indeed often suspect. Inevitably spoken in a linguistic code with which one or the other is not fully conversant. In this there may be some scale by which objectivity might be assessed such as some agricultural practices and how food is cooked but not over matters such as issues of food distribution and offerings to the spirits, ownership of land, boundaries and cooperative efforts. There are very few reasons for assuming that what is being passed to the researcher would receive the agreement even of members of their primary families, much less extended ones and their neighbours. But once information is sought about abstract ideas and practices based on them which relate to ordinary day-to-day matters much less those that relate to the spirit world, there are few reasons to suppose that the answers are not related to their needs of the moment. The 'truth' will vary almost by the minute.

There might be some similarity in the minds of those giving information to even the most personable and pleasant researcher as they would be giving information to the police. They are dealing with some sort of officially sponsored enquirer or why else would they be asking such questions which they would assume to be unlikely to benefit them as far as their previous experiences had shown. Those that give information to researchers come under several categories but they all share two common characteristics; these people are all informants and what they are doing does not fit into their usual social relationships. There is little in the provision of information by informants that could possibly fit into the requirements of science. It is well meaning inexactnesses over which there are no predefined controls. They fall into the following categories; people who are accidentally asked for information, those who are asked for information because they have the required characteristics for being part of a predetermined sample and people who provide information as part of a potentially continuing social relationship.

Finally, people who provide information from being part of a shared participation in an event in which there is little distinction between the researcher and the researched in which someone is researching their own religious community. In this there are no informants separated out by the details of their lives which they are providing. The whole situation is complicated by the biases built into the combination of their covert role of researcher and their overt social roles. This may be mitigated by the part-time nature of this involvement as being a member of a Roman Catholic congregation in southern India or a Japanese factory (Kondo, 1990) but not of a Hindu community in Kathiawar.

In the other categories the informants are just providing information to a social stranger which they would not have done in the usual course of events. It can never be the same as information taken from a security camera as can be available for crowd control at mass pilgrimage centres such as in Mecca at the Hajj, but even that would not provide anything more than primary facts of little explanatory value. So we need to look closely at why these people give both personal and impersonal information to people who are not part of their social networks. The reasons for doing this have to be sufficiently strong to overcome the nervousness which comes from talking to strangers against which most people are socialised from childhood. This is a situation which has no parallels to scientific methodology as there are numerous social fences involving social distance which have to be overcome before any such standards can be anticipated; age, sex, education, ethnicity, social status, height, nationality, religion and marital status. There are social even physical dangers in associating with a stranger.

The reasons for giving information to a social stranger will have to a compound of reasons strong enough to offset the built-in disadvantages. There will be no permanency in the balance between advantages and disadvantages as it can change from one day to the next. The informant can gain financially and socially from attachment to an outsider. Even if there is standard questioning as in a survey of religious lives in Guyana (South America), Zambia and Zimbabwe in which I contacted was asked everyone the one open ended question 'what do you do', the answers varied. Twenty minutes from a priest who did not want to be interviewed on matters which he considered entirely personal and fourteen hours on and off from another priest who taught in a seminary in Tanzania and who had parish experience in Uganda. As could be expected the answers were so varied in content that there were no uniformities except that they were all Roman Catholics and were working in a particular country. There is little in the context of research into spirituality and well-being which can make information provided by informants fit into scientifically acceptable categories. They are varied in their own characteristics and in what they have experienced and talk about.

The Nature of Truth Obtained from Sampled Informants

In the study of any population in which everyone is individually different, anything less than total coverage must mean that information is being missed. While it may be possible to interview all the members of a small self-contained group such as the members of a monastic community but then some have pastoral duties outside the monastery walls. Thus the men and women would be influenced positively or negatively by thousands of outsiders who would be impossible to contact. Even if that was attempted the overall environment would be changing while such a lengthy survey was going on.

So sampling takes place not only for scientific reasons but because of the impossibility of any wholesale alternatives so as to make the research possible and for the convenience of the researchers. It may be possible to take a slice of bread and to assert that it is the same as the rest of the loaf but that is impossible with humans. Have we any assurance that the sample has been chosen according to scientifically acceptable principles. Firstly, we may not know how many people there are in the proposed universe and to what extent their membership is stable nor do we know what are the defined principles by which the researchers and the people concerned consider to be valid membership. By what standards can we accept a person as a Hindu or Muslim when there is an absence of supporting scientifically acceptable data.

Even if we have a sample of people who state that they are Roman Catholics, their priest might say that this is not exactly correct as they have not been inside a church for at least the last ten years. Once any sample ceases to be acceptably boxed in, it is inevitable that detracting exceptions from the requirements for scientific validity for field study research reach almost unmanageable proportions. It is coming to terms with these problems which must concern any social scientists aspiring to be scientific in the accepted sense of the term (MacCorquodale *et al.*, 1954).

Ideally we know that it is almost always impossible to take details and indeed interview whole populations unless the group is quite small and well-known in its characteristics. In a survey of religious life in Zambia, 95 per cent of all priests, nuns and brothers were interviewed but we do not know the significance of the 5 per cent who were not interviewed. Since the survey was being carried out with the support and agreement of the bishops we can assume that there were unknown and perhaps important reasons for their absence. In such a survey with the sample spread over large areas of the country there are also restrictions from cost of time and transport and the physical stamina of the researcher. However samples cloaked as they may be by having to provide scientific justifications for what has been done, hide the factor of convenience for the researchers. Out of twenty four studies between 1965 to 1979 used in religion and mental health research no less than eighteen involved students and there would have also been the factor of willingness to conform to the wishes of the senior staff in the universities in which they were studying. Even if we had some reliable data, we cannot use a book of random numbers through which to choose a sample which is not biased in some direction or another. If we have a list of the houses and their occupiers in a Hindu defined part of a town, the turn-over of the population is likely to be high so that the social universe is fluid. People do not have the caged in characteristics of primates nor bacteria used in experiments (Skinner, 1938).

In going over the answers it is often the case that some can be discredited as unreliable and that is particularly likely to be the case with answers to sensitive questions. In a survey of adolescent sexual behaviour in Nigeria over their liability to contract AIDS, 31 per cent of completed questionnaires were found to be invalid (Slap *et al.,* 2003). One can presuppose that there would also be large numbers of invalid replies related to spirituality.

Similarly, if we choose more or less anyone of the same age, self-stated living place and of the same education level, then that is a matter of chance. There is always the issue of non-compliance or absence of those that were chosen to be part of the sample. It may be acceptable to ask how much was spent on food last week but questions about spirituality are much more sensitive areas of behaviour and there will be substantial avoidance or inaccuracy in their replies. There is always the fact that those questioned will know that they are part of a survey and are likely to shade their answers towards their own interpretation of that end and of course virtually nothing is known of the background of participants.

The larger the universe, the smaller the proportionate size of the sample, leaving the vast majority untouched as in public opinion surveys. It is an act of social science faith not fact that the smaller is for research purposes similar to the whole. In the absence of any definable uniformities samples can only be acceptable as attempts to be scientific. The validity of the collected data is no more than a construct of what has been recorded. So in respect of research by sampling on thinking and behaviour in relation to spirituality and well-being would appear to rest more on opportunism than scientific method. Moreover we are knowingly aware of these shortcomings which are in fact insuperable in researching human societies and their individualisms. It is prudent in this respect to remember that the work of Sigmund Freud in 23 volumes do not give a single experiment and yet he remains influential.

The Use of Religious Statistics

There is a certain reliability about religious practices, when participation is recorded by institutions, particularly when these are secular. Beyond these we have very little information that goes beyond estimates as participation is only a primary fact. We know nothing from these facts about the reasons for participation which might indeed be entirely secular as a pilgrimage-holiday tour. We can know the number of foreigners who go on the Hajj pilgrimage because the Saudi Arabian authorities will have immigration controls but they have only estimates of the numbers of nationals attending just as the Indian secular authorities who stated that an estimated 70 million attended the last *Kumbh Mela*, some of whom were not even Hindus. It could have been ten million above or below that figure; it was an informed guess made-up from transport figures, sanitation problems and crowd control realities. We have no means of knowing the number of Christian pilgrims going to Lourdes, Compostela and Medugorje as centres of devotion nor the number of Hindu pilgrims who go Banaras. All we can say that the number of pilgrims in all continents has been increasing from transport data but we know very little of the relationship to spirituality apart from the factors of easier travel and greater affluence of those travellers. They may know that they are terminally ill but we do not know whether they are praying for an easy death or prolonged life or indeed whether they are praying at all.

Overall statistics of religious practices are predominantly Christian of which the Roman Catholic Church has a standard system. Often with other Churches it is necessary for those involved to provide proof of participation as their parishes do not maintain any records. For Muslims there are 'wakf' bequests of property for religious properties which in Egypt are administered by a government ministry. Statements in documents produced by religious authorities are not valid evidence of anything beyond what they record as in certificates of baptism or marriage giving names, parents and address which is usually no more than an area.

We cannot draw any conclusions from this as to spiritual predispositions or intention. In the absence of documentation it is only in some cases that membership of a faith is recorded and estimates are likely to be larger than social realities might suggest. Situational variables are beyond anything approaching accuracy although some registers may contain details which can be used as adjuncts to particular hypotheses as to sex, age and localities of baptisms and financial support and the purposes for which special ceremonies have been held. So religious statistics are patchy indeed and fall far short of the consistency which would be necessary for any scientific analyses.

The Taxonomy of Situations

In approaching a research project into spirituality there is a decision to make whether the researchers should approach the social environments in which the practices of spirituality are assumed to be operating or to attempt to analyse the situations which give rise to these practices and ideas. These are two perspectives and would require the researchers to have a double even a schizoid mentality to give equal attention to both. The choice is dictated by whether the researchers are undertaking micro studies of the spirituality related activities of a community conveniently circumscribed in space or by appearance and for which these researchers are able to dedicate both time and residence. Alternatively the macro approach in which spiritual activities are assessed in terms of whole wider social environments.

This is a decision which may not be made on scientific grounds alone. It might be made because of opportunism, being friendly with some members of a community which has occurred by accident or at least having the overt support of a community or religious leader which might push researchers into certain locations. On the other hand some social commitment to a particular locality or social group which would allow a deeper analysis of more individual uses and understandings of the practices and ideas of spirituality which could not be done with a study involving hundreds and indeed thousands of people.

There might also be the factor that researchers with more open extroverted personalities might have an easier return on involvements with smaller numbers of informants in which there are more personal social relationships and in which the focal points are particular people. While on the other hand researchers of a more retiring introverted type might flourish in working on broader issues which would not have to rely on the creation and maintenance of what would usually be cross-cultural social relationships. So whatever the approach chosen it is not one based on scientific necessities but more on personal abilities and opportunism.

The Impossibility of Exactness

Since health and religious behaviour are closely related (Reynolds and Tanner, 1983) it is reasonable to compare the data which is available for both. Health in Western concepts is related to the presence or absence of particular diseases or malfunctions. When individuals visit a physician, they start with giving descriptions of the symptoms and not some suggestions of how they were caused and it is these that are compared with statements elsewhere. Unless the doctor has tests done, he acts on the symptoms which are more personal opinions than facts, and it surely must be the same with questions about religion.

In any analysis of religious behaviour it is a basic mistake to think that anyone whether Roman Catholic, Hindu or Muslim has a single identifiable objective or understanding or that their behaviour can be explained in terms of scientific reductionism within the cultural paradigms available to them. This is not just the result of predominantly secular social scientists finding what they expect to find but also the result of quasi-traditionalists on being asked about their religious practices more often than not reply that this is what we have always done. Giving to the enquirer what can be no more than orally transmitted memories for which there can be no substantiated evidence. Such informants are perhaps forced into creating such verbal exactnesses by the unusual nature of the questioning which is so different to how they normally interact.

Secondly, there can be no assumption that when an informant says that we do this or that this is likely to be a shared view as there will always be covert and overt factors which are entirely individual. Not only just individual but strikingly idiosyncratic as well because no one in their behaviour and thinking is a reduplication of someone else. The constant variations that go on in the one individual as the result of physiological, psychological and social changes which occur on an almost minute to minute basis.

Finally, There can be no assumption that the regular performance of certain religious rituals since a very large proportion of all religious ritual is repetitive in both form and practice, are performed with the same intention either collectively or individually. Leaving aside the creation of such rituals to deal with personal crises. The Buddhist mantra '*om mane padme hum*' which is repeatedly endlessly by many northern Indian Buddhists, can only be exact in the fact that the phrase is composed of four words; this repetition is done to acquire merit so there are cumulative changes for those reciting even if they are unaware of what specific changes have occurred in their karmic status. The suggestion that much of the repetition built into religious rituals is more or less mindless is surely a form of intellectual bias when so much of more ordinary behaviour comes from habituation.

Repetitive forms of spirituality are certainly looked down on by most theologians who do not have a karmic framework of thinking, and who counsel believers that their devotions should be consciously specific. So few of those specialists would agree even hypothetically that similar religiously motivated actions have similar consequences or come from similar backgrounds. This exactness in religious rituals can be assessed in three ways. Firstly, when the rituals come in set forms either because they are the easy to remember or they are basic rituals in which orthodoxy states are necessary. There is also the fact that many people make up their own prayer forms and continue to use them repetitively long after they have lost their initial freshness. Even without any karmic thinking most worshippers would feel that they are accumulating benefits from such regularity, so the exactness of print cannot be equated with any exactness in how worshippers approach their own regularities.

So beyond these mouthed and mental repetitions, the devout are always making their personal inputs which are outside any possible observations or assessments because they are inaccessible and individually variable. There is always the religious and indeed secular satisfactions from regularity which imposes stability on an unstable life. Worshippers may indeed be conforming subconsciously to what is required from the orthodoxies of their faith. Once it is brought forward into the conscious mind, the concept of exactness evaporates into the intricacies of individualism and the particular social environments of that time. We have to conclude that exactness is a scientific necessity but it can only be obtained in assessing religious ideas and behaviour by cutting out from consideration all the variables of personality and environment which cannot be constrained in that narrow way.

Subjecting the Inexactness of Prayer to the Exactnesses of Analysis

Since prayer is the commonest form of individualised religious behaviour it is inevitable that it should have been subjected to considerable scientific attention not so much as to its nature but as to its consequences. Those who are praying are asking for something which indeed in many cases is expressed specifically. There are irreducible difficulties in trying to connect the forms of religious understanding expressed in prayer with specific consequences. It seems clear enough that prayer in the form defined as 'every kind of inward communion or conversation with the power recognised as divine' (James, 1902:464) is extremely common in whatever form of religiousness is being considered. Not suit the major international religions, but the so-called tribal religions which have not been committed to paper or the purely personal ways of belief and practice which are only vaguely within the parameters of their surrounding cultural religious understandings.

However hard we work to find an acceptable definition of prayer in social science understandings and scientific terms which also conforms to theological conventions, it is this which has to be at the start of any such investigations. Since this is probably impossible, it might be better to think in terms of possible correlations. Even if individuals sit and physically do nothing, there are going to be assessable consequences since most of their physiological processes are going to slow down. If those individuals are asked to pray on a specific theme, then there are similarly going to be physiological and psychological changes. The difficulty there is that these changes from praying may be very similar to the effects of quietly sitting in a comfortable chair reading a favourite book.

Can we assume that people involved in experiments over the effects of prayer are doing what they have been asked to do. That is a big assumption about their ability to maintain concentration; there is always the problem of replication and the controls used for comparison. To what extent can people voluntarily produce on demand a replication of 'real' prayer carried out in churches, mosques, temples, monasteries and at the shrines of saints or ancestors who may or may not have ever existed. We really have no idea what is happening in such persons' minds when they state that they have been praying and moreover praying for a specific objective. We can suggest that it is similarly an act of faith to believe them.

A multi-facetted study of Dutch Carmelite monks and nuns whose lives centred on contemplative prayer (Mallony, 1977) based on the teaching of Saint John of the Cross were given a lengthy questionnaire on spirituality. She reached conclusions that mysticism was associated with positive mental health. There were correlations that prayer involved rational processes associated with mental distress and that mystical factors correlated with mild but not strict views of asceticism. These results were based on the interpretation of data which must have been inexact from its very nature and coercive. These questions were given to 53 monks and nuns out of the monastic situation to which they were accustomed and to which they had sworn allegiance. It cannot be considered as paralleling scientifically valid proofs as they may have been points for the everyday institutionalised conformity of those involved. It is not necessary to consider the shortcomings of the results in terms of their statistical procedures when their invalidity in those terms comes from the absence initially of definitions (Finney and Malony, 1985).

In whatever study is made the sides of any equation can never have equal scientific value. On the prayer side the data will never be exact as it cannot be in the absence of any substantive definitions and on the other side a self-sustaining statistical exactness. But surely that is not the end of any assessment of prayer as probably the commonest form of religious behaviour. Of course, we do not know and indeed can never know with any exactness what individuals are doing when they admit that they have been praying. So attempts to bring prayer within the range of social science attempts at exactness has taken away its essential element of an inward communion or conversation with the divine.

These points are made in a study of fifty novices before, after and during the retreats they made in United States and Canadian Jesuit centres when they were isolated from the outside world (Sacks, 1979). The researcher suggested that the result would be their increased cognitive integration and such results were found to be statistically significant. However, he concluded that it was impossible to identify which aspects of the retreat were responsible for these results. In what ways could the retreat process be separated out from their interaction with God and the new social environment which these men were experiencing as both might be a major contribution to their growth in self-esteem.

Right from the start of social scientists working on religion there have been attempts to quantify the results of prayer (Galton, 1872). The religious community raised the objection that it was a sacrosanct subject and that as such it should or perhaps could not be subject to empirical investigation. Nevertheless the social sciences will continue to investigate religious behaviour and thinking as important parts of contemporary life but their conclusions should be considered as valuable and indicative viewpoints which should not be seen as statistical facts.

The Problems of Units of Measurement

The scales of involvement and the resulting statistics come from the need to divide material into categories to make it more manageable and hard science is very exact in its categories of measurement. To accept the fact that all humans are biologically, psychologically and in terms of social experience different makes the use of any categories explicitly unscientific. The social science attempt to be scientific in this respect is not much more than a delusion.

The commonest unit of measurement is age but while it is acceptable that there must be social and biological changes with age, the rate at which people change is not constant. Also however ages are divided up for analysis, those who are 29 and 30 years old are likely to be in different categories and such adjoining ages are likely to be similar in their characteristics. There is a more basic difficulty that we accept that people know their ages and if they do that they are prepared to disclose them to strangers or in answering a questionnaire to be used for some unknown and socially suspect purpose. Very few believe that their answers are kept confidential by the researchers.

Other categories of measurement, if not all are equally illusionary such as membership of a faith which can be assessed according to religious records and classifications, personal affirmations which may depend on who is asking and in answering questionnaires. The differences in the implications of recording oneself as a Hindu must be enormous between a woman who performs a daily '*puja*' at her household shrine and a businessman who would marry according to Sanskrit rituals because his prospective in-laws expect it. They have found a prospective date for which they have obtained a satisfactory horoscope from the combined birth-dates of the couple.

But there are other categories which in scientific terms can have no significance at all such as asking in a questionnaire or working out from the answers to questions whether an individual is very religious, average or not religious at all. Whatever categories are recorded there is very little or no confirmatory data which would support such categorisations. Such listings remain no more than a record on paper that someone sees fit at that particular time to circle one category rather than another for reasons about which we have no knowledge at all.

We can take the Allport-Ross Religious Orientation Scale (Allport and Ross, 1967) in which all the twenty-one questions lead towards religious answers. Complex considerations which might reasonably be appropriate to be answered by highly educated or reflective persons, but would have little relevance if put to a Hindu villager, Muslim pilgrim, Buddhist monk or a temple administrator in contemporary China whose answers would probably coincide to some extent with the government's known atheistic policies. Some of the questions to be graded could be taken as verging on the insulting as 'although I am a religious person I refuse to let religious considerations influence my everyday affairs'. Some of the alternatives in the Minnesotta Multiphasic Personality Inventory were found by African men training for the priesthood as both were morally wrong as in a question in another survey involving moral dilemmas 'the prayers I say when I am alone carry as much meaning as those said during services'. We should surely accept that attempts to categorize social and particularly spiritual behaviour rests on very shaky grounds because the replies are not only unverifiable but are themselves far from concrete. It would seem no more than a poorly legitimated method of making human material manageable.

Polygenic Causality: The Problem of Heredity

Against scientific knowledge genetic investigations are often socially biased by assumptions of single factor dominance as if the consequences could be similarly socially isolated. Since the majority of societies are patrilineal, it is often difficult to break away from this particularly as the majority of social scientists at least in the past have been men. In researching cousin marriages in the Afro-Arab community in Mombasa, Kenya (Tanner, 1964) it did not take long to get the patrilineal genealogies of all existing families from informants. The matrilineal line was persistently missed out even though there was a preference for marrying cousins from the mother's side.

Leaving aside such biological connections it must be obvious that any individual is likely to be influenced if not consistently socialised by at least two families and two sets of grandparents. Social and biological hereditary factors become very dispersed. When we have children who are in practice socially shared as in a joint family house among Hindus in Patna or Pakistanis in London, the problems of causation become increasingly complicated. A five year old Zigua child in Pangani, Tanzania had only spent six months in the same house with his parents and the Gonja a Ghanian tribal community exchange children on an almost compulsory basis (E. Goody, 1970). What someone may say as their views on spirituality and well-being and how they practice, even if correctly reported, has a very long pedigree indeed. We must assume that several totally different and unrelated psychological and social systems influence the consistent mental sets of everyone who act as informants (Gottesman, 1963). So as we trace backwards the possible reasons for behaviour which we can only do with the more obvious behaviour currently known, causation become very tenuous at best and we know even less of the conscious and unconscious strength of these 'hereditary' influences.

The Problem of Divergent Causality

Hard science is based on linear causality and primary facts and while it is quite possible to connect two events in a religious context and to state that one causes the other as in the change of a woman's name after a Western Christian marriage and the requirements for inheritance and divorce in Islamic law. These are primary connections and cannot be all-embracing explanations for situations in which the social backgrounds are different.

For most people in all cultures who have understandings related to spirituality or religion, these primary linear explanations and connections are not adequate and certainly not for social scientists looking into processes of thought. At one end of the scale an accident or illness is attributed to luck rather than to statistical inevitability and at the other to moral failings such as the Oxfordshire working man dying of cancer who asked ' what have I done to deserve this'. Others will see causation in ritual pollution and the malevolence of other people, ancestors or spirits.

So primary reasons are quite as acceptable to Kung Bushmen bitten by a snake as to a Kolkota business women who has lost out on a contract. They will both seek for and usually obtain reasons which are far more complex than the simplicities of these primary connections. There are certainly some linear causal connections from these primary simplicities but in addition there are always lateral complexities which invite interpretation rather than the possible rigidities of linear proof.

There is in this the problem of boundaries, how far back and how wide should the search for connections be made. We know that biologically a mutation at very low levels of social existence can catch on and become commonplace. It is not unreasonable to keep open these possibilities and to go beyond mathematical probabilities. Tata factory workers and Gujarati farmers will almost always think laterally rather than linearly just as would have been the thinking processes of Mahatma Gandhi and Jawaharlal Nehru. It is not only in the background to any individual's particularities that there is divergent causality but in their group affiliations and social behaviour generally, none of which can conform to the requirements of science.

The Weakness of Explanatory Derivations

The explanations which individuals may give of their spirituality ideas and practices may indeed be reasonably correct according to their own thinking and also with some of those with whom they associate. It is more likely to be in partial accordance with the expectations of that person who is asking the questions or the institutions to which they belong. It will also vary with mood swings, antecedent events and also possibly the weather. Why indeed should the answers be 'rational' explanations of matters which are unlikely to be experienced in the rationalistic framework of thinking implied by such a question. Whether the questions are asked by a relative, friend, priest or researcher the nuances in the replies will vary with their differences in age, status, occupation, sex and whether they are liked or likeable. So we can conclude that there is little in such relationships and their results which could be classed as scientifically valid. 'The human personality unless one approaches it with the postulate of impoverished reality, has in its context, structures and concerns, even in individual differences as to some of its 'laws' and very much in its origins, properties and relations that make the study of personality rather more similar to such disciplines as history, archaeology or the reconstruction of a criminal case from police evidence than the mechanisms of heredity' (Meene, 1978:809).

The only reliability is that a particular person has said or written these words at that time and place but how and why these words materialised would have to be the subject of specific and detailed enquiries. Such statements could be used as the bases for finding out the linguistic codes which are used in thinking about spirituality and the statistical frequencies of certain words and phrases. But beyond this these statements cannot form the bases of any scientific analyses; they can be no more than cumulative clues.

There can be many reasons for spiritual activities other than spirituality; membership of a religious group can enhance status, contribute to political action and indeed to qualify for an inheritance. Baptising twins in Ngara, Tanzania may have been to avoid the cost of complicated traditional rituals as was suspected by the priests. The birth of twins and their probable early deaths might equally have been a jolt which turned the parents towards Christianity and of course there are other possible contributing factors. Thus we can conclude that there is little in seeking the derivations of spirituality behaviour that can be allied to scientific methodology.

Unknown Critical Events

Every individual whether contacted by a social scientist or not have experienced a sequence of critical events in their lives which will certainly influence how they react to their current situations and how they will see themselves in relation to research. These critical events can be the experience of danger in warfare, accidents, getting through an examination with conspicuous credit, getting married, being present at the birth of a child, seeing one's harvest or house destroyed by floods. While some of these are commonplace in their critical nature every person will have had their own particular critical experiences. Whatever they have been the memories of them will remain with those individuals throughout their lives and not just as Post Traumatic Stress Disorders. So we should assume that the informants used in research and on whom the researchers depend, will each have had critical events in their lives. These may have made these men and women what they are and in how they view their contemporary environments of which the social scientists are a part. In most cases researchers know little

little about the private lives of the people with whom they are closely associated for the whole period of the research.

Researchers assume that their informants are 'normal' but we inevitably make no allowance unless we are directly approached, for the disasters which have occurred in their lives; sudden unemployment, animals destroying their crops, the deaths of partners or children, the burning down of a house and all their property, the theft of their few possessions. Researchers come from assured and relatively safe backgrounds so they have no personal experience of the personal disasters which can affect the lives of most of the world. The spread of AIDS, drops in the price of cash crops, corruption in the political system and the loss of morale that can come from the failure of political inspired development programmes. The list of factors outside the control of those that are being researched must always have a lasting influence on how individuals will see spirituality and well-being. These undefined and often unknown variables affect the potential scientific value of information received.

The Unnaturalness of Data Collection

Social scientists and their work are part of the societies in which they have been socialised and also part of those societies which they study. They are not and never can be detached from these social situations which initiate research, the research environments in which they carry out their professional work nor in the consequences of what they have done and published. All of this goes on with their own personalities and personal affairs in the background influencing their activities.

It seems a reasonable conclusion that social scientists are deviants to the accepted standards of their own societies and abnormal ones in the experience of the societies in which they work. In the sense of when they are publicly active, they are not much different to other branches of bureaucracy which claim a right to invade the privacies of others on the basis that it is in the public interest for more information to be known about how people behave. In the matter of researching religious behaviour it is hard to see that this is justified unless such activities are or might potentially be dangerous to the public good or economically costly to the communities in which they operate. Most of those researched have a shrewd idea that this work is being done to enhance the careers of the researchers.

Leaving aside the infrequent collection of data about religious practices when the subjects are under institutional control and see this is valuable to their own ideals and interests. Blood pressure data related to Buddhist and Christian monastic meditation. The DNA sampling and religious affiliations of the parents of children with inherited diseases for which the Amish preference for marrying partners from within their small communities and the Muslim more specific preference for marrying their cousins are certainly religious factors leading to considerable personal distress. This information is collected either by detached observation or by methodological intrusions.

Observations in which the social scientists act as flies on the wall so that in time they are not seen to be there at all and acceptable. Many people are doing just that in the normal courses of their lives; watching others is one of the commonest and most interesting of human activities for what is in public view. Of course, there are drawbacks to this as to where and when it can be done but it cannot be classified as deviant behaviour unless the watchers behave in ways that make their behaviour deviant; a camera among other cameras is acceptable but perhaps not a single one so the observer has to socially conform. They cannot expect to be excused from what is locally considered to be good manners because of their professional requirements and of course by conforming they learn something about what those societies require of their members.

For social scientists to be unobtrusive is not at all easy when they have been socialised to behave in certain ways which may will clash with the requirements of the societies in which they work over the public subordination of women and in body language generally. However, overall participation as a stranger is not a deviant activity by definition because few societies are so enclosed that their members have no known ways of relating to strangers. The notice on a Hindu temple prohibiting the entrance of Christians as do notices on the boundaries of Mecca do not make social scientists into deviants but merely show that it is necessary to be a Hindu or a Muslim to cross these boundaries. It would thus be reasonable to suggest that participant observation of religious activities is an acceptable way of collecting data. Remembering that intruding into the social secrecies of others without their agreement is always going to be a deviant activity and as such always going to be methodologically unsound.

Interviewing might best be looked at in terms of the social distance between those involved. The prolonged discussions between social scientists and their regular informants, of which there will always be a very few preferred relationships which may continue for years. These are not much different to relationships which many people have in all societies and the fact that one partner is an outsider, does not necessarily make the relationship into a deviant one.

Formal isolated interviews for which there are no parallels in those societies must usually be seen as a deviant activity particularly when they are carried out with a sample chosen because those to be interviewed conform to certain known personal categories. In what might be called 'normal' social life at whatever level of economic and political development, interviews do not occur except for bureaucratic and institutional needs in medicine, law and in the selection processes in education and employment. It is certainly a modern activity as a way of recording personal data as quickly as possible and in isolated environments which do not resemble commonplace social relationships. There is no pretence at equality in such interviews in which those being interviewed are usually on the defensive. The interviewer is often speaking in a status related accent and using a different linguistic code to the normal speech of those being interviewed (Andrews and Engelhart, 1979). This is likely to be particularly so in religious matters as the interviewers are not often of the same religious beliefs as those being interviewed and would certainly see the subject matter in more intellectual and abstract terms than would those most interviewed.

If this is an unnatural relationship there is no particular reasons to think that the answers will necessarily be correctly related to the questions asked but more likely to be correct in relation to the situation in which they are asked. There may be a parallel in the adjudication of customary disputes, in which there is rarely such an arrangement as putting a witness on oath as it is assumed that whatever they say will relate to their position in the case which is now a public matter. However, when it comes to matters which are more private it seems intrinsically unlikely that anyone being interviewed will expose their views to a stranger. That person is not a friend, unless they see some personal advantage in providing answers, economically, politically, just out of conceit at being consulted at all by some higher status outsider or to cover up what they really feel or have done.

There may be another more important aspect which points to the unreliability of interviewing about the extremely private matter of religious behaviour of which only a small proportion of ideas and practices may be public. It is necessary to stress again that for almost all people they may never have had to express themselves about such intimate matters. More importantly they may never have thought out what they do believe in and why they practice. No matter whether the questions asked are specific or general in their answers, those interviewers have to use specific words.

It seems unlikely that interviews or the replies to questionnaires about religious behaviour are ever likely to provide data which correlates closely to the unknown and ever changing workings of the individual mind. Interviews may infer indirectly rather more than they elucidate what individuals do and think about their relationships with the divine. It seems astonishing that professionally sceptical social scientists should accept so readily the accuracy of the answers to interviews and to express their results numerically. In an inventory of the religious beliefs of college students, there is no reason to suppose that any of the individuals involved think in terms so convenient for the decimal system (Brown and Lowe, 1951). One is inclined to conclude that the numerically calculated results of large scale interviewing and administration of questionnaires may provide those involved in a sense of achievement. They have piles of paper to assure themselves that they have worked hard and got results.

The most striking fact about social science studies of religious behaviour is the repetitive use of the word empirical or the implications that their work is based on and approach the required standards of science. If the researcher records on camera the congregation at and ceremonies in a mosque, temple, church or synagogue, the result is certainly facts. Why they are there and of what they are thinking while going through the body movements of worship, there are no comparable facts. Moreover the methodologies which are used to produce facts do not do so; it is a fact that an individual may state that he has encountered the spirits of his ancestors or that the divine has talked to him but these are not facts that such relationships have occurred but only that he or she states that they have. To go further than this is a leap of imagination which may be true but it is not social science to state that it is.

It seems likely that quietly and as unobtrusively as possible observing religious behaviour is the method most likely to provide acceptable data about religious activities which are not personally known to them. There is always the fact that these observers in terms of accuracy are always a limited tool because of personal biases and the limitations of observation. It may be that we must rely on what we can learn from qualitative research methods.

3 Qualitative Approaches Towards Understanding Human Behaviour

We have established that the quantifying of social behaviour related to spirituality and well-being is unlikely to be accurate even in the collection of primary data in the senses intended by these researchers. What is being analysed cannot be isolated from other factors or indeed defined according to the standards required by science. The very process makes it certain that what is recorded is not all that likely to be a recognisable reproduction of what is being researched.

More particularly these quantifying methodologies for the collection of data have to be carried out in ways which have no known parallels in what might be called 'naturally' occurring social behaviour. It is the ways in which information is collected that may change behaviour by taking it out of the wider contexts in which it has to have occurred. These are alienating processes which consciously or unconsciously distort the data particularly over matters which most people consider to be not only private but very personal.

If the purpose of research is to attempt to reproduce and analyse human behaviour in ways that mirror what is happening, then other ways have to be used. Most socio-biologists would accept that to examine the behaviour of caged chimpanzees is going to be different to that of free-ranging ones. Why should social scientists accept as real the human behaviour confined by the constraints of methodologies based on the requirements of hard science be any different. The goal of social research is to understand behaviour in its natural setting.

We have the possibilities of catching the meanings of social behaviour by means which are different to and less alienating than the methodologies which are required by science. In fact to split the professional title of these researchers so as to continue with the social aspects of humans behaviour in relation to spirituality and well-being and to discard the word 'science' which presupposes the overall possibilities of obtaining accurate information about human behaviour which can be checked by other subsequent researchers.

Thus some of the disadvantages which we have discussed in relation to quantifying human data can be turned round to be seen as part of the normal human condition of which the researchers as much as the researched must always be a part whether they are in a research project or outside it. These may be useful ways of finding out what is going on because they are just the usual indefinable factors which make up life as it is. The variables which are to some extent modifying the behaviour of those involved as there will always be such factors as choice, luck and personality as these are the channels through which human behaviour occurs.

Cannot researchers be considered to be behaving more or less normally looking into what is going on around them, distorted no doubt by the fact that they are outsiders if not in reality but at least in their own minds to be so. Much more socially inserted into their field of research as a person than would have been the case with the requirements of scientific methodology. How else might it be possible to find out information of behaviour relating to spirituality and well-being, but it will be always constrained by the limitations of humans observation.

The Ethical Constraints on Social Science Research

Religious research even more than less complex research topics is filled with ethical issues involving intrusions into the private affairs of individuals and communities. How far can the researcher go in asking questions about what is often abnormal forms of behaviour? Questioning often goes beyond what such involved people would consider reasonable in the context of passing information on a need to know basis which can rarely include social strangers.

To what extent can researchers go beyond the normalities of participation in community life in order to see and understand more of what is going on. Such intrusions would disturb their own forms of spirituality should they be the objects of such research. To do so makes the researcher into a total outsider who is behaving badly and insensitively almost by international standards. An Irishmen, the local school teacher commented on reading what the researcher had concluded about their community "it is not your science I'm questioning, but this, don't we have the right to lead unexamined lives, the right not to be analysed. Don't we have a right to hold into an image of ourselves as different...but as innocent and unblemished all the same". The researcher created a public shame as there is 'a distinction between whispering something beside the fire or over a counter and seeing it printed for all to see. Why did you have to write it in a way that we could read it and understand exactly what you were saying' (Scheper-Hughes, 1982). Similarly, a study in Ghana concluded that a number of those people thought to be possessed by spirits were probably schizophrenics (Field, 1960). This might will have given rise to similar misgivings if those people had been able to read in their own language what the researcher's conclusions had disclosed about them for all to read.

So there is the issue over the disclosure of privileged information. If the aim of research is to influence decision-makers for the greater good of some section of mankind, what degree and amount of disclosure is justified if the result would lead to even further dissent? Are the researchers justified in asking questions about conformities to orthodoxies if the forms of spirituality practiced is seen by parts of those societies as abnormal and deviant?

There are issues over intellectual property rights which are clear enough when they have been committed to paper and are copyrighted. Many ideas which go to make up the component parts of published research work have been provided by non-literates who assumed some measure of social equality with the social scientists to whom they have given information in good faith according to their own social standards (Masoga, 2002). This is an important ethical issue when these informants subsequently become researchers in their own right.

If a fieldworker is taking details from a limited number of informants in one to one sessions in which what they say is recorded as nearly verbatim as possible, who in fact is the author of the final report. It comes out under the researcher's name, but this could be seen as a form of theft unless the producers of the information have signed release forms. In a way it is a competition for authorship and a process in which the author becomes alienated from his or her sources. A moral split from an interpersonal relationship in which both parties are constrained by mutual access to moral guide lines into a situation in which the researchers have abrogated to themselves the right to property which they do not own in this total sense; a termination of dialogue.

The Elements of Fieldwork

The three basic components of fieldwork, the researcher, the project and the people researched are not covered in equal proportions in reports on completed fieldwork. Their introductions deal with the status of the fieldworker and a list of professional colleagues for whom they feel a combination of academic political need and professional gratitude for advice over what they have written.

What else is known about these fieldworkers without whom the research would not have been planned, worked or reported on. Overall not much almost as if it was not important that they should be real people not more or less abstract entities. Their age can be guessed at, their sex can often only be known by their use of their first names in the author's title and possibly from the dedication whether they have partners, parents and children. Yet the whole report pivots round their personal abilities and circumstances; how on earth did Kumar manage her research on Banaras artisans when she was breast feeding her first child (Kumar, 1992); this information only came from a latter book on her

Banaras fieldwork. How did Colin Turnbull manage his fieldwork when he was accompanied by his male partner of long standing and working in communities which would not have been tolerant about homosexuality (Grinker, 2000).

Other than what is disclosed in their professional writings very little is available which would put these men and women into a humanized perspective made necessary by the simple fact that they did their research in entirely individual ways. There is no way in which fieldwork in the social sciences can be paralleled to research work in the hard sciences. Hypothetically the persons doing that type of research have no personal characteristics at all except for allowing personal bias and inefficiency to disturb the process. But in rather obvious terms this cannot be realistic in social science research.

In the field situation the researchers are faced with a great variety of personalized situations to which they have to react actively or passively. Whatever degree of success is achieved comes from their individual ability to cope with an ever changing variety of human activities in a strange social and physical environment. It seems likely that the results put into print have undergone some personal censorship about their version of events over the period(s) in the field. Where diaries exist, we have no knowledge as to the extent that they have been altered. There is certainly no guarantee that they are any more or less accurate than the fieldwork reported to have been done in the same period. The degree to which they coincide with actual events is certainly obscure.

The diaries of Malinowski (Malinowski, 1967) are regarded as important because of the author's pre-eminence as an anthropologist and because of their uniqueness but they have certainly been edited in deference to his surviving family. His widow refers to the removal of a few extremely intimate observations but we have no knowledge of what they may have been. An anthropologist who went to him for advice in Cambridge in 1926 wrote to his fiancée that he had been advised how to get a native mistress (Gardiner,1984).

The fieldworkers have to be seen as people who have characteristics and abilities which antedate and coincide with their research abilities. In the hard sciences the apparatus and personnel through which the data is obtained are available for public scrutiny. In the social sciences this essential element tends not to be given the importance which in their role as researchers necessitates. Everything depends on the extent to which they personally obtained and filtered the information which became available to them. It is not just methodology which is important but the ways in which individuals as personalities develop and use the methods which are available to them.

Researchers as Objects of Scrutiny

Few individuals realise the implications that as researchers away from the trails of tourism, they are always and inevitably objects of scrutiny and speculation. It is curious that this should be so when they are entering environments which are new to them just as their presence there is new to those people. They are classified as strangers whether this situation is a village, occupational group or indeed a university.

It would seem that researchers assume that because they have official and self-assumed status of social scientists that they can individually slip into a community in much the same way that a doctor or nurse might slip into a new posting to a hospital or clinic. They are often unwelcome in situations which communities or persons consider important and private (Laitin, 1986:35). Intrusion on Lutheran worship in London is no more acceptable than intrusion into Yoruba worship in Lagos.

Unless they are researching under cover in the total sense rather than merely disguising the real purposes behind their presence, they will always enter the field of their research as strangers. They remain so for most of the people they meet for most of the time even if they have established equitable relationships with the community as a whole over a limited range of rather public activities. They will always be objects of scrutiny more than just passing interest because they do not fit into the available roles in any community. They have no job and curiosity is not usually seen as a benign characteristic in anyone. Of course, there may be communities which accept a resident researcher as just another example of migratory intellectuals in business or university living in dormitory suburb.

Even if they may be accepted by the limited few who see the purpose of research and who get some personal advantages from being incorporated in such activities, for the majority they remain outsiders. They will want to know as much as possible about how their personal behaviour differs from their own. This curiosity about the behaviour of researchers will be much the same whether they are non-nationals or internal expatriate nationals. At this level the personal hygiene and body language of researchers will be of as much interest as their tentative and perhaps inadequate use of the local language and how to behave as they work on religion and spirituality which makes them seem to be no more than poorly socialised adolescents.

The greater the ethnic and cultural differences between researchers and those researched, the greater the extent of this curiosity. In the background there is always an intellectual distancing between those involved which makes the scrutiny of the researchers more detailed and perhaps more hostile. No one likes to be visited for too long by people whom they assess to be or consider themselves to be intellectually superior. Strangers who come and do not go like so many other visitors which the community may have experienced, will always be the subject to some adverse speculation. The lives of those researched whether subsistence farmers or urban casual workers which are dominated by the realities of day-to-day necessities mean that they have no reason to assume that researchers will be any benefit to them and so their scrutiny will usually be more than curiosity. In every research situation the researchers and the researched as individuals are different to most by reason of age, sex and ethnicity as well as by as many self-assumed roles as may be considered.

The social scientists at work are always going to be objects of scrutiny on the grounds of suspicion or curiosity. It is probable that only within the parameters of university life or within institutions which have used such professionals before, can they expect to work unnoticed. It is a small circumscribed world in which their work and their ideas are as subject to as much jealousy and misunderstandings as would be the case with lawyers, actresses and doctors.

Whatever these strangers who classify themselves as social scientists are up to is interpreted by those they meet in their terms. This probably means that they will not believe that strangers can be inconveniencing themselves to the extent of living away from their homes without substantial financial gain. After all in their own communities knowledge is power and information is rarely given away without something being taken in exchange. They would know that researchers are being paid to do this work (Patwardhan, 1979) as indeed they are in their own socio-economic systems. They are very unlikely to believe that there is such a thing as the disinterested search for knowledge even if it could be translated. They would sense such an idea to be hypocritical as relating to the researcher in their midst.

The Spectrum of Bias

Any assessment of bias is complicated enough without recognising that it is usually considered in the context of the researchers while it must be equally relevant to consider it from the point of view of the biases of the researched. There may be individuals but surely no communities or institutions which have not heard of or experienced enquiries about their affairs being conducted by outsiders as to what they are doing and moreover it rarely results in benefits to them.

To the understandings of 'simpler' people this seems to be the sort of behaviour to be expected from outsiders; the agents of outside institutions, schools, churches, health authorities, police, agricultural inspectors, tax collectors and the agents of political parties. There is no reason to suppose that the receivers of these attentions from outsiders see the researchers as any different until they learn or indeed never learn to see them as otherwise. So there is usually a background varying from ambivalence to newcomers to covert and overt hostility. At another level there is some knowledge of what the researchers are trying to do or find out. There may be more specific reactions that they just dislike being the objects of investigation by a young outsider whether national or non-national. These predispositions might involve a variety of social distance factors; a dislike of the educated and newcomers based on previous experiences or just rumours.

It is safe to assume that social scientists in their fieldwork are always biased. The failure to recognise this inevitability comes in part from the refusal of the social scientists to free themselves from the burden of thinking that they can ever copy the methodological approaches and procedures of the hard sciences in researching human behaviour. It is not so much that North American anthropologists will produce white American anthropology (Hsu, 1975:206) but that Chinese, Saudi Arabian and Indian ones will remain similarly structured within their own cultural and religious paradigms. It would then be incorrect to refer to this as bias when it is the inevitable result of their socialisation. Social scientists whatever their cultural origins will see the world outside themselves through these culturally provided spectacles, however much they may understand and appreciate the whys and wherefores of other types of cultural behaviour. It is theoretically possible to brain wash an individual according to the scenario of the novel 'The Manchurian Candidate' (Condon, 1959). But whether this would be possible for a researcher remains no more than intriguingly implausible. Who would agree to be being the subject of such an experiment and indeed this would result in just another form of structured bias created for a purely intellectual purpose.

It is not simply a question of getting a community's agreement to the research and the presence of the researcher in their area and from then on rapport is established. The researchers themselves change with their experience and may become so acculturated to their host's understandings that they loose detachment even to the extent of referring to them as 'my' people. Glazier's sixteen years with the Spiritual Baptists of Trinidad must have resulted in some mutual tolerance and possibly affection (Glazier, 1993). Others may find that their lack of progress makes them show their likes and dislikes. In the end they may long to get away to their own sort of people and a more self-accepting social environment. Living among strangers on whom they are dependent for information can be very stressful.

Those with whom they are working may also change in finding the intrusions in their lives much more unacceptable than they anticipated. The social and political climate may change so that they are seen as intrusive strangers allied to an alien or central government which has upset them. In socially divided societies such as India with its multiplicity of castes, religious and ethnic divisions, there are many opportunities to take objections on religious grounds to both internal and external researchers however well connected and previously acceptable.

The perspectives of social scientists affects what they see and in turn the results obtained and indeed it could not be otherwise. This is simply because they use themselves as research instruments to record what goes on around them. Even if they were some type of permanently working machine recording what they see, hear, smell, touch and taste, they would still be recording in one direction at a time rather than another. The directed camera and microphone are accurate for the direction at which they are pointed by the fieldworker but have no relevance at all for what goes on behind their backs.

The most serious problem for the national occurs when both national and non-national researchers produce quantitative data which they state has come from their examination of their fieldwork data. The examination of sets of figures which have been gathered without any personal influence on the situation is debatable but at least initially acceptable. But once we have qualitative data in which informants produce their own data for the evaluation of the researchers, then the national researcher is faced with the dilemmas of filtering this information through personal social understandings. These are biasing their conclusions more than they would possibly like to admit. Researchers cannot avoid being emotionally involved to some degree in their qualitative assessments of what they are observing . What non-nationals might describe as no more than an evaluative analysis, might will be assessed as criticism by more directly emotionally involved nationals which is either not justified or should not be publicised anyway.

The language in which they report their findings may not be their own natal language. This is often strikingly different to the researchers' own private use of the same language and the linguistic code used by their informants. At best there is a process of careful translation and at worst a built-in dissimilarity from the professional dialect in which researchers were trained and read in their textbooks. It would be rare indeed for a reader to find that what they read is what the informants actually said. It is rumoured that Mrs. Seligman on seeing a naked Nuer man on the banks of the southern Nile, remarked that it was hard for her to believe that such a man could have the complex metaphysical thoughts written up by Professor Evans-Pritchard. Leaving aside the possibly colonial bias in such a statement she has certainly touched on a valid point.

Of course, the non-national is biased by the enormous geographical and social distance between the researchers and the researched unless they are researching communities in which there may be a substantial amount of social sharing. They will still be some one's daughter or son and have the attributes of age and social status from education. If they do research in an institution such as a religious community they will still have the biases built into the roles they assume or are pinned on to them. There can only be the questionable neutrality of any social researcher's role. The indigenous social scientist is not necessarily aided by the absence of national and geographical distancing as they will always be part of the nation building process and are mentally involved. The fact that they may understand basic values is no more neutral than the more academic pretensions of outsiders (Koentjarahimgrat, 1982). There is also the bias in which social scientists in their research treat one part of mankind as an object. In its less recent forms their endeavours come from an era of violence in which the Western world's physical and ideological invasion of the non-European arena (Levi-Strauss, 1966).

Also there is the bias which comes from the excitements of exposure to new situations with culture shock almost a rite of passage for social scientists (Nash, 1963), which cannot be confined to non-nationals. Only a few social scientists spend prolonged periods of study within a single community. Family life and careers often clash with fieldwork away from home and work places. There is usually the bias which comes from the brevity of their exposure to new situations. Geertz who spent two years each in his studies of Morocco and Java (Geertz, 1960, 1968), whereas Glazier spent sixteen years in researching the Spiritual Baptists of Trinidad (Glazier, 1993). Each will have had their personal forms of bias dictated by time spent in their fieldwork. Any individual in their social environments will in the first instance see and experience their inter-relationships in personal terms. Those involved have personal names and the pronouns used are personal and not collective ones. At first it is a Baluchi named Abbul who spoke to the researcher on a certain subject on a certain date and at a certain place and it is only very much latter that the researcher may refer to 'the Baluchi', when their knowledge may still come from a very few informants. So it is only with expanding social distances that people come to be seen in terms of imputed and imposed group characteristics; Bosnians, Baluchis and Basukumas who now have the following stereotypical characteristics. All the time the social scientists know full well that the Baluchis individually may have some but not necessarily all of these characteristics. Stereotypes are maintained rather than created and used for the convenience of their users without much regard for the realities of what these people may do and think. How does this affect trained social scientists in their fieldwork. Of course, they will still experience their own particular interrelationships but whether they admit it to themselves or not, they will still tend to think in stereotypical ways about 'insiders'.

Professional training has to proceed in ways that do not coincide with the social lives of either teachers or trainees. They learn about the generalities of human behaviour not only about how Zunis or Zulus go about their lives in general but that certain behaviour is to be expected that the mother's brother should behave in a certain way. They cannot be taught what happens when here is no mother's brother in existence. Professional training as a foundation never goes much beyond the 'typical' persons whether land-owners, AIDS sufferers, cattle thieves or priests. 'they tend to overrate the influence of beliefs on behaviour, to overemphasize homogeneity, to overdo order and coherence and underplay exceptions and contractions and to emphasize structure at the cost of process (Hollander, 1967). In the time allowed it is inevitable that the teaching of information should be grouped in this way. Any teaching that concentrated on a spectrum of behaviour in which the limits are totally dissimilar would undercut the requirements of teaching.

Even though the social scientists know that there are five million individual Sukuma and that the same number of individuals live in Nagpur and that each household, housing block or hamlet will be dissimilar in personal characteristics and experience, collective behaviour will always emerge out of fieldwork projects unless the study itself is of a particular circumscribed group as with Lewis's work on a Mexican family (O. Lewis, 1959). Then of course there comes the inevitable difficulty that the Sukuma and the people of Nagpur will say that they do not behave according to the stereotypes which the socials scientists have created.

Any fieldwork which involves the forming of interpersonal relationships must of necessity mean the taking up of a viewpoint even if the researchers recognise that it is not so much that as a necessity of being participant observers. A Sukuma, social scientist would view hostility to the Maasai living to their east as part of the paradigm within which they are living. Just as Indian researchers would think within the caste paradigms of their own position. British children in the southern naval port of Portsmouth which was heavily bombed in Second World War by the Germans, see their traditional enemies to be the French because of the prolonged naval war with Napoleon in a previous century.

The non-national researchers might accept that within their own country such biases exist. They would attempt to stand outside such paradigmatic biases without realising that to become participant observers, however nominally, they must become involved in the more prominent of these biases. A researcher living with Brahmins in a Brahmin dominated Tamil Nadu village had to accept his host's objections to outcastes visiting him in their house. 'If I was to be given access to their homes and temples to which access was not given easily to outsiders, I could not violate their (religious) sentiments at will (Beteille, 1975). Social scientists in their fieldwork may have to recognise that they cannot be both 'this' and 'that' at the same time. Their view of society may always be biased not only by these more sophisticated biases but by the simple fact that they are male or female, old or young and that some of those people with whom they are working appear benevolent and others malevolent. This is just the way that humans work out their lives in collected networks of preferences and avoidances from which even the most experienced social scientist is no exception.

Bias is a hostile word and every researcher flinches from its application to themselves even though they have to admit that they see their research objectives through very individual perspectives. They cannot avoid this without adopting an almost clone-like assumptions about researchers in general. In fact we have to accept the realities of prejudice as we all have likes and dislikes in what we see and interpret and no amount of introspection is going to take this out of our perspectives.

What we have to come to an understanding of is 'the prejudices of good people'(Esmail, 2004; Seth and Seligman, 1993), which start with the nature of research. There are first of all fashions in the subjects of research; what is chosen and what is not chosen. Any look at the Index Medicus shows that certain diseases are so to speak popular and attract research funds. In the social sciences great areas of social behaviour have received very little attention such as excreting because it is seen as a distasteful topic and not likely to enhance academic reputations. Much the same might apply to corruption in less developed and developing societies of which everyone is aware but which researchers and donors avoid working on because it is both dangerous and likely to lead to exclusions from countries. Researchers are often socially and religiously blind to political matters which would adversely affect their own research interests.

An interesting comment on the nature of scientific interests was made by the Editor of the *British Medical Journal* (Editor, 2004), 'I am interested in the study showing a steady rise in the hospital admissions for acute pancreatitis because my brother had pancreatitis; it may be indeed that link had something to do with the study making it into the journal, just as it has been suggested that the *British Medical Journal* publishes on toe-nail fungus because so many of the editorial team suffer from it, and so on'. Perhaps we should accept that the choice of research venues by non-nationals may will be influenced by travel brochures and articles in the *National Geographical Journal* or indeed just to get away from their own societies and partners.

There are also difficult issues in research environments in which there is a dominant religion. In popular imagination however illogical it may be individuals even if they are obviously strangers, are either believers or not. The status of being a non-practising member of their faith is understood well enough but not that of having a detached view of any religion is not appreciated. We have seen the case of the researcher who was studying a Pentecostal community and was seen by them as investigating them with a view to their own conversion. There is always the problem when the researchers faith can be inferred from their name as to whether they are Christians, Hindus or Muslims, and whether the researchers are still unconsciously thinking in terms of the faiths in which they no longer believe or practice.

Professor Srinivas by his name was obviously a Hindu and it was assumed that he was an atheist because he did not behave as a Hindu in the village which he was researching. He was nevertheless reprimanded for not shaving after bathing which was considered polluting. Since the grape-vine knew that he was a Brahmin even though he did not keep to the required caste diet, he was nevertheless given gifts at weddings in order to obtain benefits from his religious status (Srinivas, 1979).

The assumption that a researcher is a Hindu lacks social specificity and there was a need in a Gujarat village for him to slot himself into a sub-caste so that he could be seen as normal (Shah, 1979). Such a fieldworker's attempts to get to know all sections of the community they are studying, will come up against the restrictions of caste. There are always unforeseen consequences as when a researcher was seen to break his caste by accepting a glass of milk from an Untouchable (Chakavarti, 1979), or after they have been seen talking to Untouchables they will be asked to wash their hands and feet before entering a caste household (Dua, 1979). Once Hindu researchers are identified by their caste, then caste requirements channel the ways in which they can be communicated with and their research across caste boundaries had to be carried out in permissible places for such inter-caste contacts which were rice fields, semi-public bathing and temple bathing pools and the sites of bullock races (Unni, 1979).

It seems likely that even the most liberal minded of male researchers will have a mind-set that comes from socialisation into a male framework of thinking. This is likely to be even more so when the language used by men is in many respects different to that used by women. Their informants are almost all male and even female researchers would tend to have much the same range of male informants except when they are working on matters from which men would be excluded. This exclusion from the structures of male dominance does not mean that even in the most sexually segregated of societies that women are without influence. The rise of education for women in Saudi Arabia is said to have been due to the influence of the only wife of a previous ruler. Male researchers have to learn that women have their own networks of power which should not be classified as gossip. Their absence from public political life and their silence at public meetings makes their covert influence all the more significant.

On occasions obvious blocks to the possibilities of research can be overcome by influence and persistence. A Bengali Hindu woman married to an American managed to do research in Pakistan on the few remaining members of the Red Shirt pre-Independence non-violent movement. She not only got round official objections but got herself accepted in the Muslim community where these men lived, because of an earlier contact in Delhi with the son of the movement's founder who got her a visa for Pakistan, but even with this help it took two years (Bannerjea, 2000).The point surely is that as a national she could take her time to work her way into such a project which no non-national would have had the persistence to pursue so diligently.

Restrictions from the Expectations of Others

Research in the social sciences is rarely if ever isolated from the political and popular needs of the surrounding societies. The only exceptions may be research that nationals are able to do in their own societies as part of their existing commitments or in their spare time and with their own funds. Certainly individual researchers are looking over their shoulders as to the effects of their research on others; nothing is done in a professional vacuum.

Are the results going to be acceptable within the boundaries of the field being studied and to what extent is attention paid to the sensitivities of those who have been studied. They should not be upset in ways that the researchers themselves would not like. There is an English saying that 'there is no such thing as a free lunch' and this certainly applies to fieldwork everywhere.

What is being expected of the researchers by those researched as no one is providing information for nothing. Something is being taken away and what is it being replaced by. With particular informants these expectations are higher but also handicapping and in some cases socially and physically dangerous. They are inclined to see researchers as friends while the latter would not think in terms of such close relationships. The researchers have to think rationally of what returns they can give for information so that it is often an economic issue. But there can also be restrictions on access over which neither the researchers nor the researched can be said to have much control. In one Indian case in which the ominous behaviour of a cow prevented a woman researcher from getting access to the information which she wanted (Varadachar, 1979).

Researchers have to think of their own careers and they are thus guided by the advice of their controllers who have their own specialised interests in mind and how their own professionalism can be advanced. There are upsetting topics which nationals are likely to avoid just as there are methodologies which are closed to non-nationals.

The Biases of Omission

The non-national researcher rather more than the national one are looking for aspects of social and religious behaviour which they have been preconditioned to search for by training and their own cultural socialisations. Whether they like it or not they are inclined if not subconsciously forced to see the community which they are researching as bits and pieces of some cultural whole which is beyond assessment. Other than the fact that they can see people going about their daily routines, what they encounter beyond this is connected to what their informants provide and what their own segmented observations lead them to follow up. Their field notes reflect this and as trained social scientists they are not comfortable to consciously go beyond this limited data.

There is an analogy here to the analysis of poetry whether it is in their natal language such as Japanese looking at their abbreviated 'haiku' verses or the similar choruses of the Tanzanian Sukuma dance songs. The words can be broken down into their dictionary meanings, their phonemes and grammatical connections. What they mean may be beyond the comprehension of national and non-nationals regardless of their intellectual capacities; understandings are in reality very personal.

Most researchers would agree at least in private that their own culture is at least emotionally superior to that of the people they are studying. It may will take years of close associations with the people they are researching to go beyond the closed world of information supplied by informants. It ends up as some understanding of what they may have missed rather than what they have found.

The readers of the reports of fieldworkers about the behaviour of these cultural strangers will rarely find descriptions of kindly people with some goodness in their behaviour. There will be details of quarrels and matters of dispute. It is perhaps hard to accept that the indexes of such studies whether they are written by nationals or non-nationals would be more likely to contain pages referring to sorcery, competition and bride-wealth rather than such concepts as love, kindness, consideration and altruism (Hau'opa, 1975). To a certain extent this comes from insensitivity since most people find it difficult to attribute to others the sensibilities which they would apply to themselves. It is more likely that this is a methodological omission; these attributes are not what are looked for and therefore, they do not feature in professional writings.

On the other hand there is ample work on the nature of altruism and pro-social behaviour from experimental work by psychologists working with small samples in developed societies. It is perhaps in that shared cultural milieu in which nationals are researching nationals that such benign attributes are searched for and found. In reverse there is a bias against researching 'evil', because it would be difficult to find a sample free from bias. Mao Tse Tung stated in 1956 that without investigation of the lives of ordinary Chinese, no party member had any right to speak and that this knowledge was inseparable from their direct experiences among the people for whom they spoke.

However, national researchers in less developed societies must often start with the assumption that those they are working with have positive virtues. The diminished cultural distance between upper and lower caste Hindus involves some sharing of ideas and a common humanism which would not be the case with a non-national who may miss much outside their intellectual understandings. It would be difficult to find a Kikuyu or Baluchi researching their own societies who would highlight the negative aspects of their cultures to the exclusion of more positive values.

The Issue of Representations

In the taking of photographs and the recording of activities on tape in which the operators have no role other than pointing the camera or microphone, there is the assumption that what is being recorded is as near as possible 'natural' to these situations. These machines are pointed and beyond this they do not pick and choose and so in this respect they are rightly considered to be neutral. It is not readily accepted that in the way they are pointed that they are taking up particular standpoints. It is not just a question of how the recorded data are interpreted. An informant in prison research remarked that when there was a disturbance, it was probably a cover up for something which was happening in the opposite direction (Tanner, 1970). These ubiquitous machines which are now almost part of the standard equipment of social science researchers have an underlying bias in their use. In such situations there are always some base lines of usable reality. This is what the camera saw and this is what was said into the microphone. Two anthropologists, the photographer and a specialist in religious rituals looking at a series of photographs of the initiation rites of the Sukuma form of the Buchwezi 'secret' society in Tanzania saw different things; such 'facts' have to be interpreted.

Even if we accept that photographs come from aimed cameras, they are still dated evidence of certain activities of some behaviour and as such can be interpreted sequentially by generations to come. The earlier part of the 20th century had the Western custom of exchanging postcards in their hundreds of thousands and these are available in large numbers depicting insider and outsider aspects of life including religious ceremonies and personnel in India, Burma and the Sudan as well as for North Africa and Egypt and elsewhere (Tanner, 2003) for which no other data is available in such quantities.

Even if these researchers can pick and choose what is recorded mechanically they often choose what is unusual in terms of their own cultural understandings which are perhaps concentrated around their own high social status as intellectuals. What goes on in a corner tea-shop everyday is much less likely to be photographed than a religious procession whether in Birmingham or Bamako.

The Importance of the Researchers as Personalities

Whenever social scientists in their research have any personal relationships with any of the people with whom they are working, this behaviour is governed by the patterns which are to a large extent customary in their dealings with the researched and for the researched what they consider appropriate for dealing with strangers. This is an altogether different situation to the detachment built into sampling and studies which are statistically designed to avoid more personal relationships.

It may will be that the use of quantifiable methodologies require no particular personality qualities and that their results are unlikely to produce verifiable results that do no more than correlate the practices of spirituality to identified diseases. In many cases such quantified research involves no more than minimal interrelationships with colleagues and virtually none at all with the people who are being researched. A knowledge of statistical methods would be sufficient. Quite independent of the many other factors of importance to personal relationships leading towards any understandings of spirituality such as age, sex, personal appearance, intellect, marital status and religious affiliation. There are complex and perhaps unresolvable problems in researching within Hindu culture and have the religious status of a *Dalit* and being unmarried in societies in which the unmarried adults have low status.

So we are left with qualitative methodology as the way that social scientists can endeavour to understand spirituality and well-being, People who are not necessarily articulate enough to detail their own feelings and behaviour and moreover are only likely to expose them to strangers whom they find personally acceptable. Even the medical profession is concerned that although much may be known of the molecular pathology of a condition, little is known about the reliability of clinical diagnoses or about prognosis and the factors that affect it (Rothwell, 2006).

Since most qualitative research is done with very few continuously involved informants what is experienced by the researchers and what is recorded and published is to a major extent part of those social scientists' autobiographies. These men and women are experiencing particular relationships in particular circumstances and this is personal to them alone. It cannot be categorised into a set form with its consequences because both the researchers, the researched and the circumstances in which they are relating are inevitably variable and indeed variable from one conversation to the next. This is to miss out in any assessment of the behaviour of the researched the characteristics of the researchers and this detracts from the value which can be placed on the results; a review of a play in which there are no references to the actors.

Qualitative research has to involve the development and maintenance of close personal relationships under conditions which are strange to both the researchers and the researched, yet we seem to know much more about the latter than the former. Yet while this may not have been of much importance in quantitative survey work even into religious behaviour and spirituality understandings, qualitative understandings are much more personal both in what it involves and in what is interpreted. This approach to the gathering of information is an altogether more emotional matter as by its methodological nature, it is limited to the very small number of people with whom researchers can establish close enough relationships to see and begin to understand the underside of human behaviour. This cannot be found from questionnaires, interviews and self-produced documentations. Many researchers who have had long-term and detailed research relationships ostensibly with a community end up admitting that their work there and their conclusions were in fact dependent on half a dozen people with whom they had established close relationships which were at least as personally satisfying as the research itself.

It is not only that these limited number of people with whom the researchers have established personal relationships from which data cannot be quantified but they are placed by accident rather than intention outside the professional methodological restrictions of the social sciences. Thus for the duration of the research, the researchers and their own personal circle of intimate informants become part of each others lives. Within these circles of intimates the researchers are able to go beyond the understanding of everyday affairs and to study what is involved in spirituality which must come close to the core of anyone's personal reality. In order to get this information the researchers may have to step outside their professional role and to become personally involved with their informants and not as people who might have been selected by random procedures. In these relationships the researchers become subject to role conflicts between roles which are socially well-known and for which there are established routines for their avoidance and solution and the roles professionally required. These small coteries of informants may also have role conflicts between their usual roles in their own communities and the roles which they have taken on when working with these inquisitive outsiders.

What do we know about these social scientists through whom the behaviour of others are recorded with such care and detail. Depending on the size of the report we usually know the institutions to which they are affiliated and their status designation there and for a book there is a short outline of their careers. The dedication is usually to family members and noticeably the numerous acknowledgements are to fellow professionals who have contributed in some way to the final production and who are hopefully part of that person's future career. What is often missing is a detailed list of the key informants who have spent long periods with the researcher who are virtually field assistants in terms of the time they have spent with the researchers and without whom these works would not have been completed. Rightly or wrongly these introductions suggest not only the centrality of the authors but their conformity to methodological detachment. We know very little about them as personalities acting on a particular professional stage.

We do not know the demographic profile of most researchers much less their social characteristics and how it might have affected their work and their ability to get information. It is often the case that we do not know these until these researchers have died such as Colin Turnbull's homosexuality and Malinowski's racial views. We do not know how a researcher with a severe stutter managed his work and what part his wife had in covering for this handicap. We do not know whether the results were the result of prolonged effort or indolence covered by imagination. We certainly do not know enough about the researchers linguistic abilities to initiate and understand the complexities of other cultures and those mysterious but ever present feature of fieldwork the partially educated interpreters of the language and behaviour of these alien cultures.

We do not know what they looked like as it is the appearance of these researchers which is first seen when they enter a community. We need to know how this fits or does not fit into the stereotypes which the researchers have as to whether they are likely to be people of potential understanding and sympathy; however illogical this may be, these are widely held and handicap the start of personal relationships. Some boys in Guyana were heard to remark about a researcher into religious behaviour with whom they had no previous contact 'man, he sure do frighten me bad'.

4 The Methods of Examining Religious Behaviour

Investigating the commonplace realities of everyday life such as the patterns of going to the market or the opinions of people about their political views are complicated by the methodological difficulties of sampling, the questions asked and the ways in which observations are made. This becomes much more difficult when the subjects of enquiry are more complex and private and one has only to look at any popular picture of a religious figure to realise that in the depictions of the Virgin Mary or Krishna or in Muslim calligraphy, there are complex symbolisms which have to be explained. Even more complex problems of finding out what viewers see in these depictions; what is their meaning for the peasant as much as the philosopher, the train-driver and the theologian. Both are important and to make one more important than the other is a social biasing act. The most influential man in the early elections in Ngara, Tanzania was a bus conductor because he met many more people than candidates and theologians in these terms may have very little influence.

The complexity and uncertainty of the results of research into spirituality come from the fact that such enquiries cannot start from factual definitions of what is being talked about as well as the fact that the physical behaviour of a Hindu woman carrying out some domestic *puja* is extremely varied. At the back of all such enquiries is the fact that questioning about the private nature of religion is not socially acceptable since it is usually done by obvious outsiders; a Brahmin graduate social scientist enquiring about Hindu behaviour in Banaras may have as many difficulties as a Bengali, Japanese ones doing the same thing there or a French woman living with a Brahmin family (Reymond, 1958). The highly educated have separated themselves or become separated mentally and socially from the commonality of man.

There are also problems which come from the general dislike about being interviewed on matters which are felt to be private such as their thoughts about their practices of spirituality. Most people may feel that their views clash with orthodoxy or are out of date with politically acceptable ideas of progress. Social scientists aim to use methods which are accepted professionally and which conform as nearly as possible with the standards of hard science. Many feel this is an impossibility with behaviour which is so varied and changeable. False reporting is always likely to be high, and are likely to be particularly so for answers to religious questions about which people do not have the linguistic capability of replying and in honesty probably do not have any views in the first place. Replies are often no more than to state that this is what we have always done and if you want more detailed answers, it would be best to go to professionals in religion who know about these matters. Most people answering questions on matters which are not only private but are not checkable because of this. They are also well aware of how their beliefs fit into and clash with those of the authorities running schools, churches and hospitals so that they attribute contrary beliefs to others. As an example it is widely believed that sexually transmitted diseases and tuberculosis are caused by the breaking of sexual taboos.

Questioning someone is certainly not a popular or indeed common way of one to one behaviour and has a very limited frequency in non-bureaucratic social environments. A single question slotted into a general discussion might be acceptable but not a whole series from an administered schedule or a questionnaire. Regardless of whether the questions are leading or not, all those who are questioned would realise soon enough that the purpose of the interview was related to religious ideas and behaviour and trimmed their answers to fit into that line of discussion. Whatever the questions asked they are unlikely to have previously come up in their community.

There are four ways in which we can seek to understand both the realities of religious behaviour and their importance for those involved. Firstly, there is the observable and that means that what is seen and recorded is infrequent. Secondly, there are self-reports by individuals of what they believe and do and there is no particular reason that we can regard what they say and write as accurate. Thirdly, what we infer from the information which we have gathered about religious thinking and behaviour and this is almost certainly consciously or unconsciously biased. Lastly, data which we have gathered under conditions which are reputedly as nearly scientific as possible.

The overall problem is that from whatever number of individuals data is collected we do not know the extent to which they are typical or indeed whether the term typicality can ever be used. We never know the number of supposedly similar people to those from whom this data has been collected. The constant problem is that we are looking for religious correlations to whatever behaviour we have data about. We just do not know what has been included or excluded by the definitions with which this has been done or simply because so many factors are unavailable or unattainable.

The inputs and consequences of a single event may be innumerable or just unknown. The Seventh day Adventists have a well-documented record of very little lung disease morbidity which has been repeatedly correlated to their institutional religiously motivated prohibition against smoking. This seems clear enough but there may will be other factors which have to be considered and which are not anything to do with religion. Almost all British murderers drink tea and ride bicycles but there is no connections between these facts which are as statistically solid as we can ever hope to make in our conclusions. What other factors might we have to consider in this clear-cut religiously motivated pattern of behaviour; the absence of passive smoking and living in a smoke free low air-pollution locality, a desire for cleanliness in the home, aesthetic dislike of the smell, they cannot afford the cost, they are married to non-smokers and they suffer from other diseases such as asthma which make smoking unlikely. This is not to suggest that the Seventh day Adventist related statistics are not a creditable reflection on the motivations and self-discipline but these primary figures might will be modified by such secondary considerations. Extend such questioning to what happens at Sunday celebrations of the Eucharist in Pallavaram or at the twelve yearly *Kumbh Mela* and we end up with a more complicated knowledge of religious behaviour. An understanding which has little necessary connection with secular patterns of thinking.

Methodological Restrictions on Acquiring Knowledge

Religion for most people is a necessity at some level of understanding and practice but it is not a matter to which they have given much thought and much less likely to have got their thoughts together enough to be questioned or indeed for them to be questioned at all about their beliefs. Most people most of the time give little thought as to why they do what they do, much less how they behave in emergencies; an analytical frame of mind is a rarity. Social scientists are no more likely to do this than street cleaners, factory workers and society hostesses. So now let us look in more detail at the four methods of putting religious behaviour down on paper for use by those who were not the recorders.

A. Observable Data

Whether it is deliberately done for a certain time at a certain place or the result of the accidents of the observers just being there, observation must always be flawed because it deals with a slice of behaviour taken out of context. The attendance at Mass at St. Thomas' Mount near to Madras and going on a pilgrimage can only be understood if this behaviour is seen in the context of what went before and what happened afterwards. This is how people behave even if they are not fully aware of how a religious event has been slotted into their lives.

A single observer is always looking in one direction at a time and indeed his or her ability to observe is related to degrees of concentration and how long they are able to be observing. Someone observing a religious ceremony is usually facing the focus of attention so they are seeing the backs of other participants or the minority who are facing the other way and the situation prevents them from turning round. Having a number of observers does not mean that they will be seeing the same things and coordinating their writings is a difficulty as few if any see the same things in the same way; the eyes are always being diverted. The official orthodox focus of a ceremony may not be the points which participants find stimulating. There is always the factor of what the observer can see when the ceremony is shrouded in incense and poor lighting and the observer may have been up the previous night seeing another aspect of the ceremony.

To attend the recitation of the whole *Koran* by four simultaneous readers working from a single lamp in an overheated room over sleeping children who were to be circumcised the next morning, does not make for observational accuracy then nor for the next morning's ceremony. Human observations are idiosyncratic for social, physiological and psychological reasons. The 'I was there and therefore I know' statement has to be treated with great caution.

Observers are faced with the difficulty of reaching conclusions about what numbers of people do for most of the time at religious ceremonies for which there is a known liturgy. The ceremonies of the Coptic Church in Ethiopia are long and what the priests are doing is hidden from view. So it is not altogether surprising that numbers of those attending are asleep and in some cases lying down to do so; while this may be an extreme case it is certainly not an isolated one. We have to decide what part such forms of observed attendance have in the religious understandings of such participants; just being there may have fundamental religious importance irrespective of any particular beliefs.

In many ceremonies we have large numbers of people seen to

be doing the same thing at shrines which are the centres of pilgrimage. There is little evidence that they are in fact doing this since their participation has to be individually understood and evaluated. Any recorded observations are invariably taken out of context.

Is the use of machinery any more reliable. Cameras and recording machines only record what they are pointed at and are valuable and reliable records of that; school children being photographed in the mihrab of the Ali Mohammad mosque in Cairo and for relatives and attendants at a wedding in the Azores being photographed round the alter after the priest has left, tell us just that. The limited sacredness of places in which religious ceremonies take place and how people group themselves on such occasions; these are slices out of social time and religious behaviour.

Much the same would apply to the use of security cameras which are common enough in public places such as school play grounds and public squares where religious celebrations may occur. However their use for research has the additional difficulties of how such a mass of continuously recorded data is to be processed when hundreds of people are doing thousands of different things in different personal contexts. The conclusion may be that observations are valuable in the creation of impressions and more so when the observers have had adequate experience of watching what may be strange or monotonous and the latter may predominate. It seems unlikely that observation can rarely be more than this; it is not a scientifically valid method in the context of religious ceremonies.

B. Self-reported Religious Activities

No individual however well trained or self-conscious is able to report on their own behaviour in ways which are not biased for the simple fact that their minds do not function mechanically. Social scientists are reluctant to accept that there are few if any social reasons for people to tell the truth to strangers or indeed to record them in writing when the subsequent uses of what has been written are quite out of the control of either the writers or the collators. To fill in a form is either an act of trust or obeying an instruction to which they may have only half-heartedly agreed. Why indeed should individuals give away personal information about themselves unless it is already common knowledge since they have been brought up to be cautious about giving any information away to anyone unless they are going to profit in some way from the disclosure. The frequency of religious participations is usually exaggerated in order to make the writers look better in their own eyes and what indeed constitutes participation since it may involve standing at the back of the church or being possessed by overwhelming religious emotions.

The answers to questions posed in person is a social interrelationship in which the person questioned is reacting to the questioner as well as the questions asked; except in the rare cases in which this is a relationship between equals, this is usually between people coming from two totally different worlds, they are intellectually different of different ages and almost certainly look and smell different so there can be little assumption of trust which would come from some shared aspects of identity.

Most people having working vocabularies which do not contain many words unless there is a professional necessity to have a large one as in the knowledge of local plants and their medicinal uses if they use them in their work; a Sukuma or Tamil might will know five hundred plants while having a very limited vocabulary of words connected with religion largely used by people in communities outside their own. This leads to variable understandings and misunderstandings which are usually not sorted out prior to interviews or the administration of questionnaires.

C. *Inferred Religious Behaviour*

Even the most experienced social scientist in reaching conclusions from their fieldwork are likely to go further than might be justified from what they have learnt. They are people who have come to accept the attitudes of their professional colleagues and the atmosphere of so-called scientific secularity of universities which were founded in the beliefs and practices of the European Enlightenment. The intellectual environment in which social scientists are trained whether in the East or West or in Africa is in the one methodological tradition of secular questioning.

It is a big methodological leap from observing religious behaviour to making statements about the reasons for such behaviour in one social setting much less to extend such conclusions to more than the one community in which they have been working over cultural barriers. Who is to know among the millions who go on pilgrimages are no more than religious tourists and those that are there for more ostensibly religious reasons. We know in Japan that a rising proportion of the elderly and of Chinese in Taiwan go on pilgrimage tours which in the former cases fill up the gaps created by loneliness and the latter are combined with shopping. Then in mainland China millions go to temples on their annual feast-days which involve going to the opera being performed within the temple compound, eating new food and listening to the music with perhaps a ten minute visit to the statue of the God(s) in the temple largely taken up by standing in the line to get in. The secular minded would see this as no more than secular entertainment and those of a religious pattern of thought would see the same activity as religiously motivated. It is necessary to be modest in conclusions when so much is outside the ability of anyone to evaluate with any degree of accuracy.

D. Data Based on the Requirements of Scientific Methodology

A clinical examination of a patient supported by laboratory supported facts is the end of an abbreviated story coming from its own design. We have already shown that the resulting facts no matter how internally accurate, may not give explanations which are no more than accidental coincidences.

We know that post-mortems show that the diagnoses of doctors are often wrong despite their prolonged training. As we grow older there are multiple physiological and psychological reasons for ill-health. It is likely to be much more difficult to assess religious factors since they start with the absence of definitions and even when assessments are made about humans under laboratory conditions it can never be the same as examining bacteria which can be presumed to have a greater degree of uniformity in their behaviour than could be the case with humans. Humans cannot be isolated effectively from influences outside the laboratory. However sometimes there can be a close correlation as in the connection in Egyptian Muslims between piety and the presence in humans of internal parasites. Pious Muslims pray and prior to praying they wash their hands, feet and faces in whatever water is available. It has been established that the overly pious have larger numbers of infestations (Farooq and Mallah, 1966).

The Issues in Cooperative Research into Religion

The social sciences looking at social behaviour do not have serious methodological problems in investigating such subjects as health, agriculture and urban poverty because the issues involved are tangible and definable; they are part of the 'real' world of which hard science is another aspect.

The research into religious behaviour is different since it deals with intangible personal and institutional realities which probably become established in the minds of informants long before the researchers start their work. They will have defined for themselves that these foundations are beyond human comprehension. This is not a good start for the work of social science rationalists for that is what they are both professionally and often by personal disposition.

Research has nearly always been an individual process or at least directed by dominant persons to whom their assistants are subordinated professionally and personally. Ideally understandings should be broadened by team or cross-discipline approaches. The difficulties of methodology become compounded wherever more than one individual studies the same data coincidentally or sequentially. An extreme case of these difficulties would be the work of Freeman in flatly contradicting the methods and conclusions of Margaret Mead's in work on Samoan adolescence (Freeman,1999). Husbands and wives can indeed work together but ultimately career and domestic issues begin to dominate and one partner gives way to the interests of the other as with the wife of Victor Turner (E. Turner, 2005).

There are particular difficulties in studying religious practices because on the side of the practitioners of religious faiths there is emotion. On the researchers' side a reactive emotion in which their own upbringing and training in a rationally based field of professionalism inevitably clashes with what they are observing. The Westerners watching the public possession of young Ssonjo men by the spirit of their God Khambageu during a religious ceremony is certainly going to be intrigued if not excited by what they are seeing. It is very unlikely that they accept that these men are in fact possessed by that divine figure. It is not known whether nationals find these contradictions any easier to deal with than non-nationals. It is difficult not to rationalise as forms of psychological abnormality or social deviance when thousands of people rushing into the polluted water of the river Ganges on astrologically predetermined timings, Irish people climbing their holy mountain in bare feet or indeed Roman Catholics treating the Blessed Sacrament as the real presence of Christ in every church whenever the Mass is celebrated.

Social sciences are inevitably handicapped in their work on religious behaviour by their professional search for exactness when they do not appear to apply the same approach to the emotional and perhaps secular realities of beauty in poetry, art and sculpture. They are sceptical that any one with an ounce of common sense in their heads can worship Ganesh, the elephant headed Hindu God. They are quite content to accept Paul Klee's paintings of box-like humans as acceptable modern art with significant meanings.

If there is going to be co-operation in researching anything as complex and inexact as religious behaviour, then this is going to be a handicap on what can be achieved in the time available. It becomes the working out of differences between those co-operating rather than in the interpretation of what has been observed. It becomes committee like in the amount of time required when professional reputations are at stake. With an increase in the numbers of researchers involved in a project which may be partly the result of quasi-political necessities, there is going to be an arithmetical increase in the time taken up in consultations and a reduction in the amount of fieldwork material that can be processed. A proportionate delay in the production of any results which become increasingly historical than contemporary.

There are even more handicaps if the project becomes subject to inter-disciplinary fieldwork when professionals start from foundations which in reality have very little in common other than commitment to a common project and the assumption of good-will. In research into religious behaviour it is not just a question of bringing into play other scientists from psychology, psychiatry, and medicine but of justifying the inclusion or exclusion of liturgists, ecclesiastical administrators and theologians. In such situations of co-operation it may often end up with reports from which the views and work of others has been excluded because it would not fit into majority views and that in itself is a weakness.

Faced with data which is invariably inexact and subject to indefinite numbers of influences in strength and variations, the making of sense of religious data seems to be done best by individuals working alone. Taking whatever advice and assistance they find valuable but on their terms. The devotion and application of researchers to the topic of their choice in the field of religion does not appear to go well with inter-disciplinary co-operation.

The Methodology of Comparison

If research is attempting to assess the connections between religious rituals and the well-being of those involved, it is more methodologically sound to study more than one community which have defined geographical or social limits than cultures in which there are unlimited numbers of factors of which only a few are even remotely definable. Then we are left with a social universe which is more or less definable and theoretically confined to a village near to Banaras, a housing estate near Bangalore or an urban shanty town in Bamako. The fact that we have geographically limited the field of observations tends to make researchers forget that these boundaries are being penetrated all the time by outside influences from television to visiting relatives and inspectors from government departments apart from buyers and sellers in local markets.

The objections to the monumental comparative work of Frazer (Frazer, 1890/1922) were his indiscriminate borrowings from divergent cultures and his disinterest in the status of each frame from which he took examples (Strathern, 1987). But religion, well-being and health are very divergent and if we are going to relate these three different areas of human experience, then it seems inevitable that we have to find similarities in perhaps vague terms. This may lead to corelations even though the data itself may fall short of the requirements of accepted social science methodology.

What researchers have used for their comparisons may be a matter of personal choice. Often it is a matter of what they can get a grant for and the sheer convenience of certain comparisons in parishes which are no more than a bus journey apart. Other than canonical similarities there is little to suggest that studies of Roman Catholic behaviour in attending the Mass in Trivandrum is going to be paralleled by Peruvians attending the same ceremony in Cuzco, Peru or in a London predominantly middle-class suburb.

The scientific approach requires both detachment and deliberation, not the accidents of having a relative working in Japan or the Philippines or being posted for employment in Burma and Tanzania rather than to Sri Lanka and Nigeria or indeed being asked to do research in Guyana and Liverpool, United Kingdom where that person had never been before. There is often an accidental and indiscriminate element in what is used for comparison

So comparisons are often using the published research work of strangers often obtained through computer searches. If we want to use rituals involving the Bodhisattvas of northern Mahayana Buddhism, we are going to be provided with thousands of references which are quite beyond the capabilities of any researcher to follow up both in number and published in languages which those researchers cannot read. Few researchers with Hindi as their natal language and English as their second one can read works on Buddhism published in Thai and Russian. It seems that the biases of partial understandings in the use of comparisons are more likely to reflect the accidents of the life experiences of individual researchers than the careful choice of what is used. The need for comparisons still remains important in order to find how to what extent certain religious behaviours are unusual or whether they occur to some extent in similar environments. Spirit possession appears to occur in parts of Africa and Asia so the intriguing questions arises as to whether there are parallels with Christian Pentecostalism.

Social scientists have tried to develop standardised variables with which they can assess participation in various religious ceremonies (M. King, 1966). They remain what they are, the products of Western thinking within the inheritance of Comte about Western forms of belief and practice. What they are related to explaining is congregational religious behaviour and creedal propositions which can be applied to Christianity, Judaism and Islam. These approaches have little part in Eastern and non-literate traditional religions to which the same systematic approaches cannot easily apply.

Of course, there will be those who have loyalties to the local Hindu temple or Buddhist shrine in much the same way that there are attachments to local churches, mosques and synagogues. But much religious activity are crowd events often in situations in which it is difficult to divide secular enjoyments from religious activities as in the annual pagoda festivals in Myanmar, and temple ones in China. The thousands who flock to Hindu festivals in India cannot be paralleled easily to the pilgrimages to Lourdes or to the thousands who go to throw money offerings to the Meiji shrine in Tokyo on New Year's Day often dressed in traditional costumes.

The factors used in comparisons of religious behaviour tend to be somewhat elitist because they are usually taken from written sources accredited to the institutions of the major religions and possibly also filtered through the preference of the social sciences for behaviour which can be seen as systematic. This is almost inherited from the tightness of Jewish orthodox behaviour in their rabbinic training and veneration for scholarship. These forms of comparison do not fit well into most religious behaviour whether from the East or West which are composite activities in which the religious component may only be prominent in the considerations of those looking for just that element. When indeed is a pagoda festival in Myanmar a religious occasion when there are exciting plays to watch with female dancers, gambling booths and attractive market stalls and food shops.

While it may be possible to compare the composition of Jewish congregations within a single Western culture as regards their demographic features. It would be difficult to go further than that in all the underlying factors accounting for their presence there on that particular day and impossible to compare these congregations with those in Mumbai except in these simplistic demographic terms. Indeed such comparisons might be easy in comparison to trying to get comparisons between a Roman Catholic congregation at Mass in Goa, a spirit possession ceremony in ostensibly Hindu or Muslim Bali and whatever religious activities are carried out by the Lord's Day Resistance Army in Northern Uganda.

The Availability of Data for Comparison

In comparative studies of social behaviour including religion involving both developed and undeveloped countries and parts of countries on a scale of London, Lagos and the Lisu of Myanmar and Yunnan, or the Tamils of Southern India and Sri Lanka, the number of psychological, social and economic studies may be in the proportion of 100:10:1 in terms of time consistency and coverage. On the whole the amount of material available for the behaviour of university students is relatively ample but for large blocks of populations virtually nothing is known. What there has been published in national languages for which translations into internationally known languages has not been done.

There is another factor. Frazer was not criticised at the time of the publication of his Golden Bough in many volumes because it seems likely that he had read all that there was to know about the strange customs of non-European cultures. It may even have been thought at the time that what he had written was the end of the story. Now researchers know that they cannot possibly read all the literature related to the customs of their own and other cultures. They are similarly acutely aware that there are huge gaps in what they should know about the religious behaviours of the peoples in whom they are interested.

First at one end of this scale of comparative availability there is very little available so that there is an inevitable tendency to assume that there is more cultural uniformity there than among Americans for whom there is ample evidence of individuality in what they believe in and how they practice their forms of religion. After all some data is available about the religious practices of Tamils but very little is known as to how the Lisu worship. There is the assumption of uniformity as there is no data to suggest otherwise despite the fact that we already know that one Lisu is not likely to be all that similar to his or her neighbours since their experiences of life are not likely to be similar. When a Chinese social scientist publishes a study of a Yunnanese tribe (Cai Hua, 2001; Geertz, 2001) which has not been studied before and states with ample data that this community has no institutionalised relationships which resemble marriage, we are astonished. We have to realise that comparative studies on any topic, religious or not, is going to be a lot more difficult when we use data from previously unknown but nevertheless complex non-literate societies. Much work has been done in tabulating the cultural traits of a range of societies in the Human Relations Area Files with over one hundred context categories of behaviour. This method of isolating cultural characteristics has been popular with social scientists who cannot have any primary experience and direct study of more than a very few societies and indeed only small parts of each.

Then those with research experience of cultures other than their own come to realise that whatever the culture requires and there are always people who will be quite categorical of what their own communities consider to be their predominant customs, but that is just not the situation. There are many situational elements in the carrying out of these norms in religion and every other aspect of their lives, that they can only be regarded as indications of preferences and Leach (Leach, 1967:82) describes much data as 'tabulated nonsense'. There is a wide range of sociological phenomena which are intrinsically inaccessible to statistical investigation of any kind. 'The anthropologist is constantly made aware of the difficulty of fitting items of human behaviour and experience into numerical categories. It is not that the numbers are necessarily false but they draw the enquirer's attention away from what is of crucial significance'. It is with their common rather than rare situational variations that must dominate any cross-cultural assumptions. It is prudent to remember Goethe's statement that 'dilettantes compare' (Weber, 1962, 1:lxiv)

The Research Costs of Assessing Unorthodoxy

If it is at all possible the social science evaluations of religious behaviour bases itself on what any religion considers to be orthodoxy and that is provided by the elites in any faith and by its institutions. The pragmatism of methodology may mean that it over estimates the importance of writing in maintaining religion rather than particular forms of religious behaviour. Researchers information in libraries and through photocopying and it is more comfortable than fieldwork and probably less expensive. It is not only that this results in assessing what may be rather rare characteristics since they are optimising what is expected of their faithful.

A recent survey of public opinion about religion in Iran after two decades of rigorous Islamization after the revolution which deposed the Shah and the previous policies of enforced secularisation (Kazemipur and Rezani, 2003) showed that private praying had remained more or less the same between 1975 and 2001, but that collective praying in mosques had declined. Furthermore it was the general feeling that religious sentiments or the influence of religion in the future would decline by as much as 45 per cent in which there were no differences between the opinions of the young and older adults. This means that in Iran future attempts to assess religious behaviour might have to research the private activities of individuals rather than public collective ones which would be a much more difficult task. In all areas there is so much collective worship always going on that researchers may overestimate their importance for the individual. What happens to the religious needs of the seventy million who attended the last *Kumbh Mela* before the next one comes along?

It seems more likely that most religious practices are privately performed or at least privately carried out where the more general public and certainly researchers cannot see what is happening. These practices are not recorded although they appear from time to time in what are depreciatively called 'popular religion'. Religious authorities and theologians view their existence and persistence with a mixture of tolerance and discouragement.

Researchers have to go to wherever these practices are being carried out, and to find ways of seeing and hearing them in their individualities and of course being accepted enough to being able to observe at all. Since these men and women are almost always and inevitably outsiders, this is a complex and time-consuming process. The costs may be minimal in comparison to wider ranging fieldwork. It can never have much statistically validated information which can be used in comparison nor indeed the accuracy which can come from examining documents.

This means that we have to assume that a very large proportion of religious behaviour is private and moreover that it may have a higher proportion of specifically religious intentions than public religious activities, will not be covered because of these pragmatic difficulties. Researchers do not have the human and methodological resources to cover such semi-hidden individualisms accurately. They have to rely more on theoretical assumptions and drop-in observations or content themselves with the results of longer term participant observations in individual households.

The Overall Costs of Finding Out about Religious Behaviour

It is important to recognise that getting information at all which has some validity outside the statistical limitations appropriate to clinical medicine which has its own problems, work on religious behaviour in any community has no short cuts in the fieldwork required. In a study of a small store-front Afro-American church in Seattle (Abrum, 2000) it took fifteen months of participation in their social and religious lives before she got permission to interview anyone. Even longer for her to realise that she had to let the women being interviewed set the environment and topics for what they wanted to talk about rather than what the researcher wanted. This would have denied these women the opportunity to break free from the normal restrictions of social dominances which they experienced elsewhere (Minister, 1991).

We must also consider the human costs to the researchers involved in such prolonged overtures to what they wanted to do professionally. In most cases the researchers are isolated from their colleagues, relatives and friends and have to live under conditions of social intimacy with people who are different to themselves. The greater the social and geographical distances between the researchers and the researched, the greater the strains. It is not a situation which attracts and retains older researchers with their professional and family commitments and who in the process of aging have lost some of the ability to adjust to strange envitonments which they had as post-graduates. In many ways fieldwork is the individual betting on their results attracting enough professional interest to insure employment or at least further grants.

It seems inevitable to conclude that obtaining any valid data on religious behaviour which has none of the more obviously availability which comes from more definable social behaviour, is going to be extremely expensive in human and material costs. Moreover since these topics are sensitive to the personal understandings and perhaps convictions of all those involved, the researchers have to diminish much of their own self-importance which is built into the research processes.

Let us look in more detail at the high costs of any study connecting religious behaviour with well-being and health in what might initially be seen as a more convenient environment such as the spirituality of fifty doctors who had also been hospital patients (Klitzman and Daya, 2005). Pilot interviews were conducted that led to the development and refinement of a guide to the subsequent two in-depth two-hour sessions. These interviews were audio-taped, transcribed and content analysed. Then the research team examined a subset of the interviews for the factors that had shaped the participants experiences, coded the results under two different approaches.

It is easy enough to see that to reach this degree of accuracy on highly personal opinions for which there could be no foundation definitions has been extremely expensive in material costs. It did not in the personal strains which must have occurred for the Seattle research into the store-front church and the behaviour of its members. It has advantages in that the health aspects are provided by the hospital records but that is as far as the advantages go. All the research has been taken out of the social environments in which these opinions were formed and of course we have no evidence of this other than the assumed probity of the informants. Audio-taped interviews and their examination by a committee of social science professionals may not be the ideal situation for finding out the religious behaviour of a sample of doctors or indeed tribal peoples in Orissa.

While medical data is useful it is not necessarily hard unless it comes from laboratory sources, diagnoses are often opinions and as much data possible from sources which are not possibly tainted by the needs of the research process itself such as letters of petition pinned to Shinto, Muslim or Christian shrines; the trees round the Meiji shrine in Tokyo which are festooned with written requests for divine aid (Orsi, 1996).

5 Spirituality and Positive Health

Health as a Variable Condition

Health is not a clear-cut term nor one that doctors would care to define except often in the negative sense that someone whom they examine is not suffering from any clinically identifiable disease. An American dictionary (American Heritage Dictionary, 1995) is equally unable to provide any concise definition stating that health is the overall condition of an organism at a given time, soundness especially of body or mind and the condition of optimal well-being. It is obvious enough that many people are not healthy because they cannot adequately perform the social roles which they are expected to perform. They may consider themselves fit as their incapacities are almost standard for the elderly, although they have been defined as handicapped by the society in which they live or by the bureaucracy of that society's welfare system.

In subsistence societies and in the poverty stricken fringes of the cities in the developing world, the division between the healthy and the unhealthy has very little to do with the diagnoses of scientific medicine. It comes down to simply whether individuals can contribute enough to the survival of their primary groups so that they are not a liability. In the former communities there may be some support from some close relatives but not all that much when the margins of survival are close to their daily standards of living. Sentiment or morality may have little to do with decisions about their survival. The obviously defective child would be smothered at birth among the Sukuma of Tanzania just as we know that among the Netsilik Eskimos at one time killed a quarter of their babies because if they had survived their families would not have been able to feed for years girls who have to be fed but do not hunt (Rasmussen, 1931). For these people it is a harsh world in which healthiness is tied to their survival and the moral and spiritual understandings of the small group supported no doubt by their ancestral spirits.

In the cities of the developing countries much less help will be available for many people as there are no kin nearby and much will depend on the ties that individuals can create. In Mombasa, Kenya, a room full of Kamba daily workers stated that they were all each others' mothers' brothers. They had created the obligation to help each other out of nothing more than a very broad interpretation of classificatory kinship.

In these situations the classification of healthy or not healthy is harshly and narrowly created along the lines of physical abilities and there would be no mass media created ideal model of healthiness. But in the developed world where the official and non-governmental social and religious welfare agencies provide a substantial range of support, healthiness is much more weakly defined by function. In many such societies there is legislation to protect those who by the standards of subsistence economies would be abandoned.

In these modernised or modernising societies the mass media, political programmes and popular imagination provide a model of who is healthy. The advertisements in prominent medical journals and the popular press show the pharmaceutical industry selling its version of health by suggesting that they can eliminate or control certain diseases (Moynihan *et al.*, 2002). They are always changing these images to capture the popular imagination of healthy survival (Vuckovic and Nichter, 1997).

Outside of the industry depicting health for quite legitimate economic reasons, the mass media in all societies depict people as being visually fit. This average of physical uniformity suggests that those outside these visible parameters are not healthy and handicapped. Obesity, baldness, short-sight, false-teeth and so on can be put right at a minimal personal cost. This is not a comforting approach and of course spirituality makes no such claims or suggestions.

The Elusive Definition of Health

Whereas doctors would look on health as the presence or absence of clinical conditions which denote the absence of health, they have no reason to define health and indeed could have no means of doing so. Many if not most people have clinically identifiable conditions for which they have not gone to anyone for help or advice. It is not bad enough to justify the inconvenience, the expense in time, money and social stress or because they do not want to know. Where there are no physicians or unsympathetic ones, there are always quasi-traditional and fringe specialists in abundance who often mix the spiritual and the practical. Some are just frightened of the social and physical and undignified confrontations of modern medicine which are avoided in non-Western consultations which start from shared metaphysical assumptions.

Religions in their formalities and to a lesser extent spirituality, have always in all known societies been involved in the normal processes of living—birth, marriage and death through rituals and religions are constantly managing the life events of their believers. Religions provide written and unwritten guides which tell their believers all they need to know about how to manage the normal course of their lives and its inevitable miseries.

However life does not and indeed cannot follow a normal pattern for very long and everyone suffers upsets in the way they are living and in what they plan to happen. Everyone has illnesses and accidents and although we know that we will die it is always a shock when there are deaths particularly among people we know and for whom we have affection and obligations. There are no ways in which disasters and epidemics can be avoided and their treatments or avoidances are often no more than delays in what we know will inevitably happen if not to themselves to others in ghastly repetitiveness whether in tsunamis or new diseases. Science can explain and prevention may do no more than open up further distressing alternatives.

Spirituality whether in the form of religious rituals or more personal and private spiritualities determine in part how people will cope with these crises either by resigning themselves to God's will or karmic inevitabilities or by carrying out propitiation in prayer and sacrifices. Religious beliefs can soften the blow of illness and to some degree prolong life though not just through infrequent miracles but through abstinence from alcohol, tobacco and sexual promiscuity. Many recent studies have shown that religious beliefs and practices are beneficial (Crawford *et al.*, 1989; Levin and Schiller, 1987; Ross, 1990). On the other hand as we will show latter religious practices such as pilgrimages and in-breeding within sects can spread diseases and make genetic abnormalities more frequent (McKusick, 1973).

We need to remember that scientific medicine classifies every disease very largely by its physical symptoms and attempts to cure it through drugs or surgery. These methods have been enormously successful over recent centuries in prolonging life in the developed world and in exchange for which there are decades of senescence and new diseases created by stress. Many people feel the need for therapy and they obtain it in a variety of ways not accepted by scientific medicine but which are nevertheless often accepted as successful by those who use these complementary or alternative methods. This is very much the case for the United States which has perhaps the most scientifically advanced scientific medical profession in the world.

At the same time in the less developed countries and in the less well-off and socially deprived populations in developed countries, which together make-up the large majority of the world's population, there is very little scientific medicine or only available to a small minority who can afford to pay for treatment. On the other hand Chinese and Indian societies have culturally well-established medical systems of great antiquity and of substantial contemporary popularity.

In many contemporary societies the explanations for disease

and misfortune are a mixture of social and religious factors, attributable to the annoyance of ancestors, witchcraft, family quarrelling and the consequences of sin. Scientific medicine have no cures except in terms of psychological weakness and a general subconscious contempt for such seemingly illogical thinking. There is however truth in such beliefs that social disruption and social isolation can be very debilitating and lead to lowered resistance to lurking diseases (McGrath, 1988).

Only recently has Western scientific medicine tried to take account of social factors in relation to sickness. It is poorly equipped to do so because doctors no longer have the time for individualising the treatment of their patients. They tend in any case to see them in their offices rather than in more homely settings. A traditional healer would take some time to find out the circumstances of each patient and not to see ten to fifteen patients per hour (Nunley, 1996) or to rely on multiple drug prescriptions (Channavasavanna, 1988). This has left a psychological and social gulf between what people need and what the medical profession provides. Sufferers are filling this with a wide range of quasitraditional and contemporary innovative healers involving personal spirituality and more participation in public religious rituals. The Western medical profession has a blind spot in relation to how patients cope with severe injury and loss (Sherrill *et al.*, 1988) because on the whole they are agnostics by scientific training and personal disposition.

So we can see that the relationship of well-being to health is likely to be no more than a predominantly self-assessed state which depends on how particular individuals evaluate their own social situation at any one time. Anxiety about the proliferation of AIDS and the number infected would both affect any sense of well-being. In large populations affected by famine or civil war there are likely to be very few who are clinically healthy. The fact that they are alive might make them see themselves as well as they could expect to be given the circumstances. This might be the only way that they could see their own conditions.

A community might consider itself in an overall state of well-being when they are experiencing nothing particularly wrong outside the normal range of misfortunes which they would all expect to suffer from on a regular basis. Invade a community with professionals and this state of acceptable misfortune might swell dramatically. A leprosy expert visiting Tunduru district in Tanganyika in 1949 doubled the number of lepers in just a few days of inspecting groups of adult men. The Rockfeller Foundation funded a survey of the handicapped in Uganda in the mid-1960s. In addition to the ones who were helped by non-governmental organisations like the Save the Children Fund and the Salvation Army, it found a quarter of a million people who were unable to contribute fully to the subsistence survival of the primary groups to which they belonged.

Thus we must accept that whatever its relationship to clinical medicine may be, health is not much more than the condition in which people manage to get on with their lives since they are not suffering from anything that impedes this. Nevertheless there are certain practices involving spirituality and religion which either handicaps this ability or promotes the possibility of self-assessed well-being and even the likelihood of not suffering from certain clinically identifiable diseases. There is a substantial amount of hard data which illustrates these effects beyond the less exact but equally viable conclusions of psychology.

Health as an Idealization of Self

For those involved in scientific medicine with its known successes and its confidence in its abilities to be able sooner or latter to reduce if not abolish human physiological sufferings, health is a somewhat narrow conception; the absence of any defined illness or physical handicaps. In this these professionals may be no different to the similar ways of defining malfunctions that electricians and computer technicians use in their professional work.

To what extent do people see health in such terms? At one end of the scale subsistence farmers experience health as no more than the absence of any condition which prevented them from cultivating. At the other end of the scale are the Westerners living in societies with comprehensive welfare systems which can provide them with a significant amount of curative or at least maintenance medical care. The question of livelihood comes in much later in any considerations of their personal health.

Neither of these groups see health in quite the same way as that of the medical professionals. For the subsistence farmers there is a recognition that some mass diseases have been controlled but even that has been severely eroded by the appearance of AIDS as a new mass disease. They are unaware of the recognition of other new diseases. They recognise that they all get old with increasing disabilities and die. This is probably not seen as any absence of health, just part of the inevitabilities that terminate living whatever they do about it. Whatever is done before then combines a mixture of indistinguishable secular and religious actions which they hope will lead to some restoration of reasonable functioning consistent with the realities of their lives.

To what extent does the Westerners cushioned protection from these realities of life differ from the experience of misfortunes which can so easily overwhelm the lives of subsistence farmers. It has been suggested (McGuire, 1988:238-44) that health for middle-class American healing groups is not so much a medical issue which can or cannot be ensured by medical processes. For many such people health is an idealization of a kind of self and healing is not so much a physiological process, but the cultivation of a subordinate relationship to a transcendent deity. Many forms of contemporary religious healing cultivate a flexible self open to new possibilities and potentials.

This is surely relating health to forms of spirituality and it may be that contemporary Western societies have approached the limits of rationalization about what can be done to the body and see bio-medicine as limited in what it can do. They need more than ever before emotional experience and styles of moral evaluation and legitimation in which there are changes in the very practices by which the self is symbolised, shaped and expressed (McGuire,

1988:251-2). If this is thinned down to more individual feelings, it may be that these people just as the Sukuma of Tanzania or the Santals of India have realised long ago in the pragmatics of their lives. The practicalities of health and its maintenance have always, are still and will always be severely limited and no more than delays in the processes of progressive dissolution.

Thus the definition of health is not so much correlated to short-term solutions but relates to wider conceptions of the individual, the family and communal requirements and the ways that they fit into the overall order of the way in which the universe is conducted. It is doubtful whether any society has ever really thought that there was a clear alternative between the acceptance of biological inevitability and seeing the individual as part of the context of some wider divine order into which they can aspire to integrate themselves. It is in practice a zig-zag interrelationship varying in space and time. There is always the predominant factor that health unless it is subject to clinical evaluation from start to finish, can never be more than a personal evaluation of their own condition at that time and under specific circumstances.

Spirituality and Health

Spirituality can involve activities which are consciously chosen from a cultural menu or it can involve no choice at all except in the sense of doing or not doing what is culturally prescribed as the right thing to do in the circumstances. In this situation there are the religious standards at which this behaviour is directed; abstention from food during the daylight hours of the holy month of Ramadhan for Muslims, the vegetarian diet required of Hindu ascetics and the processional gymnastics of Tibetan Buddhists. However it can be assumed that quite often these requirements do not exactly fulfil what individuals may need because of demographic or circumstantial factors. All these are physical activities which have assessable physiological consequences which are combined with psychological returns such as feel good factors and on a down scale into indifference. Our available data is overwhelmingly based on scientific procedures; behaviour which is complex and possibly undefinable tied to results which are defined but these are correlations not cause and effect relationships. Such results may will exclude psychosomatics and a whole range of possible psychological factors.

Physical behaviour may be intermittent rather than regular and the devout consistently overestimating the regularity of their own devotions. There are likely to be attitudes of mind which are continuous in their subconscious latency and which the individual will have from being socialised into a particular culture. There may will be a social and religious framework that leads to either passivity or activism in response to misfortunes and pain. If children are brought up within a social system that involves ancestors, free-ranging spirits, witchcraft or an endless succession of lives, these are not likely to be shaken off by a few years of education. A study of Ghanaian students found that only the sociology ones took a critical view of traditional ideas about witchcraft and other such matters (Jahoda, 1968). There are bound to be spin-offs between the rational behaviour necessary for survival and other contributory spiritual activities which dove-tail into this.

Since spirituality must affect both mental and physical processes we have to consider what people do and think that affects their survival as biological units which contribute to their own survival and that of the species. The latter is a very long-term and detached approach which would be unlikely to be a factor in most people's thinking outside links with their ancestors in Japan and sub-Saharan Africa and the survival of particular famous families with hereditary names and inheritable wealth.

Then there are negative issues to consider when behaviour based on religious requirements contributes to the lengthening of life leading to economic distress and social ignominy. So data relating health to well-being has to be assessed not only in terms of clinical evaluations but in the effect of prolonging life would have on the well-being of the family. It is thus quite understandable that the elderly in Japan go to specially empowered temples to pray for a quick death that does not involve them in being cared for by their few children and the distress of physical dependency.

It is in this context that the manifest and latent functions are important and who is evaluating these issues? If an enduring spirituality practice does not fulfil its manifest functions of family solidarity by the obligation to care for the elderly, then latent functions come into play and attention to a God or Goddess that is known to ensure what the Japanese elderly would call a benign death, come into prominence. There are spiritual, social and economic issues supporting these changes in the form and ideology of spirituality. If such a practice is seemingly dysfunctional for some parts of society, but still continues, then its persistence implies that it still has uses somewhere (Merton, 1967). Divination attracts young educated Japanese women because of their liminality in male dominated employment and the opportunity it provides to their test ideas and opinions with a diviner who is a stranger (Kawano, 1996).

The practices of spirituality are too individual to have any widespread commonplace positive or negative influences on health beyond the one person who has taken up a particular activity which they may have thought up themselves in combinations of otherwise commonplace activities but religion with its institutionalised practices certainly can have. Hinduism provides religious backgrounds for male dominance and there are thus consequences against the health of women; they eat last and when girls are ill there is a delay in getting medical assistance which would be called much sooner for their brothers. In Islam male dominance has been off set by the property rights of women who have set up their business in Saudi Arabia. The 'zar' cults of spirit possession in the Sudan and East Africa are similarly outside the control of men despite its opposition to acceptable Islamic practice (Kenyon, 1999). In addition in Iran women have developed their own religious teaching institutions and virtually monopolised certain shrines for their parallel devotions (Kamalkhani, 1991).

The Field of Enquiry into Spirituality and Health

The scientific enquiry into the realities of any such connections is not whether they exist or not since it is obvious enough that the workings of the mind and body are connected but whether much can be achieved by trying to make water-tight connections between activities that are ostensibly based on spirituality but involve non-religious factors and health.

Available data there is dominated by Western small-scale studies which are always compromised not so much by methodological criticisms as by the time between research and results and environmental circumstances; their results are historical rather than contemporary. There seems to be a sub-strata in human behaviour which keeps in existence a need for forms of spirituality which in the Western world fill the cracks left over from the unfulfilled hopes of pragmatism. There is thus the assumption that the spirit world in some form or other exists seems to be a constant with individuals and the societies in which they live. Since what this is remains beyond definition, it may not be sensible to try and assess this side of the question by scientific methods. We have to start from the statement that if something is believed to be true it is real in its consequences. So on one side of the equation there are powers and influences which have been constantly assumed to exist. The powers of God, ancestors, spirits, *karma* and luck or whatever but acting on this reality, not assumed but known to exist. Men and women have consistently used up varying amounts of time, energy and resources to have these powers on their side rather than acting against their interests.

The difficulty is that there are no boundaries to these assumptions and when they come into play in the lives of individuals and the groups within which they live, the amount of time involved varies. When we consider health we are on firmer but still imprecise grounds in that this is assumed to be the absence of any pathological and psychological diagnosed states hostile to well-being. It is possible to relate this quite clearly to some spirituality practices as in the passage of contaminated moisture on the surface of a religious image between worshippers who queue up to kiss it. But then the Sukuma who claims to be possessed by an irritated ancestor might be diagnosed as schizophrenic by a Western psychologist. In Tanzania he or she would be seen as having a normal and perfectly understandable temporary religious affliction which could be cured by customary procedures (Field, 1960), probably more effectively than by Western sophisticated procedures which are not all that successful with curing this disease.

There is always then the problem of attributions since we know that of those who seek the resolution of their misfortunes through spirituality a high proportion will have them solved without recourse to either secular or religious activities. So we are always left with a very small proportion of human activities which can be linked tightly enough with the practices of spirituality to constitute scientific proof rather than strong suspicions of correlations. Much ingenuity and effort has gone into trying to create such water-tight situations for the study of prayer. It is not so much that they show some significant connections but that they have small overall significance except perhaps for those who would be praying anyway. The practices of spirituality always take up a small proportion of total life experiences if they are assessed in time and motion terms and even if this is related to the obviously devout.

Even those leading lives directly dedicated to spirituality whether in a Chinese Taoist or Benedictine monastery, Hindu *ashram* or in yogic isolation actual involvement in devotions has to be part of a daily programme with long periods of sleep, eating, washing, excreting and even gossiping. The underlining of spirituality is occasioned more by their geographical isolation and special costumes. Periods of meditation may be labelled as the practice of spirituality but in reality they may be physiologically and psychologically indistinguishable from dozing. The time spent on activities which can be isolated as religious or spiritual might be no more than 10 per cent of the waking time of cloistered monks and nuns. It is the possible hidden intention behind the cooking of lunch which makes it a spiritual activity.

Insofar as we can link the practices of spirituality with health, we can expect to find small pieces of primary data and large masses of information in which the correlations cannot be made to be more than suppositions which come from both the mind sets of the researchers and those who have undergone these experiences. There are personal and subtle distinctions between being a tourist and being a pilgrim in any assessment of the Hajj, the *Kumbh Mela* and going to a famous Roman Catholic shrine. All of which involve millions of what must be individual experiences diminished by an assumption of overall uniformities.

Much is always made that the practices of spirituality are in some general way related to weakness of character or limited intelligence. These will be reduced if not eliminated by education and political authoritarianism whether in a Communist state or in equally authoritarian Shia Irán or Sunni Saudi Arabia. It seems clear enough that in the absence of any ability to define spirituality and to constrict its meanings and functions within definable boundaries that almost all people have some elements of indefinable spirituality in their lives. Leaving aside whatever elements are due to fear and mental illness, we must surely assume that whatever their functions may be, the overall self-assessed effects are benign.

The Narrowness of Spirituality and Disease Correlations

There is little doubt that there is a correlation between something called religion and in our case spirituality and increased or reduced morbidity for certain identifiable diseases but that does not establish any exclusive causal connection. Long periods spent in kneeling leads to arthritis of the knees which we would expect to find in floor cleaners and gardeners and worldwide almost all thieves drink tea or coffee but there is no connection between these activities. It is only too easy to create correlations out of an attitude of mind (Jones, 1994). The amount of physical as much as psychological data making such connections with religious activities is enormous (Reynolds and Tanner, 1995), so we have to start with this evidential reality which can only be nibbled at by methodo-logical and philosophical criticisms.

Pilgrimages spread diseases but take out the word 'religious' and substitute 'petrol', and the same result comes up. If football clubs became widely popular, it would seem likely that their members who play regularly and competitively would have low levels of smoking and drinking. The amount of time spent in this activity and its correlates would be about the same as that spent in devotions by the devout. For most people who have beliefs in spirituality its practice except in emergencies has low priority. It would be unwise to give its consequences priority over the time taken up in using public transport or slumped over a television set or computer.

What we have surely are forms of observable social behaviour which enhance or reduce the possibility of getting and keeping the symptoms of a few identifiable diseases. We do not know what we do not see and most observations are made from the backs of churches and temples or in specialised experimental environments. Overall with the built-in biases which come form specialised intellectualism and not by those who believe in what is going on there.

We do not know and indeed cannot know the frame of mind in which people carry out these particular activities labelled spiritual. To what extent are there parallels to the comment of the Quaker about the silence in which he sat at weekly meetings waiting for someone to feel impelled to speak. It was then that he sorted out his business problems for the coming week and no doubt his wife was thinking about the Sunday lunch and the laundry that she would have to do on Monday. We know that people over-estimate the regularity of their attendance at devotions so there may be a correlation between spirituality and the ability to lie convincingly to oneself.

We are observing the behaviour of people in order to connect the practices of spirituality with health in largely controlled and quite permanent social situations; Roman Catholic religious, temple priests in south India, Seventh-day Adventists with their distinctive diets and the Amish who are all within long-term social and geographical environments which will inevitably have had and continue to have physiological effects. We are authoritatively told that the requirements of spirituality are the basic reasons for this distinctive behaviour. The Seventh-day Adventists are the healthiest dispersed Christian sect in North America followed closely by the Amish whose health record is handicapped by the appearance among them of numerous hereditary defects caused by their high rate of endogamous marriages. But whatever the overall labelling of their lives as being guided by spirituality. It is the practicalities of their lives which have had the effect of lowering their morbidity rates and giving more than just the appearance of being healthy. It is the regularity of their lives and their concern for each other just as it is for the Canadian Hutterites which is appreciated by their members and retains them when the attractions of the more secular surrounding world appear to be otherwise so irresistible. They are indeed more pragmatic over what they do than subsistence farmers in Africa and Asia. They can see the advantages of their exclusivities and peculiarities in a high standard of living and day-to-day mutual help. For the Amish it pays off to look odd and be the subject of tourist interest.

It may be that these established correlations between certain forms of spirituality in defined environments with detailed morbidities since the Amish for instance have no objection to being studied in detail by unbelieving outsiders because their style of living and believing has been defined as divinely ordained. Conclusions from their study have limited applicability to the outsiders surrounding them because of their very peculiarities. These situations are as common to the peculiarities of tennis players and those who pray and go on pilgrimages. Researchers by using the terms 'spirituality' and 'religion' are not necessarily putting their data and understandings into some special category which can be comparable to the concise but often temporary definitions of health status, any more than such terms as 'socialism' and 'capitalism'.

So it would seem that any correlations which exist and which seem water-tight, will relate to specific conditions. The practices of spirituality cannot by their undefined nature be correlated to the generalities of health. Thus when we follow the hypothesized pathways by which dimensions of religious involvement influence health (Levin, 1996:858), we are going to find that the same commitments in different environments are going to have different effects on health. There are many possible correlations between religious behaviour and health which alone or in combination may have effects. The promotion of health related behaviour as on average the religious smoke and drink less, may make health more likely because of the social support from religious fellowship, the psychodynamic benefits of ritual, the consonance of particular theological world views with particular salutary health benefits, faith in the fostering of learned optimism, hereditary transmissions such as the Tay Sachs deficiency in Ashkenazi Jews, and the possibility of super-empirical and supernatural connections and multi-factorial connections in which the possibility of religious correlations become cumulative.

Whatever choices of spirituality behaviour which an individual may make or be socialised into, this becomes a pathway which will have some effect on their chances of getting or not getting a disease. Embracing someone for a religious purpose may pass on germs to and from someone outside the community or increase immunity within. We may have to conclude that there is a narrow range to the spiritual influence on physiological health and that psychological connections are another aspect altogether.

No studies as far as is known have dealt specifically with the fact the particular practices of spirituality may protect against specific diseases and that it fails to protect against others. In these respects a faith may prolong the lives of practitioners who may not be believers who might otherwise have died. It is this unusual morbidity profile that attracts the attention of epidemiologists to particular religious groups and of course they still die from other causes. But there are difficulties in relating a particular disease to mortality rates because very often people do not die from that disease and another one is given as the primary cause such as pneumonia or heart failure. We do not know how this affects statistics relating mortality to spirituality.

More importantly the lengthening of life in economically well-developed societies has always led to prolonged and debilitating diseases later in life which their earlier protective spiritual and secular practices have to some extent made inevitable. Although it is clear that the mortality rates of the Latter-Day-Saints and the Seventh-day Adventists for tumours related to both alcohol and tobacco are lower than national averages, the rates for malignant melanomas and lymphomas among the former are higher (Domagic, 1992). A further study of 22,940 California Seventh-day Adventists pointed out that non-fatal events for various diseases were not measured (Loma Linda University, 2006). It seems on the whole that some practices of spirituality either protect or enhance the possibilities of certain morbidities. In the latter case we have the shortening of life as in the Jonestown mass suicides but in the former the physiological success of a particular form of spirituality practice. This has always meant the lengthening of life and with this the probability of a long period of debilitating senescence. It seems to be the case that in taking a particular disease it is possible to reach numerical conclusions which are out of their wider contexts so we may be reaching conclusions from observed social behaviour of which regularity is the commonest feature while not being able to assess the contribution of hidden faith.

The Spatialisation of Concern for Health

The consideration of health according to the Western pattern of scientific thought has become essentially separated from the social environments in which its clients spend their lives in part because of the work study approach as part of modern management techniques. Medical institutions have become market driven in their concern for costs so that these institutions have become the sites of consumption rather than more than of care (Cartier, 2002). With this general shift to spatial dictated care there comes the tendency to emphasize right and wrong, a binary approach to decision making leading to a neglect of its socially situated characteristics as well as the particularities of individual experience (Malpas, 2003). This is particularly significant if we accept as we must that every person's perception of their social environmental reality is different and that we are all 'uncommon persons', not only in our individual needs. This is also relevant as to how the institutions promoting health should treat us but find it difficult to do so when decisions have to be made in terms of any general sets of procedures with standard determinate outcomes (Kaufman, 2002). In such contexts the ideas and practices of spirituality and religion provide a more personally relevant approach to the relief of everyday distress and its extremes.

The Continuation of Acceptable Health

Few if any individuals have continuous good health as it is a fluctuating condition between severe impairments and temporary inconveniences. The former make it impossible for these individuals to function in ways that they see and are seen as appropriate and may involve in modern societies their segregation in special institutions. The latter in societies which do not have these supportive institutions, may be involved in progressive neglect. There is also substantial social difference between being ill in-between periods of intense agricultural activity and being ill at harvest, weeding or planting times. Inability to work continuously in the urban-industrial environment may be far more distressing.

It is also a subjective condition in which individuals may feel ill while being clinically well and indeed may feel well when they are clinically ill as in old age when individuals may suffer from a number of degenerative malfunctions. There are no possible cures and yet those involved are happy enough with what they are still able to do. There are also other subjective functions of disease in which individuals are pragmatically malfunctioning but are able to use this to manipulate their status in society and in their families; they rule from their beds. It is inept to see ill-health as a scientific fact except in cases of clear incapacity when common-sense makes any clinical opinion superfluous. It is this inability to do what one wants to do or is required to do socially that is the major source of personal anxiety whatever the supposed cause or social realities of the situation.

How do individuals cope with these anxieties over health which in most societies probably only receive some clinical attention when they are classified as mass diseases. For most diseases for most of the time there are no cures and only what might be called delaying action over the ultimate inevitable death. Modern medicine in its overall efficiency can only be classified as palliative in epistemological terms. It is in the realisation of this very personal situation that individuals find public religion and private spirituality to be personally significant.

A high proportion of health seeking behaviour and the use of commercial products have no known clinical significance and rely for their success as placebos. Much the same would apply to the use of traditional herbal materials of which subsistence farmers and herdsmen have a comprehensive knowledge. An average Sukuma in Tanzania with no specialised training may will be able to identify and name as well as knowing the medicinal uses of at least five hundred plants, shrubs and trees which at the very least might have some homeopathic effects. A modern urban person whether in Mumbai or Manchester would only know a few patent medicines.

The dividing line between any understanding of the pragmatic results of this using of quasi-traditional materials which are combinations of animate and inanimate products usually in minute proportions reminiscent of the ingredients of the witches brew in Shakespeare's Macbeth and which have spiritual and modern medical connections is obscure. Of course, the latter practice procedures and use medicines in minutely measured quantities but their association with spiritual understandings is not clear although their procedures are just as ritualised as those of Sukuma diviner-herbalists.

To use or not use a particular quasi-traditional medicine or modern patent medicines which are bought and consumed in enormous quantities. This is based on combinations of spirit-possession, divination, local gossip, local commercial opportunism, clinical experience in local terms, the understanding of the social situations of those they consult and the metaphysical elements which must encroach to some degree on the social understandings of all illnesses and misfortunes. Much then may depend on the individual's frame of mind and their ability to do something combining the practical and the spiritual.

The Reduced Risks of Disease from Religious Behaviour

We can be certain that there is no clear cut division between a religion being closely correlated to a particular disease and not having any such connection. Before cholera inoculations and small-pox vaccinations became available pilgrimages spread both these diseases, but not everyone died. Huge numbers certainly and there must have been parallel patterns of contagion from market trading. Why did not they kill whole populations and we are left with the need to always keep in mind to what extent religion and spirituality act as partial preventatives.

An American study (Friedman and Rosenman,1974) showed higher rates of coronary artery disease in 'Type A' people who were characterised by forceful driving personalities, competitiveness and adherence to deadlines, than in 'Type B' people who lacked these traits. Christian beliefs if taken seriously should make people less competitive and Christian churchgoers have been found to have less heart disease (Comstock and Partridge, 1972). Overall religion and perhaps spirituality seem to protect believers against stressful ways of living and 'Type A' behaviour (Levin *et al.*, 1988). Christianity regards gluttony as sinful and this would reduce the intakes of fats and sugars. Islam has prayers involving substantial physical exercise which help fitness. Buddhism emphasizes the contemplative life and disapproves of any activity which could be called competitive. Right from the start there should surely be the assumption that behaviours based on religion and spirituality are likely to be benign since for these behaviours to have an overall hostile effect on human life would go against the fact that people would not have persisted in patterns of behaviour that were damaging. As an example religious commitment having an impact on diet and it was found in a study of well integrated elderly Americans in Virginia with strong ties to religion who were not members of sects with strong rules about food, tended to have better diets than those who were less well integrated (Mcintosh and Shifflett, 1981). Perhaps we should start with an assumption that it is only extremes of behaviour based on religious ideas that are likely to be damaging.

Christian Sects and the Prevention of Disease

It is hard to identify behaviour of people who belong to the larger religions because they are spread into very many social, political, economic and geographical environments. It is in the smaller more exclusive groups that we can identify the correlations between particular religious behaviours and some specific diseases. Whatever the statistics demonstrate, there are always the problems of the reliability of the data about actual practices related to a religion. There are substantial differences between the presumed physiological consequences of being a zealous Hindu living in an *ashram* and an internationally connected Hindu businessman living in Mumbai. What these people say they do and what they actually do may be very different.

Some forms of cancer are known to be environmentally induced of which the best known example is lung cancer which can be caused by inhaling tobacco smoke into the lungs which also increases the incidence of heart disease. The risk of lung cancer among Seventh-day Adventists is about half that of demographically similar populations (R.L. Phillips, 1980). And the Mormons of Utah have a 35 per cent lower cardio-vascular mortality than the national averages (Lyon and Sorenson, 1978).

Let us look in greater detail into the health records of these smaller Christian denominations. It is known that alcohol and tobacco contribute substantially as causative factors in certain diseases that affect the liver and respiratory tracts. So there is particular interest in the disease profiles of the Seventh-day Adventist Church and the Church of Jesus Christ of Latter day Saints—the Mormons—which prohibit the use of alcohol and tobacco.

Some 70 per cent of the population of the state of Utah are Mormons and cervical cancer in Utah is 26 per cent below the national average. This lower occurrence is accounted for by the Mormons having rates 50 per cent below the national and Utah non-Mormon averages. Jewish women also have lower rates (Kennaway, 1948). This is a reflection on the stability of Mormon and Jewish marriages since cancer of the cervix is associated with women having early sexual experience and multiple partners. While this is a clear reflection of the observance of religious values in sects with comprehensive social coverage, the correlations are not always so clear. The Mormon rate for cancer of the colon in Utah shows their rate to be 37 per cent below the national average and that of the non-Mormons there 15 per cent below. There may be environmental as well as religious factors involved as there is little difference in meat, fat and fibre consumption between the Utah population and that of the United States as a whole (Lyon and

Sorenson, 1978). A national study of cancer mortality rates showed that high concentrations of Mormons were associated with the lowest rates in contrast to areas with high concentrations of active Jews which had the highest (J.W. Dwyer, *et al.*, 1990).

The Mormon Church prescribes the use of tobacco and alcohol but total abstinence is now only required for church elders (Bush, 1986). An analysis of cardiovascular disease deaths showed that they had a 35 per cent lower rate than the national average, while the Utah non-Mormons were not significantly different. There were similarly lower Mormon rates for hypertension and rheumatic heart disease (Lyon and Sorenson, 1978). A study of age adjusted death rates for active Mormon men in California and Utah aged between thirty five and sixty four years was 38 per cent below the national average and their remaining life expectancy was seven years greater than for United States whites (Ernstrom, 1978) and this was confirmed by a latter study (Lyon *et al.*, 1980). There are always other non-religious factors to consider which could affect the incidence of disease. In comparing Mormon and non-Mormon wives it has been shown that they had fewer hysterectomies and breast X-rays but they more often lived in rural areas and were exposed to fewer occupational hazards (West *et al.*, 1980).

The second important question is that of causal factors. There are some clear and simple correlations which appear to have general validity. All four well-known Christian sects, the Amish, the Seventh-day Adventists, the Hutterites and the Mormons, have well observed rules against smoking and their lung cancer rates are strikingly low (Troyer, 1988). The statistical picture is clear enough but other factors may also be significant as amongst the Seventh-day Adventists of whom only 4 per cent were smokers (Fraser *et al.*, 1991). The number of college educated people is twice the United States national average and the dietary pattern may contribute. Their typical vegetarian diet has about 25 per cent less fat and 50 per cent more fibre than the average non-vegetarian diet and the unsaturated to saturated fat ratio is double the average (Hardinge *et al.*, 1958, 1962). The fact that they also avoid coffee drinking which is regarded as a stimulant could account for a proportion of their reduced bladder cancer risk (P. Cole, 1971). Also there was a gradient towards higher blood pressure with increasing egg intake (Snowdon, 1988) and for those drinking tea and coffee.

The correlations for a vegetarian diet are beneficial for blood pressure, coronary heart disease mortality rate, and diabetes but fair to poor effects on the risks of breast cancer, cancer of the colon and osteoperosis (J.T. Dwyer, 1988). The consumption of meat, eggs, milk and cheese by Seventh-day Adventists did not have a negative association with any cause of death. Most figures demand complex interpretations. A study of twenty three thousand Seventh-day Adventists (R.L. Phillips, 1980) in California showed lower rates for leukaemia and colorectal cancer in men but not in women but higher rates for stomach cancer. This same study showed that 93 per cent of men born Seventh-day Adventists had never drunk alcohol and that the few who did drink either as born or converted members very few had taken one or more drinks per day for twenty years or more. Similarly very few reported that they had smoked sixteen or more cigarettes for twenty years or more. For men there were lower incidences of bladder, lung, mouth, oesophagus and larynx cancers but here a few more men than women drank but in both sexes only one per cent smoked. But smoking apart there are other differences which may be related to their diet and overall life style. Whatever suspicions we may have as to the reliability of statistics based on self-reporting, there does seem to be a significant correlation between these and rates of certain diagnosed diseases.

Clearly the dietary pattern of these people reduces the risk of getting certain diseases and delays the appearance of coronary heart disease but there is always the need to consider that any disease will appear in a social environment. In the case of these people, their distinctive overall life style will have been a significant factor in their morbidity (Fraser, 1988). It was found in a Norwegian study that only the religiously zealous members of this faith had the lower rates (Fonnebo, 1991). A study of Californian Seventh day Adventists showed that just over half did not eat meat but a much higher percentage did not drink coffee (Wynder *et al.*, 1959).

Attendance at Religious Ceremonies and Health

Medical surveys have occasionally tried to relate health to the frequency of attendance at religious services if only because it is usually easy enough to count the number of people there. The snag in this is that nothing is known of the religious attitude of mind in those that attend and the surroundings which might or might not differentiate it from an equally regular attendance at pop concerts and sporting fixtures. A study in the State of Maryland, United States compared women who attended church less than twice a year with those who went at least once weekly; 1.88 per cent of the former had confirmed or suggested cervical cancer compared with 0.64 per cent of the latter (Kinsey *et al.*, 1953). This confirms other conclusions that the higher rate of church attendance and lower rates of extramarital intercourse are correlated. A further study (Comstock *et al.*, 1970) found more reported cases of tuberculosis among those who went to church less than twice per year compared with those who went weekly and others correlated this to lower blood pressure (Levin and Vanderpool, 1989). A more carefully controlled study in Melbourne, Australia (Kune *et al.*, 1993) of patients with colorectal cancer showed that self-reported or perceived religiousness was a significantly protective factor reducing the incidence to 70 per cent of that in non-religious patients. We do not know whether these assumptions of religiousness was before or after the diagnosis had been made.

Can anything be concluded from such a broad range of association when the Ethiopian church services are long and Islamic daily prayers take up only a few minutes. We would expect the blood pressure to go down with doing relatively nothing in the former and some exercise in the latter. It would seem likely that progressive debility and serious illness would mean that many would progressively fail to maintain their previous regularity, but one such study found no such reductions (Comstock and Partridge, 1972). The clergy go to the bedridden sick and communities organise transport for the infirm. It is also likely that viewing religious services on television counts as attendance for some people who may even dress up for the portrayed services. Islamic prayers have always been predominantly a private affair and thus easily adaptable to circumstances.

It has been argued that these analyses correlating attendance at church ceremonies were typically uncontrolled and that it would only represent a proxy for functional health aspects in older Mexican-American Catholics (Levin and Markides, 1986). However subsequent studies over epidemiological factors resulted in conclusions that religious attendance had significant effects on the life satisfactions of elderly people. This association remained significant for women despite controls for age, marital status, social class and health status (Levin and Vanderpool, 1987).

We can conclude that 'religious attendance seems to possess a positive value system in terms of influencing attitudes and behaviour change that may form the framework for the prevention of deleterious health habits and thus have a positive impact on health status and well-being' (D.G. King, 1990). The reported relationship between religious attendance and well-being remains significant and may indeed have positive correlations to physical and psychological health.

The Health of Religious Specialists

If the rules and practices of a religion have any effects on the health of its followers, then those who adhere most strongly should show these most clearly. Those professionally committed to a faith as monk, priest or *sadhu* are useful in this respect since they are clearly identifiable and have usually a known number of years following the particular practices of their faiths.

In the nineteenth century the British clergy lived longer than that of the general population for males of the same age range. Many factors may have contributed to this and may will continue to do so as there are the benign effects of income, diet, good housing and regular employment but of course selective recruitment of healthy individuals to the clergy. Aspirants to the Roman Catholic clergy receive both physical and mental health examinations if only because their training is an expensive process. However the average life expectancy of Roman Catholic missionaries has been found to be less than the average for their home countries with variations between temperate Asian and tropical and sub-tropical African countries (Boldrini and Ugge, 1926). Now they have short periods abroad and can be flown home in emergencies as well as having higher standards of living.

In general these committed men do not have a uniform pattern of living and of course only the Roman Catholic priests are celibate. Others may will be cared for by wives who have their own forms of religious commitment to include the keeping fit of their pastor husbands. Greek Orthodox priest tend to marry the daughters of other priests and this physical and social environmental commitment may will run in families. Studies of monastic life allows a more controlled evaluation comparing the nutrition of Benedictine monks in Holland living on a mixed 'Western' diet with that of Trappist monks in Belgium who had frugal vegetarian diet which found more obesity among the Trappists (Groen *et al.,* 1962). A further study concluded that the prolonged consumption of a diet low in animal protein had no deleterious effects on the health of a Trappist community; it would be bad for children but these men were already mature adults when they entered monastic life. A further study showed that monks had a markedly reduced coronary heart disease mortality rate but was associated with a higher than average cancer mortality rate (Keys, 1961). In a further study of morbidity among Dutch Trappist and Benedictine monks found (Mackenbach *et al.,* 1993) that they suffered less than the general population from heart disorders, asthma and bronchitis but to be twice as likely to suffer from sinusitis, migraine, arthritis and rheumatism.

So there is no clear answer to the question of better health for these men committed to a socially enclosed religious life. They tend to live longer but their mortality from heart disease is high especially among Roman Catholic priests. Are there any differences in the health profile of nuns amongst whom cancer of the cervix is extremely rare (Towne, 1955). A twenty year study of their blood pressure showed that it remained virtually the same while that of women living in the community increased progressively (Timeo, 1985). British nuns eating little or no meat had incidences of breast and colon cancer no different to that of the general population (Kinlen, 1982).

Religious Involvement Leading to Longer Life

It is clear enough that certain practices whether they are religious or secular will shorten or lengthen life. We know that extreme asceticism will harm just as excessive promiscuity which might be associated with Tantric cults in Hinduism. Numerous surveys have established that religious devotion, special diets and the avoidance of tobacco and alcohol diminish the morbidity of people who are devoted in the whole of their lives to certain religious commitments. Seventh-day Adventists who can be expected to live longer than Irish Roman Catholics drinkers. Nevertheless this may be an unrealistic grouping for the whole small population of Pitcairn Island in the Pacific are Seventh-day Adventists just as there are devout Roman Catholics in Ireland who both drink and smoke. One can expect a moderate life to assist longevity but much must always depend on factors in the social and geographical environment which may assist or handicap this moderation.

Perhaps this should not be seen in just medical terms. A study comparing the lives of Israeli Jews in kibbutzim collective farms which were secular and those which were based on Judaism (McCullough *et al.*, 2000) found the latter finding strength and comfort from religious attendance and simple membership. Other studies have shown that the benefits drawn from religious practices provide much more than just the social contacts involved (Oxman *et al.*, 1995). Social resources are likely to decrease with age so that religious involvements often become a durable substitute or supplement for inadequate social and coping resources. Those without any strength or comfort from religion had almost three times the risk of death and not feeling deeply religious was associated with an increased risk.

So we find that religious social involvement reduces the risk of cardiac surgery (Oxman *et al.*, 1995), acts as a buffer against coronary heart disease (Goldbourt *et al.*, 1993), reduces overall mortality at least in the United States (Hummer *et al.*, 1999), and in Israeli kibbutzim (Kark *et al.*, 1996). Religious beliefs and practices reduce the possibilities of stroke (Colantonio *et al.*, 1992), suicide by Muslims rather than Hindus (Ineichen, 1998) and acts as a buffer against the impact of stress (Kendler *et al.*, 1997. Pressman *et al.*, 1990). The drawback to all these studies and there are many others is that they are from samples of Westerners from Europe and North America. Since in many cases Easterners, Latin Americans and Africans have a much greater overall involvement with religion, it would be reasonable to expect similar results from Indian, Chinese and Indonesian samples if they were available. These would be severely modified by the greater prevalence of untreated diseases which would be subject to modern quasi-traditional treatments of varying efficacy.

In this Western context religious faith and practices may positively affect health by way of other parallel behavioural features relating to the surrounding political and social environment in which many anxieties are reduced by the structure of their societies. It is to some extent public knowledge that this is related to a better health and a more healthy way of living in general. It is largely a question of whether individuals make the choice of this option. But there is a wider coverage for these not overlarge health statistics, as religion provides greater satisfaction and meaning to life, a sense of general well-being and feelings of peace; it is in this context that we need to look at miracles.

The Proportionate Reality of Health Promoting Benefits

In the influences of spirituality practices on factually based health it is too easy to get carried away by the horrors disclosed by newspaper headlines rather than the less accessible even inconspicuous advantages of other aspects. The recent stampede during the Hajj pilgrimage to Mecca which caused about a thousand deaths. In proportion to the two million pilgrims who would have performed the same ritual at the same place on the same day, we are left with a casualty rate of less than one per cent. They have died in possibly the place they would have chosen to die anyway if they had the choice and the benefits accruing to the others from participation.

Islamic suicide bombers who kill themselves and others in order to gain the benefits of paradise are small in number and have a large number of victims who have nothing to do with these beliefs. This practice whether in New York, London, Israel or Iraq can only be classified in negative health terms in much the same way that the early mediaeval Roman Catholic Flagellants in Europe spread the Great Plague in their ostentatious marches between cities (Ziegler, 1970). Those Hindus bringing back holy water from the Ganges after the *Kumbh Mela* spread cholera into their home areas up to the time that mass inoculation became available (Banerjee, 1951).

In other sectors spirituality and religion causes medical hazards and reach the public simply because of their abnormality. The refusal of Jehovah's Witnesses to accept blood transfusions for themselves and the publicity given to legal cases when parents refuse to allow them for their children to be inoculated against certain mass diseases (National Immunization Programme, 1999). However the numbers involved are very small indeed and is more a cause for medical ingenuity than for public concern. Much the same applies to Christian sects in the United States which have obtained legal exemption from compulsory inoculations or the handlers of poisonous snakes relying for the protection of their faith in the Holiness Churches of the southern United States (Schwarz, 1960). We must look at the health issues in the practices of religion and spirituality in terms of their generalities in large populations rather than as incredulous reactions to abnormal behaviour which goes against secular common sense.

As against such extraordinary behaviour we should consider activities such as the Islamic and Christian prayer procedures. These have the benefits of physical exercise with their standings, kneelings and prostrations which in the former involve the devout in seven cycles performed five times per day. While the washing of hands, face and feet prior to prayer in unclean water can be a hazard. The Christian practice of embracing others during services as assign of peace is more likely spread infection than might occur in Islamic Friday communal prayers in which there is no obligatory touching and no sharing of any communion cup.

Complementary and Alternative Medicine

Taking the perspectives of different cultures leads us to conclude that what is in Western societies seen as complementary and alternative medicine is the mainstream of activities elsewhere to which Western medicine can only be called their complementary and alternatives. Whereas in Western developed societies this is added to or considered supplementary to the dominance of scientific medicine but overall these societies which are rich enough to have developed these complex and expensive systems of medical care may be less successful than the expense would justify. Paralleling this there is an enormous expenditure on complementary medicine which has nothing much to do with spirituality and not much to do with scientific medicine either except in shared aims for human improvement with its copper bracelets, supplementary vitamins and herbal remedies which are believed to have the effects justifying the expense.

In the less developed societies and in the East generally there is a massive amount of quasi-traditional medical treatment and systems of medical understandings of great antiquity to which scientific Western medicine is supplementary. It is not just a question that scientific medicine is not available, too expensive or just plainly mistrusted. There is in the East alternative systems of care with a substantial literate intellectual backing for their methods. According to contemporary Indian understandings, a coherent body of theoretical and practical methods with direct affiliation to spirituality; a true alternative.

Then there are the medical systems of tribal and quasi-traditional systems not based on any literate continuities which in their local specifics follow unspecified but acceptable cultural parameters. These systems continue to run parallel to whatever scientific resources are available and of course keep sufferers in contact with their possibly unexpressed religious beliefs.

Then in the Western developed world which has wide-ranging and costly available scientific medical systems, there is not so much the use of alternative systems but stuck on pieces of other systems often in conjunction with newly created spiritualities or spiritualities borrowed from other cultures which may have psychosomatic rather than clinically expected effects.

Healing in the Modern City Context

There are comprehensive modern studies of the range of alternatives chosen by ordinary Western people to deal with their health problems such as that of McGuire (1988) who took a cross-section of middle class people living in New Jersey, an east coast city of the United States most had steady jobs and were found that they engaged in naturopathy, faith healing, transcendental meditation, occult therapies, psychosynthesis and American Indian healing methods. Nearly a half of this sample considered that they belonged to main-line religions. Another study of a sample in California found that they engaged in yoga, transcendental meditation and Zen Buddhism (Wuthnow, 1977). Both these studies showed that these modern educated Americans tended to be using in bits and be using in bits and pieces parallel religious systems dealing with different aspects of their lives. This is similarly the case in sub-Saharan Africa among practising Christians; the same private bricolage responding to and put together for individual needs.

These modern activities allied to spirituality served personal needs within and are a product of their social environments. They may choose one of the many alternative options commonly available in cities for reducing the problems and anxieties which they feel have not been coped with by other more established institutions. For some religious practices take a more persistent and all-embracing hold which can have a health promoting quality. A reasonable example of the religious factors affecting health are the Latter Day Saints, the Mormons who prohibit the use of tobacco and alcohol. Not only does this show up in lower mortality rates in Mormons than non-Mormons living in the same are but these rates are lower in Utah State where they comprise the majority of the population than in Missouri State where they do not (McEvoy *et al.*, 1981).

Outside the Western world fringe healing groups are the main feature of spiritual understandings in the absence of centralising institutions. In Western societies they are decidedly on the edge of acceptability since they lack a formal priesthood and institutional arrangements. They have no canonical literature to ensure uniformity or conformity beyond their culturally acceptable boundaries. There is certainly no uniformity in their rituals in which they resemble the propitiation ceremonies of subsistence farmers in Africa. Yet they remain both popular and widespread in all contemporary societies either connecting them with some parts of supposed traditions or as supposed alternatives to the inactive rituals of available institutionalised religious procedures.

They are certainly popular and widespread in modern Western or so-called Westernised societies as their large and varied populations make these possible alternatives widely available. Prayer and ritual procedures are a cathartic exercise occurring between like-minded people who give each other support in times of crisis and difficulty. By making their anxieties public in small groups of like-minded people they achieve at least a mental resolution or some direct relief which they would not get from either the orthodox medical world nor indeed from the orthodox religious one. A worried American mother engaged in faith healing described how she was soaking up her daughter's long standing eczema in prayer. Again the orthodox medical profession has no space for the worried relatives of a sick person and even when it does this is restricted to parents or partners. In Western fringe groups and elsewhere in quasi-traditional treatments the family, often extended to quite a large number of relatives, offer comfort and hope and even in some cases the nursing and feeding of the sick and distressed. The difference from orthodox religion is also apparent. A mother could go to her local church, mosque, synagogue or temple and pray for her daughter in private. She would be unable to make her distress the central concern of the priest, imam or rabbi or the whole congregation, whereas in the faith healing group however defined, this is precisely what she can do.

While most of this involvement in less organised religious movements are on a come and go basis, some become personally involved in cults in which a set of ideas is taken up by a social group under the supervision and leadership of a person whose personal charisma has attracted a group of followers (Galanter, 1999). Some cults are disastrous such as the one led by the Rev Jim Jones in Guyana in which the whole community of nearly a thousand committed suicide (Lasaga,1980; Hall and Galanter, 1999). Such occasions attract attention because of their abnormality in the opinion of outsiders while obscuring the benign results of others. In the former case what seems to go wrong is that the allegiance demanded of followers by the leader is too extreme attempting to control every aspects of their lives. Cults can however be less extreme and can bring a sense of security and meaning to people who have lost that in their ordinary lives such as the seemingly extreme detachment and repetitious ritual of the Hare

Krishna sect in some Western cities which is reputedly successful in reducing hard drug addiction.

Perhaps what modern religious healing groups and the quasi-traditional ones in economically developing societies, do most of all is to put people back in charge of their own health and distresses. The whole person is involved in an understandable social context and can perform certain actions in their rituals such as in yoga or repetitious devotions or clear their minds as in meditation or ritualised dozing as well as in what is in effect group therapy. Each of these innumerable and varied techniques brings its own kind of benefits, spiritual and physical and those benefits are not obtainable through the orthodoxies of either medicine or religion.

Traditional and Modern Medical Ideas

While modern medicine is to some extent an outgrowth of Christian religious concern for human suffering, its demonstrable effectiveness came more from the masked secular stimulus of the European Enlightenment and its selective effect on death rates is not much more than a century old. Before this and today in many parts of the world local quasi-traditional religion and indigenous medicine are still used for the treatment of human misery in which illness and misfortune are indistinguishable. Quasi-traditional healers since they are not united through any system of professional training are relatively free to innovate combining their own ideas of treatment with seemingly successful approaches which attract the attention of clients and provide for their own livelihoods. Every conceivable way of dealing with the problems of their clients continues to be tried in some societies somewhere. Herbalism, exorcism, spirit possession the propitiation of ancestors and unrelated spirits or the confession of sin. These are all group categorisations for an enormous variety of practices tailored to suit clients and situations of which no record is kept except in unreliable memories and personal feelings about their success or failure. All these methods share the same characteristics of dealing with the whole person as a single unit rather than taking what is believed to be wrong out of its social context into the abbreviating isolation of the consulting room and hospital.

It is now becoming recognised that these quasi-traditional healers whether they are diviners, herbalists or shrine priests have an important place in the public health systems of most developing societies (Ademuwagun, 1969). First there enormous numbers of these locally accepted 'professional' diagnosticians in all cities rather than in rural environments responding to the rising population numbers and their corresponding anxieties from these new environments. Even in the mid-1950s Mwanza town in Tanzania had ten times the number of quasi-traditional healers than could be found in the surrounding villages. In 1973 it was estimated that there were 15,168 quasi-traditional healers in Lagos for a population of 665,246 (Harrison, 1974). It must be accepted that these men and women have developed valid and successful skills in dispensing curative and preventive treatments and in providing rehabilitative care usually combining physical and spiritual anxieties. They belong to the same cultures as their patients, sharing common beliefs and values about the probable religious origins of their misfortunes and using the same symbols of communication. Since their standing depends on their reputations passed on by word of mouth, the successful ones have skills in interpersonal relations including counselling with sympathy, identification with their clients and very possibly genuine concern. They are usually not in a hurry to get on with the next patient. Yet despite these advantages there has been little overall utilization of their services because both sides of this divide between Western and quasi-traditional medicine start from different premises. They do not see any immediate advantages from cooperation. When an Ethiopian theological student in London had a nervous breakdown, his friends told his supervisor that there was little that the British National Health Service could do to help as 'he was mad in an Ethiopian way'. The doctors who have received lengthy training in Western scientific methods and thinking consider that their methods are effective in an all-embracing way. They are far from ready to accept these corner-shop 'untrained' healers as even in some vague way their professional equals (Lambo, 1971).

There is another important aspect which highlights the value of these quasi-traditional healers because good doctors cure rather than cures make good doctors. Certainly Western drugs and some methods such as injections and the use of the stethoscope are popular and inspire considerable confidence but that is only part of what is being considered by ordinary patients. The whole Western scientific processing of the sick and upset is off-putting with the disinterestedness of medical personnel in patients as people as any visit to the waiting rooms of any hospital shows readily enough. Peasants and the urban poor are often dealt with on conveyor belt approaches by subordinates (Alland, 1964). The choice is often between the local quasi-traditional healer with whom relationships are culturally understandable and inexpensive in time and money and the local dispensary with few medicines often in short supply and only available through corruption. It is the former who provides the physical and psychological health service for most of the population most of the time (Imperato, 1977).

The rituals which accompany Western medical treatments and examinations which are regarded by its practitioners as an essential part of medicine such as the uniforms of nurses, the decoration of hospitals and the professional assumption that doctors are sexually detached, are often both direct and cursory. In most contemporary societies it is not possible to find out what is wrong with a patient in less than an hour of somewhat evasive conversations. A concentration on the clinical and biological misses out the social and religious diagnoses of these quasi-traditional healers which may be nearer the point of what is wrong and is thus mutually amenable to changes of mind and social and religious readjustments (Bibeau, 1979).

Even medical institutions run by Christian bodies and without direct missionary intentions to convert, may seem very secular to people from other religions or tribal backgrounds. Even sympathetic doctors and nurses may not be able to bridge the gap between their patients and their beliefs when they are committed to one faith with its symbols on the wall. The patient can at least assume that there is a religious dimension but that it is a leap into the unknown even with the charitable work of Mother Teresa and her nuns among the abandoned of Calcutta. It is perhaps an unfortunate fact that however charitable the grounds are for the work of medical institutions, it is not an obviously sympathetic environment for the social and religious problems surrounding the illnesses of their patients. It will not include any understanding of the significances of a culturally alien spirit world whose existence is not accepted by them either professionally or personally.

Newly emerging Christian independent Churches with a wider understanding of the intellectual backgrounds of their followers have been better able to deal with their spiritual needs in ritualistic ways which are culturally unacceptable to Western theological thinking. A long queue of people wait to go through the laying on of hands for the reduction of their illnesses and other miseries after Legio Maria Masses in Nairobi. This is a rare breakaway sect from the Roman Catholic Church has gone against all the changes in liturgy inaugurated the Vatican Two conference retaining Latin and indeed increasing its previous ritualism to excess.

The extent of cooperation between quasi-traditional healers with their social understandings and spiritual connections and government agencies varies from place to place. It is always low because for any formal cooperation would risk alienating the medical profession and international understandings. The recent situation in South Africa where a very senior politician took an unscientifically supported and traditional view of the origins of AIDS highlighted the built-in difficulties of any such cooperation.

Some Malaysian healers have attended government sponsored courses on elementary medicine and hygiene (Bolton, 1968). More significantly they have been used by businesses which have had their production workers possessed by spirits leading to the mass hysteria of women employees for which scientific medicine had no solutions (Ong, 1985). In India there has been some involvement of these traditional healers in family planning (Neumann and Bhatia, 1973).

What may have happened generally is that these men and women are politically and socially powerful because of their connections with the spirit world. They are pragmatically and humanely useful since these governments are unable to provide adequate and revenue supported countrywide medical services. Their work is tacitly allowed to continue probably because they are too widely active and popular at every level of society for any politically based bureaucratic control to be a practical plan (Jansen, 1974).

It is valuable to compare the healing practices of a Coptic Christian priest (Giel *et al.*, 1968) and a Muslim sheikh (Workneh and Giel, 1975) in Ethiopia. The people consulting both these religious practitioners for solutions to their problems which could only be broadly described as medical. They were suffering from physical and mental illnesses as well looking for solutions to social misfortunes. In the one healer there was a combination of roles which in developed societies have turned into specialisations expensively isolated from those who have troubles in terms of time, motion and resources. This brings out in yet another form the fact that spirituality cannot be isolated from any of the other factors which comprise the experiences of individuals. In both situations the cures were gradual and consisted of combinations of medical treatment, social explanations and psychological advice supported by the confidence of the patients which came from their religious faith. Both these men had a particular form within which their consultations took place which allowed them to provide their own personalised interpretations. The Coptic priest in trance states combining his charismatic personality and suggestive questioning. The Muslim sheikh was equally dogmatic telling his patients that they could only be cured by having faith in Allah and hitting the afflicted part with his hand.

The Understanding of Miracles

Whatever the scientific realities of any particular case, it is perhaps more satisfying to conclude that any cure or solution is miraculous than to attribute it to rational causes. What is considered miraculous varies in time and with social environments and events which the people themselves attribute to divine actions is probably as globally common as it has ever been. These researchers looked at these patients in ways that were perhaps inevitable with professionals trained in Western scientific methods starting with the assumption that cures were unlikely to occur. They were perhaps reluctant to state that these diverse religious therapies appeared to 'work'. The Ethiopians involved and indeed their families, friends and neighbours probably took an alternative approach assuming that such procedures would work and that when they did not, there must be other factors which prevented the wanted solutions which of course were always readily available.

In important ways religious practices as much as religious convictions gave their participants the confidence and courage to carry on with their lives instead of giving way to despair. It is here that we should consider a most important aspect of religion and its relationship to medicine. It is only the Roman Catholic Church which records 'miracles' which are proved to have occurred at such shrines as that of Our Lady at Lourdes; abrupt events which have gone against medical prognoses and they are few indeed.

The English medieval concept of a miraculous cure was widespread and well documented (Finucane, 1977). The tomb of St. Thomas Becket at Canterbury was associated with 1141 miracles between 1171and 1189 and that of Godric of Finchale with 244 although he was never canonized. The point surely must be that then as now there are many supplicants at the tombs of Muslim and Christian saints who feel 'miraculously' better and have no interest in having what they personally believe to be true authenticated by what they see to be suspicious outsiders. Given the workings of the mind and the individual understandings of personal spirituality, it would be surprising if the majority of supplicants did not feel better after having gone through religious procedures. Miracles and belief in miracles continue to be a modern phenomena. A woman who had been surgically sterilised and the procedure anatomically confirmed latter came to want a further child became pregnant and produced a further child for which event the medical report was headed 'mind over matter' (McKelvey and Dornan, 2004).

We have only covered a small range of the correlations between religious practices and disease of which there is an enormous amount of medical data. Disease is only one conspicuous part of any assessment of health. Obviously we all die of something which perhaps in younger persons would be called a disease rather than the wearing out of the physiological body. So we can to some extent reduce the risks of incurring some diseases but equally there is always the obvious chance of thus increasing the likelihood of others. We need to look at the possible ways in which religious practices may at least temporarily subvert the processes of nature. The use of prayer, the commonest of all religious activities whether it comes within the orbit of what might be called orthodox understandings of religion or the largely unseen and unknown practices of spirituality.

If we mean by a miracle that there has been a sudden and radical change in a physical condition recorded by a physician both before and after such a event, then they are rare. So infrequent as to positively discourage anyone from putting their hopes in such occurrences. The chances of such an authenticated miracles at the shrine to Our Lady at Lourdes has been put at 300 to I against (Garner, 1974). We should look at miracles in the context of faith rather than in that of clinical medicine. To the modern analytical mind this seems little more than an example of the credulity of the uneducated and ancient mind. If the records were similarly available there would be comparable figures connected with Buddhism, Hinduism, Islam and Taoism but such a conclusion might be a part of modern secularist thought. There is no easy psychosomatic explanation for these records of the sudden total disappearance of crippling physical disabilities or the restoration of speech, vision and hearing to the previously blind, deaf and mute.

Divine healing has a long modern history starting with a Divine Healing Conference with international attendance which was held in London in 1885. During the recent charismatic revival in the United States there were thousands of testimonials to divine healing cures published. It would be inappropriate to lump these into the same category of credulity if that is indeed the appropriate explanation (Harrell, 1975:87). The range of illnesses healed was as broad as medical science but the largest numbers cured were headaches, nervous conditions and alcoholism. These people did not just believe that they had been cured through some divine intervention, they knew it to be a fact. As Garner writes 'and so the sick leave Lourdes still with their bodily ailments, all but a few. But they are cured—cured of despair, of sadness of their inability to accept mortality.' What is the definition of health? Optimum adaptation to one's environment. In this sense, nearly every pilgrim, bodily sick or not, who goes to Lourdes receives a benison of health (Garner, 1974:126). It is in the development of such an understanding that we will latter look at spirituality and well-being after an examination of prayer.

There are ways in which religion and medicine can be integrated to the satisfaction of both sides of this continuously difficult relationship between science and religion. In Thailand there has been an on-going difficulty of finding bodies for the training of medical students and indeed for finding parts for transplantation because of the Buddhist belief in transmigration. These problems were overcome by calling the individual body 'great teacher' instead of referring to it as a medical object. Before for the start of the course there is a dedication ceremony attended by faculty members, students, relatives and Buddhist monks in which this title is conferred on the bodies, thus giving the deceased merit and a relationship with the students. At the end of the course there is a further ceremony including a procession with Buddhist monks to the cremation site in which the bodies are carried by the students and pamphlets distributed with a picture of the deceased, details of their lives and expressions of gratitude from faculty members and students as well as condolences to their families (Winkelman and Guldner, 2004).

Pilgrimages

The visiting of important places of religious significance has been common enough ever since records were available.Its significance has always to be seen in the social contexts and personal psychologies of those involved. There has often been a tourism element and in Taiwan religious pilgrimages to well-known temples are combined with shopping (Yuan, 1988). In Japan such tours are a commercially created and are a welcome break for the monotony of the lives of an increasingly aging and isolated population (Woss, 1993). In India the monotony of subsistence farming is broken by a web of social occasions combining thousands of religious fairs with pilgrimages (Bhardwaj, 1973). In fact pilgrimages are virtually a universal global activity of increasing rather than decreasing popularity because of greater affluence and the ease of travel apart from the best known ones to Mecca, Jerusalem and Banaras. These are all dwarfed in popularity with the *Kumbh Mela* pilgrimage to the Ganges at Hardwar, every twelve years to which an estimated seventy million people came on the last occasion of which a proportion may not have been Hindus.

Modern Western Europe has no fewer than six thousand active shrines which probably receive more than eighty million pilgrims per year. Lourdes alone has some 4 million per year and the newly created one at Medjugorge in Croatia more than a million in addition to these Roman Catholic shrines there are re-established Protestant ones (Nolan and Nolan, 1989). In Hispanic Latin America there are nearly a thousand pilgrimage sites drawing visitors from outside their areas (Nolan, 1991).

The pilgrimage involves almost every aspect of human individual and group physical and psychological activity. Climbing mountains often with bare feet, crawling to shrines on their knees, going round shrines with the movements of a caterpillar, drinking and soaking oneself in sacred but polluted water, kissing of religious images as tangible expressions of their underlying beliefs. All this along with the camaraderie of a shared experience almost as a holiday atmosphere in which the expenditure of time and effort was balanced by spiritual returns. What is the definition of health? Optimum adaptation to one's environment and in this sense, nearly every pilgrim, bodily sick or not, who goes to Lourdes, Mecca, Banaras and thousands of other shrines receives some benefits.

Other Systems of Spirituality and the Maintenance of Health

What we have seen so far is the relationship of Western scientific medicine to various religious activities which have a sufficiently distinctive practice to justify the assumption of a connection rather more than a correlation. In this context it cannot be suggested that the 'religions of the book', Christianity, Islam and Judaism are providing alternative ways of contributing to health. They have each contributed different elements to modern medicine but this is a study of contemporary influences of religion on health not of the history of science and religion. All three have histories in which the behaviour of their believers and theoreticians have had some influence on health but they had little understanding of the bases of disease. These results must have been more or less incidental rather than the results of thoughtful understandings of disease. To impute more than this to the events of history is to distort the nature of the progressive accumulations of scientific progress even to accepting its fashionable nature (Kuhn, 1970).

All we can say is that these religions have practices which affect health but none have alternative systems of medicine which their believers can choose to follow. There may be some relatively minor differences in behaviour between hospitals run by Jewish and

Roman Catholic charities but their medical activities are virtually the same. So anything medically specific to these religions remains in the behaviour of cults and sects which reject some aspects of modern medicine such as the refusal to use blood transfusions by Jehovah's Witnesses, but such believers do not follow coherent alternative systems of medical practice. The Hutterites of Canada who have a more comprehensive communal life than Israeli kibbutz communes, have no hesitation in using modern medicine for their members.

On the other hand in the East there are coherent alternative systems of medical understanding and practice which have not only survived but are popularly used by enormous numbers, institutionalised and receive official support. In contemporary China according to the World Health Organisation, 95 per cent of hospitals have units for traditional medicine just as many do in Indian hospitals. Thus in both China and India there are two systems of medicine in public use and in vague equality with complex written backings and not as a parallel system in which quasi-traditional medicine is used in secret.

6 Spirituality and the Risk to Health

The Enhanced Risk of Disease from Religious Behaviour

Infectious diseases and harmful behaviour need certain conditions in which to thrive for which the latter prosper in small communities. On the other hand most diseases need large populations in order to survive as in small populations they either wipe out the host populations and hence themselves or they produce immunity in the population so that people survive while the disease agents die out. So infectious diseases tend to do best where they occur in large populations. Where there are shifting communities and in situations where individuals are moving around rapidly into new areas where there are new people arriving and the disease agents can find new people to infect. Therefore religious occasions which bring people together over social and demographic boundaries are likely to help the spread of diseases. Religious exclusiveness which tends to cut people off from each other and to close group boundaries will hinder their spread. Religions tend to be socially expressed whether institutionalised or not. Spirituality in so far as it is separate to religion, tends to be isolated in individuals; it does not necessarily have any need to be expressed in group activities.

Besides infectious diseases there are deficiency and genetic diseases. These can be increased by religious practices. The total Vegan upbringing of young children by the Black Hebrew community in Israel (Shinwell and Gorodischer, 1982) has been shown to retard their growth and to produce in them a wide range of deficiency diseases. Similarly the overall refusal of the Faith Assembly in Indiana, United States to use medical assistance has resulted in significantly higher infant and maternal mortality rates

(Kauntiz, *et al.*, 1984). With respect to genetic diseases the Amish with their persistent inbreeding have produced a large proportion of children with defective traits (McKusick, 1973). Several normally rare recessive gene disorders regularly occur among them. Some 12 genetic disorders were first identified among the Amish and a further 18 have been studied among them.

Fatalism

If religion imparts fatalistic ideas, these must lessen the conscious and subconscious efforts of individuals to overcomes their diseases and misfortunes. Other individuals may feel that they need not attempt to cure them. However this has to be assessed in the social environment in which it occurs. There is an enormous difference in what sufferers can expect to happen after disease or disaster in the towns and villages of Britain and Indonesia which cannot be isolated as attributable to religion. There is a saying attributed to the Prophet Muhammad that as plague and death in battle came from God, it must be seen as martyrdom (Dols, 1987). The Ottoman Empire was notorious for its fatalism when confronted with the plague (Slack, 1985). Christian thought at one time held that predestination alone explained why plague was irresistible and that providence alone offered the only effective consolation for those afflicted or threatened by the plague (Slack, 1985). This contrasts with the action of the Swedish Lutheran Bishop and his Church who maintained that spreading of the plague should be equated with murder and that practical measures should be taken in addition to repentance and prayer (Ottosen, 1988). Hinduism as a religious way of life teaches no gospel of mercy to those outside the caste in which individuals are born. Since an individual's earthly condition is largely determined by one's previous existence and Hindus as well as Buddhists and Taoists are religiously preoccupied with changing their future 'reincarnations ', the doctrine of *karma*, their minds are deadened both culturally and religiously to the states of mind and body of 'outcaste' human beings (Shils, 1959).

Under modern conditions the fate of children with malignant disease can still be thought to be in the hands of God and beyond the control of the treating doctor (Bahakim, 1987). This same fatalism can lead to Muslims and indeed Christians having fewer emotional reactions to the loss of their children (Bedikian, *et al.*, 1985; Bedikian and Thompson, 1985). A study of this loss among American families found that there were differences in the aderenocorticotropin endocrine reactions to bereavement according to their religious beliefs; Protestants attributed the loss of their children to their own moral faults and had higher excretion rates while the Roman Catholics who believed that it was God's will had lower endocrine reactions (Hofer, 1979).

A study of the impact of genetic disease in Saudi families (Panter-Brick, 1991) showed that all parents believed God determined their fate in granting health or illness. One mother said 'the disease runs in my family, but only God knows why some children are fine and others are not'. The researcher concluded that 'Parents...used religion as a vehicle for expressing their feelings (Insh'Allah or God willing being one common expression). Many popular attitudes towards health and disease were rooted in the body of Islamic teaching elaborated in the *Koran*, narratives of the Prophet Muhammad's life (hadith) and the writings of theologians....They believed their burdens were willed by God and should be born patiently (*Koran*.LVII vv.22-3. Naught of disaster befalleth in the earth or in yourselves but it is in the Book before we bring it into being....Grieve not for the sake of that which hath escaped you). This helped parents to overcome feelings of anger or helplessness..... Mothers would say 'I must accept His will'. The more devout families perceived suffering as a test of their faith....Religion also made possible the denial of responsibility..... Lastly, religious beliefs allowed hope for the child's survival and did not prevent parents from seeking a cure. According to an authoritative Hadith 'the Prophet said' O servants of God, seek medical treatment. God has put a remedy for every malady, clear to whoever knows it and unclear to whoever does not know it'. It seems more than likely that the majority of men and women are fatalistic. Some diseases can be cured but are replaced by others and accidents are so sporadic and inexplicable that statistical chance is a singularly unsatisfactory explanation for personal experiences of what may happen next day or round the next corner.

The Spread of Mass Diseases and Pilgrimages

It is easy enough to catalogue the spread of plague and other diseases through religious practices before there was any knowledge of how infection was spread, so it needs to be assessed in modern circumstances. Some modern behaviour can still provide opportunities for the spread of plague such as the Hindu practice of feeding some hundred thousand rats in a Bikanir temple in memory of the Goddess Karni Ma. It is pilgrimages that provide the optimum environments for the spread of infectious diseases.

The best known of the world's pilgrimages is the one to Mecca with its annual concentration of Muslims in a small area of Saudi Arabia for which the whole country is annually mobilised to receive some two million foreign and national pilgrims. Four transport companies alone in 1974 were providing 2550 cars and 2957 buses with another two thousand ordered (Bushnak, 1978). The preventative medical problems have increased with the enormous increase in the number of pilgrims arriving by air. In the past the difficulty of getting there made sure that the weakest pilgrims were weeded out en route and the incubation period for some diseases passed before they entered the country. The use of modern transport has meant gross congestion in and around Mecca with the resulting problems of inadequate sanitation since numbers of pilgrims have no experience of public control over excretion, noise and physical exhaustion. The Muslim year follows a lunar calendar for their devotions which means that periodically the Hajj pilgrimage takes place in the hottest time of the year. There is the strain of a physical as well as a spiritual experience and there have been regular mass deaths from stampedes. While the standards of health care have improved and many countries now send their own national medical teams to cope with the health problems of their own peoples in their own languages. It is still a health hazard as one range of mass diseases are replaced by others. There are still the inevitable consequences of overcrowding in stifling heat. Taking home water from the spring of Zam Zam may also contribute to the spread of disease as it has done with other pilgrimages particularly in India.

In almost every country there are festivals related to religion which attract large numbers of pilgrims with secular as well as religious interests. In India alone there are some four hundred religious fairs (Bhardwaj, 1973) attracting thousands of pilgrims from outside the focal areas. Every twelfth year at the *Kumbh Mela* enormous numbers of pilgrims congregate on the banks of the Ganges at Hardwar and the provincial government estimated that some seventy million people came to the last gathering. Since 1950 inoculations against cholera have been compulsory but in the last year before this some 52 thousand died from cholera (Banerjea, 1951) and there are now thousands of mobile lavatories. The Ganges which is considered a holy river from source to the sea is heavily polluted and it would be hard to think of any better way of spreading water born diseases than the religious practices of these Hindu pilgrims ceremonially bathing in the river, drinking its water and taking home samples as gifts to their relatives who have not been able to make the pilgrimage.

Christian pilgrimages may also spreads disease as at Lourdes the ill and often incontinent pilgrims are bathed in the shrine's spring which has its water only changed twice per day. There are altogether thirteen tubs which at peak times immerse about eighty-five pilgrims an hour (Marnham, 1980) to a total of over seven thousand on a summer's day. A devout theory holds that the microbes die in the Lourdes water and words to that effect appeared in a recent Guide to the Grotto. The same idea holds for those who immerse themselves in the polluted but sacred Ganges. This claim for the water at Lourdes was based on experiments in the

1930s which found that the water was polluted with colon bacillus, staphylococcus, streptococcus, pyocyneus and other microbes but showed that experimental animals were unaffected by these bacilli which came in the Lourdes water. The fact that there is pollution in this water is not of any importance to those who come or are brought to Lourdes with this bathing intention as the key event of their pilgrimage. There are parallels to this in the holy water at the entrances to Roman Catholic churches in which those coming in dip their fingers and this water has been found to contain typhoid microbes (Losito, 1946). The national Christian shrine in Mexico City as well as Hindu shrines in India have numbers of pilgrims approaching these centres on their knees often for long distances causing abrasions. Ireland's holiest mountain has pilgrims in bare feet climbing to the summit. These activities show that an element of deliberate asceticism is part of all pilgrimages.

Missionaries as Sources of Infection

The movements of small number of people dedicated to particular faiths have often gone out to new places of residence to spread their beliefs and this combined with their different standards of living has meant that they bring in diseases as well as taking foreign ones back to their own localities. Whereas in the past Roman Catholic stayed abroad for long periods often with only one leave after twenty years, now missionaries and their families come and go much more frequently. Missionaries on leave in the United States have been shown to have high levels of intestinal protozoa and helminths (McQuay, 1967) as well as hepatitis (Frame, 1968). Missionaries were found to have a rate of 1301 per thousand as against 24.2 for the domestic population (Kendrick, 1974).

Missionaries are also known to have affected the health and survival of those they have sought to convert. American Protestant missionaries and their supporters flying light aircraft have been persistently in and out of isolated communities in Brazil which have grass air strips. A Yanomamo village of 179 people suffered 40 per cent mortality with no children there under the age of ten years because of infectious diseases brought in by missionaries (Chagnon, 1977) as was also the case for the Wai Wai of Guyana (Guppy, 1958).

Infection from the Practice of Cannibalism

If individuals eat parts of a fellow human being who is suffering from any transmissible disease, then they are likely to be infected depending on how these parts have been cooked. In New Guinea there is a severe degenerative disease of the central nervous system known to medical science only from 1957 and named 'kuru' after the valley in which it occurred. The doctors found that the women there ate the flesh of deceased men who were not killed because the community felt that this retained their spirit through the fecundity of the women. Quite reasonably it was concluded originally that this disease was passed on genetically through women; the decline of the custom led to a decline in the disease (Glasse, 1967). The people regarded the disease as being caused by witchcraft. Most women were cannibals eating anyone but close relatives whereas men did so less often as they thought it robbed them of their vitality and protection against arrows in tribal warfare. Overall men seldom ate the bodies of women because women both living and dead were believed to be physically dangerous to men and were best avoided in many circumstances. The women prepared the corpses for eating, working bare handed, squeezing the raw brain tissue into a pulp before cooking and it was in the brain tissue that there was the highest concentrations of infected doses (Gajdusek, 1973). The point to remember in this example of bizarre and dangerous behaviour is that given the premises, the behaviour is logical. No more illogical than the practices of the Faith Assembly in refusing medical treatment or the Bikanir Hindus preserving rats in a temple in honour of the Goddess Karni Ma.

Diet

A good balanced diet heightens resistance to disease and a poor one lowers it. How do religious dietary rules affect resistance but there are also periods of religious celebration which affect health by their overloading of the digestive systems. The Christian period of Lent in Western societies is no longer a period of marked deprivation since now believing individuals deprive themselves of some luxury but not of staple items in their diets.

On the other hand the Muslim holy month of Ramadhan is a lunar month of no eating between sunrise and sundown. Not too difficult when night and day are equally divided but much more difficult in the northern and southern hemispheres as the month of fasting works its way round to very short nights so that fasting might be for eighteen hours. Muslims suffer more from lack of water particularly when they live in environments which are periodically very hot. Some devout believers do not even swallow their own spittle in day light hours. In young Muslims it has been shown that there are significant increases in the intakes of protein and carbohydrates together with a reduction in the number of meals taken combined with an increase in family meals leading to an increase in body weight (Frost and Pirani, 1987). In both Britain (Aslam and Healey, 1986) and Kuwait (Aslam and Assad, 1986) Muslims have changed their drug dosage timings during Ramadhan. Many Jews discontinue medications during the eight days of the Passover (Chusid *et al.*, 1982). There are widespread exceptions for the old, sick, travellers, pregnant women and nursing mothers as well as those involved in war. With these reasonable exceptions in mind, there are not likely to be adverse effects on health, although in the first days such fasting combined with staying up late to eat twice in the night and to eat breakfast before dawn might be related to accidents and lost business opportunities.

The fasting rules of the Ethiopian Coptic Church are much more extreme than this and can become a health hazards. Their regulations prohibit eating before mid-day and the eating of any food of animal origin except fish at any time during the 110 to 150 annual days of fasting. One result of this is a clinical condition known as 'injera' gastritis caused by the required diet of baked flour pancakes. The lasting effects are especially visible in young children who receive a quarter less of an adequate intake of protein especially as they receive no milk and animal protein. This is an ominous change for the worse in the already inadequate diet of the poor (Knutsson and Selinus, 1970).

Whatever may have been the ethological basis for male dominance it is certainly maintained in all religions and is shown in the distribution of food. The men of the household are fed first and when there are shortages boys are given preference over girls. This is as much a feature of traditional societies such as the Orang Asli of Malaysia (Bolton, 1968) as it will be in the urban slums of Mumbai, Lima and Nanking. In the distribution of meat from sacrificed animals, the preferred parts go to men in patrilineal relationships to the donor and there are often discriminatory taboos which affect the protein intake of women of childbearing age and children.

The general restrictions on Muslims not eating pork which is often rationalised on the Prophet's foresight over that animal's uncleanness is probably of little health concern as there are no restrictions on eating chickens which have dirty eating habits. It is difficult to assess the Buddhist and Hindu vegetarian aims since their overall health status is more strongly governed by poverty and the agricultural cycle than by their food intakes which in agricultural communities is likely to be reasonable in the months after good harvests but increasingly inadequate until the next harvest comes around. Vegetarianism on the basis of religious convictions would seem to be usually based on the economic status allowing choice.

However in Western style Zen Buddhism believers practice their own system of macrobiotics which is thought to create a system of spiritual awakening or rebirth by a largely cereal-vegetarian diet combined with the avoidance of many fluids (Ohsawa, 1965). This diet is believed to help in achieving a general state of well-being and is regarded as a preventer of as well as a cure for cancer, mental diseases and heart trouble while medical consultancy should be avoided. 'We shall demonstrate the macrobiotic preparation of delicious aesthetic meals that cure all illnesses (present and future) giving at the same time longevity and usefulness to everybody, at no expense and with no special training'. Individuals who follow such a diet for long periods are in danger of serious nutritional; deficiencies including scurvy (Sherlock and Rothchild, 1967), anemia, hypoproteinemia, hypocalcedemia and actual starvation. Cases have been recorded in which infants were receiving only 40 per cent of nationally recommended dietary intakes (Robson *et al.*, 1974) and severe malnutrition occurred (I.F. Roberts, *et al.*, 1979).

There are other diseases of developing societies which are to some extent caused by religious rules such as Kwashiorkor in Africa which comes almost entirely from the absence of sufficient protein in the diets of children. This absence of protein is often the result of religious taboos on the consumption of meat, chicken and eggs by children and also by their mothers. This debilitating condition may be fatal and also as a precondition for other diseases. Ganda women do not eat meat and subsist largely on a diet of cooked bananas and vegetables and as a staple diet for children and this often leads to Kwashiakor (Welbourn, 1955).

The religious correlations to defective diets seem to be either situations in which the predisposition to inadequacy is beyond the control of individuals either because these practices are nearly culturally universal or are the results of their environments and so are unavoidable. They are also the results of deliberate choice by individuals who join religious cults which have restrictive diets as part of their commitments and are thought to lead to religious and moral improvements.

ceremonies. If in this matter we set on one side the effects of religion on any sense of well-being, 'Christian ideas on cleanliness must be counted a step back from those of civilised people either pagan or Jewish. The Christian rejection of washing (because of the idea that nudity and mixed bathing led to promiscuity) and tolerance of filth (and Saint Jerome felt that) the man who bathed in Christ needed no second bath'(Darlington, 1969:299-300). So people who cleaned themselves up before going to church do so for social reasons rather than because of religious obligations. Christians have no global reputation for cleanliness.

Whereas washing is normally thought of as a cleansing activity, it is not always the case. Much depends on social, religious and the availability of water. Islam is quite distinct in requiring washing before participating in the obligatory five periods of praying each day. The *Koran* commands 'O you who believe; when you rise up to pray, wash your faces and your hands as far as the elbows and wipe your heads and wash your feet to the ankles' (Sura, 5;7). This is certainly a hygienic process in its frequency and universality but much depends on the purity of the piped and flowing water provided at every mosque. In Yemen and Bangladesh where this water comes from water storage tanks there is the risk of contracting infections from guinea worms (Underwood and Underwood, 1980). In Egypt the devout who washed themselves in open water had higher levels of bilharzias infections than the less devout (Farooq and Mallah, 1966). It has been suggested than the lower rates of infant mortality among the Jews of New York in comparison to the Roman Catholic Italians may have been due to their ritualising of cleanliness.

Contact with Religious Objects

In almost all religions there is some contact between believers and what they believe is sacred; there is touching, kissing and eating from certain utensils. Muslims as part of their Hajj pilgrimage to Mecca kiss the stone in the 'kaaba', the so-called navel of the universe. Orthodox Christians kiss icons, venerated pictures of sacred figures and Roman Catholics kiss the foot of a wooden Christ during the Good Friday services even though an altar server wipes it with a cloth between kisses. Recently in St. Petersburg thousands queued all day in order to kiss an icon which was on loan for a short time from the United States. In such practices it can be assumed that potentially harmful microorganisms are deposited on the objects of devotion by some of the devotees and that these are transferred to subsequent touchers. In Greek churches it is possible to see that the glass covering an icon becomes misted over from the kisses it receives and there is no wiping of the surface.

The sharing of the communion cup from which some Christian denominations ceremonially drink as part of their key religious ceremony has come under experimental study to test the possibility of transferring infections (Gregory *et al.*, 1967) which found that wiping the cup between drinkers had little effect on lowering the bacterial count. Another survey (Hobbs *et al.*, 1967) found that it reduced the bacterial count by about 90 per cent. The wine in the communion cup killed certain microorganisms within two or three minutes but Microbacterium avium was undiminished after an hour and Staphylococcus pyogenes was completely protected by the saliva droplets in which it was suspended. More recent studies have held that the communion cup cannot pass on either Hepatitis B virus or the HIV virus (Gill, 1988). This is still a potential dangerous process of sharing the communion with persons infected with new forms of tuberculosis (Kingston, 1988). Much might depend on the position of the infected person in the queue and the extent of the lips contact with the cup's rim.

We can see from these examples that religious practices may spread diseases wholly accidentally but in making these connections that microbes can be transferred from one person or surface to another person in entirely scientifically acceptable ways. We have to be careful not to ignore the ever present psychological and social element which can influence the individual aspects of epidemiology. In a recent study of 28,169 Chinese Americans (D.P. Phillips *et al.*, 1993) it was shown that they died significantly earlier than matched white controls if they had one of the particular diseases associated with their birth year phase. Chinese astrology holds that a person's birth year phase such as the Earth makes him or her specially susceptible to tumours. This study showed that such people did in fact die 1.3 to 4.9 years earlier than the controls if they had 'their' kind of disease. The explanation appears to be largely psychosomatic and that an element of fatalism or loss of the will to live may will speed up the course of those astrologically connected diseases.

Enhanced Mortality and Religion

It seems unlikely that any major religion will have consistent behavioural factors which lead to increased morbidity and mortality; their active members are in too many different social environments. However in the smaller sects there will be some behavioural consistency which will relate to adverse factors. In the southern United States there are some small Christian Protestant sects that believe that if they are free from sin then they can handle poisonous snakes and drink poison and they will not be harmed. It is not surprising that some die as the result of these dangerous practices (Schwarz, 1960; Alther, 1975).

On a larger scale the Church of Christ Scientist despite prohibiting the use of tobacco and alcohol having a mortality rate among college graduates which is higher than among comparable graduates who are not Christian Scientists (Simpson, 1989, 1991). In a comparison with Seventh-day Adventists who also do not use alcohol or tobacco, they still had a higher mortality rate (Simpson, 1991), the difference being that the latter have no objections to use of medical services. Another survey showed that Christian Scientists had death higher rates than the national averages for malignancy and heart disease and that 6 per cent of their deaths were preventable had they taken advantage of currently available medical services (G.E. Wilson, 1956).

Religious Violence

If we can accept that people will not continually behave in ways that threaten their own existence and their community we can surely conclude that some types of destructive behaviour will be unlikely to catch on socially. So there is ample data of the destructiveness of religious beliefs and practices held by small sects which underline their distinctiveness by such behaviour. They are statistically insignificant and their main function is to provide researchers with isolatable behaviour. There are few reasons for seeing religious and spiritual ideas and activities as in any way functionally hostile to human survival in any comprehensive sense. However religious violence is another matter altogether.

It is perhaps generally assumed in developed societies that religion as a motivating force is of diminishing importance and at most one confined to personal behaviour and its choices. This comfortable theory based on rational man ignores the destructive power of religion in contemporary wars and civil wars which would include crusades, martyrdoms, terrorism, sacrifices and of course genocide.

Historically religions have been extremely destructive of human populations and their environment apart from their responsibility for the spread of disease (Reynolds and Tanner, 1995: Chapter 13). In 1893, 33 thousand pilgrims died in and around Mecca and the dead remained unburied (Izzedine. no date). It is not so much the numbers who have been killed historically for religious reasons but their proportion to whole populations. The Taiping Rebellion in China, 1851-64 under a leader claiming to be the brother of Jesus Christ (Boardman, 1952) may have killed up to 20 million people so that in some cities only dogs survived (Wakeman, 1966). Tamurlane killed from piety (Groussert, 1970) about 80% of the populations along the belt of Arab-Iranian civilisations (Lamb, 1932); his men are said to have piled 70 thousand heads outside the walls of Isfahan. At the Christian siege of Damietta in 1219 only 3000 Moslems out of a population of 80 thousand survived

(Oliver, 1894). These are very high proportions of these populations significantly reducing their pressure on their environment.

More recently the Turkish killing of some 35 per cent of Armenians in 1915-17 (Boyajian, 1972) does not quite reach up to the same levels of environmental relief although the figures will be higher if emigration is included. The killing of over 10 thousand Mahdists in the Sudan at the battle of Omdurman in 1893 (Levy, 1974) would probably be about the same level of population reduction. Some better-known historical massacres would have had little environmental effect. The St Bartholemew's massacre of Protestants by Catholics in France only killed 1% of that population (Benedict, 1991). Much the same applies to Jewish pogromes in Russia and Poland over the end of the last century rising to an estimated 60 thousand killed in 1917-21 mainly by the White Ukrainian Army in 887 major and 349 pogrammes [Encyclopaedia Judaica, (1971).13.694-701]. Finally, the Holocaust killed off whole Jewish communities in a return to the population obliterations of Tamurlane, with an estimated six million Jews killed in all between 1933 and 1945.

A study of 106 wars between 1820 and 1952 (Wilkinson, 1980; Richardson, 1950) showed that differences of religion were frequently cited as a cause of fighting in 35% of inter-religious pairs with different beliefs about the world in general having been the cause of fighting in 16% of all belligerent pairs. Three quarters of all inter-religious pairs had a Christian member and 90 per cent of all fighting between co-religionists was Christian. Only 10 per cent of wars had neither a Christian nor Moslem component. This has led some commentators to conclude (Wilkinson, 1980; Wright, 1964) that Christianity and Islam strongly incite their members to fight those of other religions or incited those other religions to fight them or that these two faiths especially incited their members to fight one another.

Are current religions associated with warfare to any lesser or greater degree? Lebanon (Christianity *versus* Islam), Israel (Judaism *versus* Islam), Sudan (Islam *versus* Christianity and African traditional religions), Sri Lanka (Buddhism *versus* Hinduism), Iran/ Iraq (Shia Islam *versus* Sunni Islam), Afganistan (Islamic civil war), Yugoslavia (Christianity *versus* Islam), Cyprus (Christianíty *versus* Islam), Ulster (Roman Catholic *versus* Protestant Christianity) and south-eastern Russia (Christianity *versus* Islam). This list could be extended further by including conflicts in which Christianity fights Communism, as well as in Kashmir, India and Pakistan (secular Hinduism *versus* Islam) where there have been three wars and continuing tensions. The attack on the World Trade Centre in New York in September 2001 killing some three thousand people was religiously motivated as was an early gas attack in the Tokyo subway by members of a Japanese sect. Thus it would seem that there has been no let up in what might be categorized as wars in which differences of religious beliefs are at least one of the principal motivating forces. There are newspaper photographs of weapon training in mosques and mullahs with their kalashnikovs just as there are pictures of Christian priests shooting in the Lebanese civil war with pictures of Our Lady on their rifles.

Some of these current religious wars are no more than continuations of older quarrels dating back centuries as in the ex-Yugoslavia where Christians and Moslems are still reacting to each other in terms of past Turkish dominance. Others in the Lebanon are continuations of circulating tensions between Christian, Druzes, Jews and Muslims in which each religious community has been the object of periodic massacres. The present latent, continual and widespread tension between Greece and Turkey in the Aegean and Cyprus dates from the Middle Ages.

Have there been any changes since 1945? In the past Christians have been ahead in bellicosity with Islam some way behind but this balance appears to be changing so that Islam is becoming the most bellicose religion, whether or not terrorism is included in Israel, Egypt, Algeria in which religion is the main category distinguishing protagonists. In sociological terms Islam with its small range of religious requirements fulfilled by action rather than attitude combined with belief in heavenly rewards, appeals far more cogently to those who have not benefitted from economic and social development. Islam is likely to appeal much more in the future and to cause more ideological trouble than the ex-Christian societies of the West which do not appear collectively to believe in anything sufficiently strongly to fight for it on religious grounds except for a few small fundamentalist groups.

The incitement to violence is obvious to any reader of the sacred literature of both Christianity and Islam. They are full of violent language; the battle and victory against sin is one of the commonest. This forms an important current part in religious nationalism (Juergensmeyer, 1993). 'Onward Christian soldiers' and 'Fight the good fight' are still popular Protestant hymns in English. Overall there are no grounds for thinking or planning on the assumption that such quarrels essentially based on religious differences are becoming less vicious and destructive.

In terms of biology the destructive effects of warfare are surprisingly short-term; nature recovers remarkably quickly. In the tropics a battlefield is nearly unrecognisable after two years; the effects have to be looked for. In deserts warfare does not matter and indeed it is probably the best place for fighting as groups of breeding males only destroy themselves in waterless wastelands of stone and sand. In terms of species survival, warfare is no more than a hiccup in time, much less destructive of environments than the proliferation of the omnivorous goat. In many situations religious violence gives religious and spiritual motivations to those would otherwise have overriding interests in life.

Such violence may also have direct personal value for survivors as it reduces population pressure by destroying surplus numbers of young men who are then not able to reproduce. The killing of an estimated hundred thousand men in the Iraq-Iran war could be seen as an environmental success allowing those countries a breathing space to develop more for the maintenance of their too rapidly expanding populations. However as in the current Afghan war dead fighters would have their widows absorbed into polygynous marriages ever since the battle of Badr in which the

Prophet Mohammad encouraged the surviving men to marry the widows of those killed for their new faith. Christian warfare has the advantage of leaving large numbers of non-breeding widows. The rapidly expanding population of Sri Lanka correlated to the 1947 DDT campaign against the malarial mosquito which doubled the island's people in 17 years. The civil war between Buddhists and Hindus could also be seen as environmentally advantageous for the population as a whole except in the sense that the killing has not yet reached high enough levels to relieve overcrowding.

Finally, warfare moves populations away from the areas of warfare into refugee camps in which they would die in larger numbers than they do but for aid motivated at least in part and in origin by Christian obligations to help those to whom they are not related. In this sense Christian aid prolongs the population in marginal areas incapable of sustaining high population densities as in Somalia and Darfur. These camps disproportionately kill off the old and the young. The women there who live on nutritionally low diets for prolonged periods are unlikely to become fertile since their menstruation becomes irregular or stops altogether.

The significance of contemporary religious warfare on population levels has perhaps not been fully recognised because the totals are not high enough to merit mass media attention. If the Ulster Protestant *versus* Roman Catholic figures for 1969-81 were applied proportionately to the United States, they would have had 282 thousand killed, two million injured and if applied to mainland Britain 75 thousand killed and three-quarters of a million injured (Hickley, 1984). If economic waste is related to what might have been done to the environment in Northern Ireland the totals are equally horrendous. Over a hundred churches damaged or destroyed 1971-82, 28500 shooting incidents, 7200 bomb explosions plus 3200 bombs defused, 2300 deaths (O'Malley, 1983). This is a civil war between two Christian groups, more or less fundamentalist Protestant Christians led by their clergy who talk in terms of 'no surrender' and Roman Catholics who take little notice of their own clergy's admonitions to stop this violence.

The effect of this prolonged real violence and its potential to occur anywhere at any time must have handicapped the possibilities there of anyone seeing their well-being insured in terms of public religion.

Religious terrorism in which the initiators give their lives in a struggle on God's behalf (Rapoport, 1982) thus gaining immortality as with the Hamas bombings in Israel has little direct effect on the environment as the two religious communities involved are already segregated. Since the United States State Department estimated that only 8700 had been killed by terrorism 1968-95, the numbers killed are too small to have any effect on individual well-being beyond those directly involved and the devastation is local and temporary except in the creation and prolonging of an atmosphere of fear. The crashing of aircraft into the World Trade Centre and the Pentagon killed off only a small number of fecund men and women.

Religious violence if it does not kill, separates populations. Like moves towards like and in anticipation of the 'other' taking over their property and land, as much as possible is destroyed. In Israel Jews have destroyed property in areas to be taken over by the Palestinians, and evacuating Christians in ex-Yugoslavia have burnt their houses rather than let them be taken over by the incoming Muslims. The effect of the Greek Christian attempt to dominate Cyprus and the mainland Turkish counter-invasion, effectively divided the island with very few Christians in the north and even fewer Muslims in the south. Much the same as in Asia Minor where Greek Christian villages are still empty after the flight of their inhabitants in the early 1920s.The result of these population movements of 20 years ago in Cyprus is still visible in the north with empty farms, closed shops, idle factories, and desecrated Christian cemeteries. The forced evacuation of Cretan Muslims in the mid-1920s is not so visible except architecturally. In both these cases there were low numbers of killings but the previous well-being of shared communities has been replaced by well-being that comes from open communal hostility. In Belfast 70% of the population lives in religious ghettoes of their own choosing after decades of mutual harassment. This division in Israel as in what was once Yugoslavia has been carried out by the power of the part religiously motivated gun.

The more passive influences of religious practices on individuals and groups (Reynolds and Tanner, 1983) tends to preserve them socially and biologically and for them to see well-being in terms of religious exclusivities. Religiously motivated 'zoos', small enclaves of accidental preservation and uncertain well-being separated from the hostilities which they have created for themselves.

Human societies quarrel over immediate issues that are popularly understandable and indeed find it easier to fight than to compromise. They find it easier to see their quarrels and difficulties in terms of race (visibly different), ethnicity (tribally different), nationality (politically different) and religion (ideologically different). These themes are easier to understand and are more satisfying tools for mobilising effort than the passivity of religious moralities, and personal ways in which they are expected to relate to their neighbours who are different to themselves. This is all the more inevitable as all humans are socialised from childhood to distrust, dislike and avoid outsiders.

Very few people in the contemporary world have any sense of material security, certainly not in the sense of institutionalised supports that are perceived as guaranteed for a lifetime. Even in national states that can economically provide comprehensive welfare systems, it is doubtful whether more than a small minority see themselves as secure since the concept of security changes with economic and social development and involves more psychosocial factors for which there are no answers. Even the most comprehensive and effective welfare system does not eliminate threats from without and indeed such threats are inevitable for all human beings. Most people live under economic and social threats from people whom they assess as being different to themselves.

It is trite to state that security for individuals is for them to live out their lives without being faced with insurmountable difficulties; that is to say that outsiders are defining what is reasonable security.

Most people are prisoners within a particular social system and outsiders tend to state that once a people are past Maslow's Stages 1 and 2 (Maslow, 1970, 1943), then they are materially secure and should thus be able to consider their well-being as involving people different to themselves.

In theory secular rather than religious governments should be better able to restrict religious violence and to appreciate and promote the long-term value of a benign environment for their citizens. In practice there has been a growth in specifically religious nation states where once there were only the Vatican and Saudi-Arabia; now there are several Islamic Republics and of course Israel which despite its secular constitution is seen as a Jewish state by the entire Muslim world. While Western secular states have a reasonable record in withstanding the demands of Christian pressure groups or more specifically preventing fundamentalism from turning to persistent violence. States with Muslim populations have had a continuing problem with violent fundamentalists who would be almost by definition oblivious to compromises.

At levels below that of the nation state, religions are not structures administratively or theologically capable of taking action to improve or indeed prevent the decline of the sense of general well-being not based on their exclusive principles. It is not their job and moreover there is no public demand for any such change of focus. All religions focus on the individual's behaviour in relation to God(s) and their fellows; these are primary considerations. The foci are individually eschatological rather than related to this life collectively for their own societies much less societies with which they have no contacts at all.

Religious emotions are to a large extent out of the control of religious authorities who usually do not incite their followers to violence. With Christianity in the past and with Islam today there seems to be an inbuilt aggressiveness. With the contemporary and continuing male dominance in Islam there seems to be a correlation with aggressiveness. Religious aggressiveness seems to have struck a sympathetic chord within the individual and collective psyche which is usually outside the practical control of religious leaders their public utterances and dogmatic beliefs have laid the foundations which others have found so useful to develop into aggressiveness.

In any society in which religion remains even of quasi-importance, much less dominant such as in Islamic states and in right-wing Hindu parties in India, threats to religion, however interpreted or rationalised, can easily become popular rallying cries. Hindus and Muslims have been at each others throats for centuries in India with a regularity which defies rationality. Statistics show that it has been an almost seasonal activity. Protestants and Roman Catholics in northern Ireland seem to show the same persistent hostility to each other sparked off by the so-called marching season of Protestant parades as if this violence coincided with climatic and agricultural cycles. In such situations elected governments as much as oligarchic ones, respond to the need to be easily popular by supporting such causes or use them as a way out of other difficulties, which may be as much secular as religious as in the recent Iran-Iraq war. The Shia Iranians responded to Sunni Iraqi aggression in a specifically religious way; it was perhaps accidental that they fought over oil-less desert and this has now been transferred to Iraqi towns. There is little reason to suppose that the majority of the world's population grappling with persistent short-term insecurity will be any less likely than in the past to see their spiritual well-being and secular interests as best protected by violent confrontations based in many cases on religion.

7 The Importance of Prayer

Prayer paradoxically is both the most public and at the most private activity in spirituality. Our knowledge of prayer does not come just from the statements made in answer to questions, but from the fact that these attempts to reach the spirit world are carried out in public. In almost every cultural setting we can see if we wait long enough that someone is going through the procedures which have no parallels to their everyday practices. The Great traditional religions have particular systems and set procedures for prayer and provide variations for most eventualities but beyond these the Little traditions of popular religion (Redfield, 1956) have innumerable procedures involving prayer whether in Rome, Beijing or Djarkata as well as in the villages of Kathiawar and under the shadows of the Himalayas.

The Nature of Prayer

For those who want to know more than their own culturally restricted and personal understandings of prayer, there is an automatic handicap. Almost all social scientists have been trained in the Western linear pattern of thinking which is tied to print. We start by looking into the books connected to religion which will tell us what particular faiths have defined as prayer. The necessary required wording and the personal state of mind in which these prayers should be undertaken. So we start with the restrictions imposed by print and more importantly in an acceptance of the contemporary Christian requirement that these prayers should be deliberately written in language understandable by the majority of believers. These prayers in print are theologically based and institutionally promoted and imposed on a believing public as part of their membership of a particular faith. This contemporary readability in a large number of different languages is particularly Christian and the other religions of the book who are also nominally monotheistic retain their core beliefs in their own sanctified languages.

However, in the Eastern religions there is no minimal requirement that their prayers and religious understandings should be readable and understandable since they are written in archaic languages or in specialised linguistic codes. The basic prayer in Buddhism '*om mane padme hum*' repeated endlessly by the devout has only the meanings which they personally impose on it. Even quasi-traditional religions have their spirit possessed diviners talking in 'strange' languages or glossolalia which have to be interpreted. There is thus a restrictive approach to any understanding of the human use of prayer lodged between the requirements of printed orthodoxy and the individual outpourings in prayer based on personal necessities. It was noted long ago that prayers begin as spontaneous utterances and degenerate into traditional formula (Tylor, 1873:2;371).

The Universal Utility of Prayer

Prayer is certainly the commonest type of spirituality in the estimation of observers as well as in the understandings of the people themselves in all cultures. It is a multi-dimensional phenomenon for which there can be no definitions which do not exclude as much as they include. Early social science assessments (Calkins, 1911) divided prayer into forms of adoration, contemplation, fellowship, penitence, petition and thanks giving while more recent studies have divided prayer into sixteen categories (K.L. Ladd and Spilka, 2002). When we go beyond the repetitive use of approved orthodox prayers, we have nothing beyond self-reported data as to what personal needs people attach to these commonplace and repetitive forms.

While attempts to define do indeed produce answers it would

seem that the essence of prayer is that it is ambiguous in what it aims to do and in the forms which it takes since every word in such definitions are themselves subject to definitional problems. Whether we use the definition of prayers as being inward, outward or upward (R. Foster, 1992), we are still left with the perennial problem of the differences between prayers. Printed religious traditions, written petitions at shrines which are usually brief and give no indication of the intellectual standing of the writers and prayers that individuals say that they use which are perhaps unlikely to be the actual forms which they use in personal emergencies. The channelled ambiguities of praying must account for both its popularity and its persistence because it will always use the semantic style of the person praying. Even with glossolalia, talking in tongues, the phonemes are those of the person's natal language. Overwhelmingly anything can be put into prayer and probably just as much taken out; it is a utilitarian process based on the universal existence of hope.

The principal caveat which detracts from the theological evaluations of prayer is that in terms of Maslow's hierarchy of needs (Maslow, 1970), it is only at the higher levels that it becomes sufficiently detached from immediate wants to fulfil at least some of the aims and principles of those charismatic philosophers and theologians who have supplied the bases of the great religions. At the lower level of needs in which the vast majority of people are permanently or at least very regularly situated, most prayers are likely to be directed at material ends for a tolerable standard of living.

The Problem of Spiritual Efficacy

Everyone knows in their day-to-day lives that what they do with particular intentions does not always succeed. Their plantings of seed may not sprout, their business projects will not always succeed and almost certainly they know overwhelmingly that their hoped for personal relationships will be fraught with persistent uncertainties. If this is so in the so-called pragmatism of their daily lives to what extent can we apply these uncertain calculations to the expectations of their practices of spirituality.

Is there not a basic problem that we are assuming that those involved in praying are making locutionary acts intended to have consequences. Those involved perhaps even a majority are involved in illocutionary acts which have no intention at all behind them other than their performance is an end in itself. This would certainly apply to the endless repetitions of '*om mane padme hum*' by northern Buddhists, a phrase which is more or less meaningless in itself. This interpretation might also apply to the repetitious nature of Islamic prayer routines. Thus it would seem that a very high proportion of ritual acts particularly praying are illocutionary logically entailed to keep the system going but involve no specific intentions. In such situations the question of efficacy, if that word can be used at all, starts and stops with the 'mechanical' performance (Alston, 1964). So there is a division between purposeful performance but purposeless prayer and those that are purposeful in having a specific intention. Most prayers in a sense may will be purposeless.

It seems reasonable to assume that individuals in all cultures have a single cognitive system and apply the same concepts of rationality to their relationships with the divine as they have with their fellows. The expect a high rate of success in their petitions forwarded through their systems of spirituality but that is exactly the same framework of optimism with which they approach family, business and the marriage arrangement for their children. They also know from experience that if they should become ill that there will always be a substantial chance that they will get well and a similar substantial proportion that get worse and die.

Some Chinese see the actions of the Gods in response to their petitions as not much different to the reactions of contemporary bureaucrats to their requests left with higher and virtually invisible authorities. Much the same applies to petitions left at temples usually sent upward by fire and incense or in other cultures left tied to trees or stuck on temple walls. Both systems are the same and the results consistent or inconsistent depending on the formality of the approach (Groot, 1892-1969).

How do these petitioners account for the failure of their prayers. It may be that the petitioners have got it wrong and that the faults or failures are due to their own shortcomings. There may have been some errors in the formalities required for Chinese petitions. Then the Gods or ancestors although approached in what the petitioners see as a very personal and suitably humble way, might will see it as lacking in the required respect for approaching the Divine. Individuals know that the higher the official the larger the numbers of petitions which they will receive. What might be seen as their arbitrary decisions are based rightly or wrongly along with the petitions of others relating to the same problem; difficulties are usually interpersonal. Any decision of the Divine is bound to upset one side or the other. The Gods or whatever may be will make their decisions for reasons of which the individual petitioner can have no idea.

The act of requesting which is the essence of prayer assumes that as in secular life that both parties have a common interest. In practice prayers are not sent into the ether in the hope of it being picked up by something rather in the same way that currently messages are sent out into space in the hope of getting a response from another occupied planet. Most Chinese religious rites show a similarity to the secular act of requesting 'chia' in which the speaker believes that the other party has an interest in getting and carrying out his or her request (Ahern, 1979). They assume that the entity to which the petitions are addressed has an interest in complying as the link is already there.

Most of the ritual acts which we carry out as part of our own spirituality have no objectives on which we expect to see any concrete results. They are either thoughtless in the sense of not having any identifiable pragmatic element or rather that their efficacy and primary purpose is to make the user feel satisfied and in this it is almost universally successful. Burn an effigy or kiss the picture of a loved one. This is obviously not based on a belief that it will have a definite effect on the object which the picture represents. It aims at some satisfaction and it achieves it. Or rather it does not aim at anything; we can act in this way and then feel satisfied. The description of a wish is the description of its fulfilment. And magic does give representation to a wish; it comprises a wish (Wittgenstein, 1971).

The Varieties of Prayer

There can be little doubt that the majority of prayers occur in the mind and are not spoken much less written. We can know little of this and even if some people speak their prayers in answer to questions we have little assurance that this is what happens in the privacies of their minds. So any attempts to categorize prayers rests on theologically based ones and those provided by institutionalised orthodoxy. As in Christian prayer books containing prayers for special occasions and crises. A more valuable alternative are the prayers stuck on boards in churches, tied to sacred trees or on boards outside Shinto temples in Japan.

A useful initial categorization is to divide prayers between those that are inward on behalf of the person praying, outward prayers for others and upwards towards a relationship with a spiritual entity (R. Foster, 1992). It seems likely that the majority of regular prayers and those that are the result of theological thinking are upward. This division was expanded latter (K.L. Ladd and Spilka, 2002) to suggest that inward prayers were spontaneous, outward ones engaged the physical world and the upward ones included sacramental praying incorporating the use of words provided by others in order to connect with divine spirits.

A study of prayer subjects which were used in undergraduate courses in a mid-western American university found sixteen types of disclosed prayers which do not fit readily into such broad all encompassing classifications as adoration, thanks giving, confession, rest and dividing petitioning prayers into a fourth dimension of intercession. The objectives of praying written into north Chinese prayer slips addressed to Gods and Goddesses were 97 per cent for the healing of disease, 90 per cent over marriage, and then in diminishing numbers over the anxieties of travel, law suits, children and family problems, the recovery of lost articles, business worries, crops, animals and official status (Hayes, 1924). Those on racks outside the Meiji Shrine in Tokyo included one from an ophthalmic surgeon asking for help in improving his operating technique. It may will be that categorizing prayers misses its essential individuality when personal circumstances must inevitably be considered. It seems likely that the majority of personalised prayers are petitioning for something specific. Some 40 per cent of Americans in one study claim to have prayed for material things at one time or another (Poloma, 1993).

Although it has been suggested that the ascendancy of science and technology in modernised cultures has reduced prayer for material needs. It is thought to be childish and immature as requiring an image of God as willing and able to intervene in the daily affairs of individuals (Poloma, 1993). This may be an intellectually detached and inadequate view of prayer. These modern advantages are spread thinly among the world's population and even where they are available, they are not invariably successful. People still die just as crops and businesses fail. Whatever the practical effects may be, prayer is certainly believed to have the desired effects and those who are disabled in some way are more likely to claim that some healing has taken place. Prayers for healing appear to contribute to greater life satisfactions and some betterment in the sense of realistic well-being for those in poor health.

Of course, there are small minorities of Buddhists who pray for the goal of *nirvana* and the social ideal of world renunciation (Spiro, 1971). But the vast majority of their prayers are for material benefits. In the Buddhist and Hindu context this requires careful definition since there must be many who pray for economic success as in the petitions to the elephant headed God Ganesh in India.

Prayers for recovery from physiological and psychological distress is similarly a material aim. Clearly the materially deprived whether relatively or comparatively poor are likely to use petitioning prayer to improve their conditions but any distinction over an education, ethnicity or intellectual divide may be unwise. There has to be a distinction between the intellectually competent who may will be non-literate and those who are uneducatable and in the category non-Western in the sense used in some surveys of Asians and Latin Americans who have long standing and persistent religious cultures which have survived parallel to contemporary theologically westernised Christianity to which they may overtly belong. It is a confused situation in which much depends on personal crises and it seems unlikely that the most intellectualised white American would not pray for the survival of their children or that pregnant women who believed that they were not well, would not pray for their unborn children (Levin *et al.*, 1993). Prayers for a purpose are perhaps by definition petitionary.

Prayers which are a regular feature of personal spirituality are likely to be ritualised and provided by the religious system to which individuals belong. Indeed it would seem that in the usual course of spirituality even personally composed prayers become standardised very quickly. Their use takes on some at least of the characteristics of the mantras of Eastern religions. All religions which have become institutionalised have set forms of prayer which are not only part of their regular ceremonies but are likely to be used in private devotions. They have within them by definition some elements of divine power, and of course they are easier to use than personal compositions. There is also the feeling that the saying of these orthodox prayers makes for some accumulation of spiritual benefit. In the recent past the devout Christians certainly totted up the number of ceremonies they attended. There is still the saying of the repetitive rosary by Roman Catholics and Muslims. More specifically in the Eastern religions there is the accumulation of merit which is thought to help the individual's karmic future.

Meditative prayers in the Western developed world would

appear on the one hand to be an important part of the activities of religious professionals and of the religiously minded who have the spare time for this time consuming activity and who go on religious retreats, periods of reflection in special residential centres. This prayerful stillness does not appear to be a prominent part of the religions of the book experience. On the other hand it is a prominent part of Eastern religious experience and these religious professionals concentrate more on their own spiritual development than in providing any pastoral services as understood in Western societies. It is suggested that meditative prayer is in effect encouraging a withdrawal from the practicalities of living but it may have some effect on their sense of well-being.

The Users of Prayer

The users of prayer fall into two not exclusive categories. Those that believe that they can actively communicate with some entity in the spirit world. These entities have a reciprocal interest in listening to these prayers to which they may or may not respond. This is the commonplace view which is almost universally believed in, but it is in this majority behaviour that there is the relationship to magic. There is the belief that the unknown transcendent power can be manipulated by petitions and material considerations.

Alternatively there are those who see prayer as a method towards self-improvement through philosophic and intellectual efforts. It is intended as the means by which individuals can gain some direct experience of the spirit entity at which their prayer is directed and that this can change the very experience of reality. In this group there are the professional practitioners of religion who devote their lives attempting to attain the ideals worked out in theology. Many people have some fringe knowledge of these ideal states but to attain them requires detachment from the day-to-day realities of living. To lead a life of prayer requires the spare time to work at its attainment and the support of others either at a very low standard of living as a Hindu mendicant or Buddhist monk dependent for survival on his daily begging round for food or in religious institutions requiring economic independence. The pursuit of spirituality in subsistence communities has to pay off; if they cannot work, they die.

It is perhaps too simple to state that people pray when they are in trouble and want relief. A study of American undergraduates and seminary students found that they saw prayer not as an acknowledgement of defeat in the face of personal difficulties but as a means to overcome them (Welford, 1947). Prior to cardiac surgery the vast majority of patients intended to use prayer and this provided a positive attitude with a direct impact on optimism as measured by organisation, affiliation or subjective religiosity. The better educated and higher status employment with no mental problems were optimistic but prayer was most frequent among those with lower socio-economic status, minority membership who felt themselves to be oppressed (Ai *et al.*, 2002).

To Whom are Prayers Directed

There is a division between prayers directed at theologically acceptable targets which is clearest in Islam and Judaism but less clear with Christianity with its dogma of the Trinity, the dominance of the Virgin Mary as the object of prayers and as the centre of pilgrimages as well as the numbers of officially recognised Saints at whom prayers may be directed. Outside these theologically acceptable figures to whom prayers may be focussed there are within these three faiths large numbers of quasi-official sacred sites which are connected to s(S)aints about whom little is known and whose tombs are the centre of popular devotion, thus making religious devotion more accessible.

However in the Eastern religions outside the narrow theology of the 'religions of the book', there is considerable prayerful devotion to persons and objects which in the Western sense have no serious theological backing, such as charismatic humans thought to be holy, mythological figures, and places inhabited by spirits and ancestors. Hinduism apart from the overarching concept of Brahma to whom prayers are rarely directed has large numbers of Gods and Goddesses which are virtually mythological constructs as well as an enormous numbers of local deities all of whom in statues and pictures are accompanied by very complex symbolism. Buddhism which has no God, has created divine attributes for the Lord Buddha as well as creating saints, the Boddhisattvas who have delayed attaining Nirvana to help humans just as Burmese culture has the 36 'nats', national spirits who provide such help to petitioners with all manner of misfortunes. Shintoism in Japan is reported to have several million deities as well as such objects of prayer as aborted foetus to whom prayers for forgiveness are directed. China has innumerable local rather than nationally recognised deities such as the Green Dragon King mixing history with mythology. A contemporary religious poster in Shanghai contained more than twenty images of divine figures. Then in these cultures there are ancestors to whom prayers are made which is also a feature of quasi-traditional non-literate cultures. Half of the verses in Berawan prayer in the Philippines are devoted to insuring that the recently dead know exactly what is happening and why (Metcalf, 1989:266).

So outside the orthodoxies of the three 'religions of the book', the objects of prayer vary between the devotion of millions to the major deities down to lesser local deities and ancestors as well as to spirits inhabiting trees and springs which may all be prayed for more or less at the same time. In addition it is difficult to separate out the objects of prayers which are generally or isolatable in relations to individual, familial, communal and national interests. David Hume, the early English philosopher, contrasted the monotheism of the enlightened few in the Western world with the implicit polytheistic tendencies of the uninstructed 'vulgar' masses. Throughout history people generally have failed to perceive the design of a single deity in the rational order of the universe because of their lack of training in abstract contemplation and their anxious tendency to personalize gods, the unknown forces that govern human fortune and misfortune (Hume, 1757).

Problems of Prayer Experiments

In all experiments to prove the efficacy of prayer there are numerous methodological problems which are probably beyond solution even though the objects of these experiments were sufferers under the close medical supervision of medical staff. It is asserted that in double-blind studies that not only did the patients not know that they were being prayed for but the staff knew nothing of the experiments. A hospital is a closed community and news of such work must surely have got around and possibly leaked to patients in wards or in the gossip occurring in any institution.

There can be no parallel to the closed nature of laboratory experiments as the social boundaries of those involved can be penetrated by innumerable outside influences. In prayers for those who are ill, prayers may appear to act but medical treatment is still being continued so that may have suddenly become more effective. Prayers for business success in India and Japan may appear to have been successful. These may have happened because of economic factors which have very distant connections with the petitioner or in fact were damaging to others who may have been equally active in praying. There is the well known prayer of the Christian priest in the last century on the Isles of Scilly whose inhabitants always hoped for shipwrecks from which they might profit. While he was not praying for shipwrecks but if they should happen could they happen on the shores of his island.

We also have no means of knowing about the extent to which these sufferers were already praying for themselves and in one study (W.S. Harris, *et al.*, 1999) this must have been inevitable as the patients were known to be at least weekly church attenders and stated that they prayed daily. Whether they knew that they were involved in these experiments or not they were already believing in the success of prayer. If they were about to undergo surgery or were terminally ill it would be more than likely that their families and friends were also praying for them. For instance in Britain there is a Crusade of Prayer run by the Roman Catholic Cenacle Sisters in which thousands of people write in asking for the sisters to pray for others about whom they are concerned. These are not only for the more obvious familial targets but also for office and factory floor staff who are ill.

In one study (W.S. Harris *et al.*, 1999) those who were praying were told of the medical progress of those they were praying for so that they may have increased the intensity of their prayers or in some cases given up some measure of their hopes. So the exact nature, sincerity and duration of prayer are obscure nor do we know the extent of extraneous prayer penetrating the experimental group. Although people involved were asked to pray for particular but unknown sufferers, it is an assumption of trust not something that can be proved or disproved that they have done as they agreed to do and that all their periods of prayer were of an equal intensity. If prayer is a power then it must surely have been augmented and diluted in these ways.

Then the intentions of the experimenters may be an influential factor in any connection between those praying and those prayed for and the possible consequences. Few if any researchers are likely to enter experiments on the efficacy of prayer without some preconceptions, as they are not experimental machines. Surely the modern fieldworker is likely to approach the subject of prayer with some possibly rigid professional scepticism since they are often agnostic. In effect their approach overall might be similar to Christian commentators on Islamic prayer procedures in the 19th century who recorded its mechanical nature (Thompson, 1856:296) and endless repetitions 'accompanied by almost none of the virtues of true piety' (Olin, 1860:105-7). So if prayer is a material force, there is no reason to suppose that it can be confined experimentally to a single prearranged social dimension.

Thus the intentions of the experimenters may influence the outcome as well as concern over the validity of random numbers.

Overall the mechanisms of influence remain unknown which of course is the underlying reason for the experiments in the first place (Olshansky and Dossey, 2005). In the assessment of well-being and attitudes to spirituality of individuals involved in experiments, there are leading questions such as 'I believe in God, I believe that He is personal and concerned with individual lives. I further believe that he is responsive to prayers for healing' in which those interviewed had to agree or disagree (W.S. Harris, *et al.*, 1999). This of course discloses the line of thinking within which the experiments were being conducted.

There are also ethical problems in setting up such experiments which divide sufferers into one group that is prayed for, ostensibly for benefits rather than to prove the futility of prayer and another group which is going to be ignored. To use a control group for anyone who believed in the power of prayer was the equivalent of denying them treatment. In one study this issue was solved (Byrd, 1988) by obtaining the consent of all the sufferers who were to be involved with the guarantee that at the end of the praying for period, those who were in the control group would have a similar period of praying devoted to them. But of course this reasonable ethical requirement meant that the experiment was no longer blind as the sufferers all knew that they were all going to be prayed for in the end.

In a criticism of this coronary care study (Byrd, 1988) the points of difficulty were all brought together (Dossey, 1993) which may have discouraged further experimental work on those who were suffering. Work only continued on distant influences over fit humans and non-humans. This has produced evidence that distant thought can not only influence humans but also mice, chicks, enzymes, fungi, yeast, bacteria and cells of various sorts (Braud, 1990; Braud and Schlitz, 1989). The reasons for criticizing that study were the subjects who were prayed for were all 'born-again' Christians and that there was an hidden agenda that the researcher wanted to prove the superiority of his own faith. There were no safeguards to determine if the praying group had really prayed or not, little was known of the prayer strategies used so that there may be differences in the praying experience of those involved, the prayers had personal knowledge of the persons for whom they were praying which might have diminished the significance of the results recorded. No attempt was made to assess the psychological coping mechanisms of the patients and whether they or their relatives were also praying; a long list of methodological shortcomings (Dossey, 1993).

The Occasions for Prayer

There can rarely be any important occasion which is not accompanied by prayers. The saying of grace over meals, prayers before sessions of legislative assemblies, football games, examinations, executions, marriage and many forms of commitment involving the taking of oaths and they are accompanied by reverent gestures.

We can only know for certain what we see as most prayers are said privately within the head and we can only know about their extent there if people choose to tell strangers about it. If it is visible it has to have physical form and these forms are dictated by culture. Special ways or sequences for attempting to get in touch or actually achieving contact with entities in the non-material world.

Most Christians bow their heads and close their eyes and on more formal occasions kneel and clasp their hands together in front of them. Members of the Kimbanguist Church in Zaire before praying take off their shoes, watches, bracelets and hats (Ndofunsu, 1978:592). Some people get possessed by a spirit in order to communicate with them which is common in quasi-traditional societies in Kenya, Khartoum and Calcutta, Hindus chant their prayers and Buddhist mutter theirs. Devout Sunni Muslims prostrate themselves five times per day in a series of physical movements and the Dervishes, a sect of Shia Muslims whirl round and round. Orthodox Jews sway their upper bodies backwards and forwards as they pray and Quakers do nothing at all just keeping silent. Amongst Chinese Taoists prayers can be produced by slot machines and with Japanese Shintoists there are racks of written petitions outside popular shrines and on trees considered holy by Greek Orthodox Christians. Except in the forms of its diversities, prayer is seemingly a commonplace visible activity part of the regularities of life accompanying linear and cyclical rites of passage and unexpected as well as inevitable difficulties in the lives of everyone. It would seem to be self-evident since virtually everyone in every culture has prayed at some time in their lives and their languages provide for this.

Prayer for the prolongation of life and the avoidance of sufferings is universal. It is only recently with the growth of concern for and scientific research into psychosomatic diseases that interest has been shown in the possibilities that prayer could be an effective agent for the reduction of pain and the lengthening of life. All religions, both Eastern and Western, based on written texts and the traditional ones in Africa, Asian as well as the popular practices everywhere within Christianity, Islam and Judaism, have always had no doubt at all that prayers worked both mentally and materially. Broad-minded theologians might even think that scientists have only recently showed an interest in this because they have generally seen religious ideas and practices through their secular limitations.

It may be likely that this widespread and now publicly recognised use of prayer as part of the holistic care of the sick individual will build up the reputations of religious institutions, as nearly 80 per cent of north Americans believe in the power of prayer in the course of illness. Seventy-nine per cent of family physicians there reported that they had a strong religious or spiritual orientation of whom almost all attended a religious serviced at least once a month (Daaleman and Frey, 1999), yet only 10 per cent ever enquire about the spiritual practices of their patients (Dossey, 2000). Perhaps it is quality rather than the quantity of prayers that count which may be the basic methodological problem.

Hopes about Prayers Helping Health

Praying is such a commonplace activity in all cultures that those involved expect it to have positive effects and thus find evidence enough in their own minds that it does have distant consequences. Here we are immediately confronted with the division between what can be pragmatically proved and effects which those involved just feel have been beneficial.

There have been a limited number of deliberate experiments to prove such physical connections. Limited not so much by the disinterest of the medical profession or perhaps their dislike of the consequences of any positive proofs of such a connection over which they might have little control once such conclusions go beyond vaguely defined correlations. The principal difficulty must be that of setting up any clearly controlled experiment which meet the requirements of science. The basic requirement in such experiments is that the people prayed for should not know that they are being prayed for and that those praying should not know the persons they are praying for in any personal sense. Thus it would seem that these foundations for such experiments immediately start outside what most people would consider the basis of praying, a more or less cooperative effort.

In a coronary care unit in which the prayed for and control group were followed for ten months, the former had significantly lower severity scores and did better in twenty out of twenty-six medical categories under which they were assessed (Byrd, 1988). A doctor involved after there results commented that it would be as rational to prescribe prayer three times daily as medicines. A smaller British study of chronically ill rheumatoid arthritis patients found that the former had significantly less severity scores but subsequent checks showed that the controls did better perhaps because of waning interest by the prayers (Joyce and Welldon, 1965). An American study of children with leukemia in which the prayers were kept up to scratch by regular reminders of their experimental obligations showed a marked delay in the deaths of the sample in comparison to those in the control group (Collipp, 1969). These and other studies producing results have had too small samples for any wider statistical significance.

Even if the results were significant it has to be seen in terms of costs and benefits since we are not considering cures as would be the case with miracles but improvements in some symptoms and delay in the deaths of those who are terminally ill. Even in those experiments which appeared to show a causal connection between prayer and consequences, there are always suspect elements such as the intensity of the praying on the one side and the elements of religious and other hopes on the other.

Perhaps this is too narrow an approach and the definition of successful praying should be whether those prayed for feel better within themselves and leave open the question of the causative agencies. Scepticism apart much remains to be explained in the persistence of miraculous cures although they have been shown to be extremely rare when classed as the spontaneous regressions of cancer (WH Cole and Everson, 1966).

Recently the charismatic movement in the United States has produced many thousands of testimonies to divine healing which have been published (Harrell, 1975). We are left with the conclusion that the sense of well-being can be created by prayers and not necessarily those of committed believers. This is a relatively frequent occurrence but in the context of scientific analysis it is both rare and has marginal effects.

Doubts about Prayers Helping Health

Objections to the possibility of praying being a positive enabler of healing starts with Western materialistic understandings which is tantamount to excluding it from the possibilities of research. An unusual advance conclusion from the scientifically minded, perhaps more specifically that even if distant healing does work it cannot be replicated in clinical settings. The objections to the possibility of prayer working are not just based on the post-Enlightenment requirements of rationality but on the general assumption (Benor, 1991) that much of the representations for healing from praying rests on people who are strangely different and in terms of the researchers social understandings, seemingly abnormal. The powers of such people are in these terms questionable perhaps even feared because they are not subject to well established professional controls and more particularly outside consensus ones.

The most significant basis for doubting the possibility of distant healing being recognised as effective must be that despite the enormous amounts of time spent in praying, it has attracted little almost negligible scientific interest. Some of the research is so open-ended in its conclusions as to fail to produce any hard data. 176 cases of spontaneous regression of cancer were found in 100,000 cases (W.H. Cole and Everson, 1966). Regression followed intercessory prayer, conversion to Christian Science, mud-packs, vitamin therapy, force feeding, electric shock treatment and the administration of insulin. The writers concluded that almost any treatment seemed to work some of the time. Spontaneous regression was purely a random event entirely beyond the control of the individual patient.

Then there are always the necessary criticisms about the inadequacies of the methodology in which those tested are not similar enough to be the basis of conclusions even on the bases of sex, age and assessed intelligence (Rhine, 1962; Stevenson, 1970). Although in mitigation it must be said that almost every study of human behaviour is going to show methodological drawbacks and this can only be overcome by the replication of research under the best conditions possible within the endless variability of human behaviour.

Prayers Aimed at Causing Misfortune; Amoral Spirituality

It is an interesting aspect of spirituality that prayer and indeed all aspects of its practices are apparently almost always thought to be a 'good thing' and that through this no one should benefit from evil intentions. If there is belief in the power of prayer then there are surely no reasons why it should not be used against other people's interests who are obstructing those of the prayers. In warfare there are repeated prayers for victory and this must be at the expense of the defeated. Few people think deeply enough to recognise that prayer does not have a single all embracing value. A prayer to make a person better begins and ends with that person but on the other hand a prayer for business success is probably only possible at the expense of business rivals.

The power of prayer in its most extreme form is the belief that it can kill as well as heal in the so-called 'voodoo' or hex death in which an individual is thought to have been prayed to death. An individual dies apparently of natural causes because he knows that another individual with sufficient spiritual power has fingered him to die for covert or overt reasons (Lex, 1977). This has been reported to have occurred in a wide variety of contexts and places (Cannon, 1942).

Yet life at all levels and in all societies is now as it has always been highly competitive and not just in the morally suspect aspects of uncontrolled capitalism. The livestock herder, the subsistence farmer, business men and women, employees in factories and offices, as well as the sales force will always be in competition over grass, land, even rain, promotion in which there is always a pyramid of opportunities and the need to gain a greater share of the market.

Why should we imagine that spiritual power should always be benign when almost all Africans from below the Sahara believe that certain individuals have just such a power to transmit on demand evil towards others. The reality of witchcraft, malignant practices to get the better of rivals. A student lodging with a distant relative when he first attended college found himself unable to concentrate when sitting down to study. He consulted a diviner who was able to see his hostess placing various transformative objects in his room because she had wanted her own son to succeed in school and had previously similarly sabotaged other young men staying in her house (Geurts, 2002:198). In contemporary Italy there are a range of practices to prevent the effects of the 'evil eye' which presupposes that someone is using this way of imposing their ill-will on the children of other women. These are surely aspects of Christian idealism within which they are supposed to pray. If people pray for their own interests it is likely to be of sectional value to the individual, family, lineage or clan at the expense of other individuals, families, lineages and clans. Brothers will always be in competition over inheritance disguised as it will always be by overt fraternalism. In a community where there is a shortage of land, there will usually be covert friction disguised by overt friendliness; since hostility cannot be expressed openly, it seems likely that the ancestors themselves will be involved in furthering the interests of their favoured descendents. Beyond this there are diminishing circles of lukewarm spiritual practices in which there is a vague hope for blessings to be spread generally over secondary and tertiary relationships.

Is it not implausible that people should practice forms of spirituality which would benefit their direct rivals. Most people assume that there are many people to their knowledge who hold unpleasant thoughts about them even if they do not turn this into action as one of the constant realities of social life. There may be Sunni who pray for the Shia in Iraq or Jews for Muslims in Israel but they are certainly very few. It seems doubtful that there are Christian Sukuma praying for their neighbours the Maasai with whom they have had mutual cattle raiding for generations. But what about primary relationships where we know that in all patrilineal cultures there has always been rivalry between brothers over their father's property and even over the possession of ancestral relics which give legitimacy to the position of family head. In China and Taiwan the specialised system of geomancy which includes the siting of graves for the benefit of the deceased's children. One son may manipulate the burial of his father for his own benefit even to the detriment of his own brothers; the commonplace supremacy of self-interest (Freedman, 1966:143).

Leaving aside the enormous numbers of people who are

involved from time-to-time in the promotion and prevention of good and bad luck, a form of popular spirituality which occurs before competitions, examinations and marriage ceremonies, and in Taiwan there are utilitarian cults. The growth of the Eighteen Kings and other cults is not a new religion but an adjustment of spirituality to new social and economic conditions. These cults are individualistic and utilitarian viewing the economy as a place where success has less to do with good social relations than with self-interest and competition. This religious embodiment of individualism has grown at the same time as Taiwan's small enterprise capitalism has thrived (Weller, 1994).

We should accept that there are in most if not all cultures, the accepted moral rationalism to use the practices of spirituality for entirely selfish ends at the expense of others. The available cake cannot be enlarged and can only be divided in unequal shares. This is not just in the ownership of property and business success but amongst the Sukuma there is the idea that there are not unlimited amounts of rain which can fall on everyone's fields but a limited amount that can be directed on those of the petitioner but not on the fields of the next community. Further that even in cultures which have systems of spirituality based on moral principles there are likely to be many individuals who put into and get out of such systems personal advantages which are at the expense of others who are socially close to them. Not just part of a distant social world to which they may feel that they have no realistic moral obligations. These are well outside the higher stages of Maslow's hierarchy of needs and thus their own priorities have precedence.

The Scarcity of Miracles

Miracles attract the attention of the Western mind because should they exist and there is ample evidence that they do occur according to the standards of the record keepers. Their occurrence goes against the principles of the Enlightenment, but more particularly attention to them seems to be a matter of concern to Christians and to be related to petitionary prayer. There do not appear to be any parallel records for miracles to have occurred in Buddhism, Hinduism, Islam and Taoism perhaps because there have been a more commonplace and accepted occurrence there.

The records of miracles are principally connected to Roman Catholic places of pilgrimage and that Church is certainly not in any hurry to agree that any particular spontaneous regression is miraculous. The standards for acceptance were laid down by Cardinal Lambertini in 1735 as the disease must be serious, incurable and unlikely to respond to treatment. The disease which disappeared must not have reached a stage at which it would have been resolved by itself. No medication should have been given or if prescribed would have had only unimportant effects. The cure must be sudden and reached simultaneously and it must be complete and not partial. Certainly in the past many more miracles were recorded at shrines which should not have been accepted by these standards.

If we take the Roman Catholic pilgrimage centre at Lourdes as an example there have been some sixty four authenticated miracles out of some 6000 cases which have been presented to the Medical Commission for scientific assessment since 1868 (Dowling, 1984). The point must surely be that at least 6000 people who had gone to Lourdes in hope of a cure believed that they had been cured and believed strongly enough to put themselves forward as the centre of a claim. Moreover that many more would have come away from the shrine convinced that they had been helped even if they had not been medically cured. In fact miraculous medically inexplicable recovery from a probably fatal illness is rare although quite a number are recorded in medical literature such as in the compendium 'Spontaneous Regression'. However this may be something in the nature of a minimum number because little systematic attention has been paid to the concept. Remissions are often regarded as a result of misdiagnoses, difficulties over research as analysis has to start after the event, clinicians are nervous of reporting their cases because of the fear of criticism. The data is often more psychological than physical (Hirshberg, 1993). So far there is no solid body of evidence that explains the occurrence of these phenomena (Challis and Stam, 1990).

It is prudent to remember that no one knows the incidence of the diseases involved since their diagnosis and definitions are the creation of the Western medical system which is only applied efficiently to a small proportion of the world's population. Thus one is inclined to presuppose that the occurrence of spontaneous regression is higher than the records show and may be correlated significantly to various mental states.

The Effects of Prayer — Physiological

This is easier to assess because at least one end of the equation is scientifically firm while the praying end is inaccessible to science. A tremendous number of repeated visits to temples in India and to holy men are asking for blessing on a marriage and that it should result in a son but the sex ratio in both India and Britain is about the same 106 boys to 100 girls (Sheldrake, 1982). Similarly an experiment of praying for children with leukaemia who continued with their routine medical treatment and about which neither the physicians, families of the children nor the children themselves knew that they were being prayed for weekly by a church based prayer group showed no significant differences between those who were prayed for and those who were not (Collipp, 1969). Patients with rheumatoid arthritis divided between those who were prayed for and those who were not as well as a control group were involved in an experiment which lasted eighteen months. In the first nine months the prayed for group improved and in the second nine months the control group improved more and the researchers concluded that there were no statistical significance in the small numbers involved (Joyce and Welldon, 1965).

In a study that involved one thousand patients in a coronary care unit there was an eleven per cent reduction in the medical symptoms for the prayed for group but the length of hospital periods was not accorded and there were no significant difference from the control group. However as we have already described a double blind intercessory prayer experiment with nearly four hundred coronary patients (Byrd, 1988) showed that those who were prayed for had less need of medicines and the use of the mechanical ventilator, less occurrences of pulmonary oedema and fewer deaths. Another study (Benson *et al.*, 2006) in six United States hospitals with patients involved in cardiac by-pass operations randomly divided between those knowingly receiving intercessory prayer, received no prayers after being told that they might or might not be prayed for and those who received prayers after being told that they would be prayed for. The praying was started fourteen days before the operation and complications within thirty days were noted. The recorded outcomes were that just over 50 per cent in both groups receiving prayers had complications and that 59% of the patients who were certain of receiving prayers had complications. Major events and 30-day mortality were similar in all three groups. The researchers concluded that the differences to other prayer experiments might have been due to intercessory prayer not being appropriate for reducing post-operative complications and the percentages could have been different if a wider range of symptoms had been chosen and the thirty day cut-off period might not have been appropriate and relevant to the effects of prayer.

However results are more precise when the objective of the prayers can be defined with some exactness. An experiment with rosary prayers and yoga mantras (Bernard *et al.*, 2001) showed that both caused striking, powerful and synchronous increases in existing cardio-vascular rhythms when recited six times per minute. From this the researchers concluded that the use of the rosary in both Christianity and Islam introduced from the East might be used widely in health practice. These results might have come from the rhythmic regularity of the procedure which could just as well as been secular.

A study of over three thousand patients with blood stream infections were prayed for under double blind conditions with a control group of similar numbers (Leibovici, 2001). The mortality of the prayed for group was 28.1 per cent and that of the control group 30.2 per cent and the length of stay in hospital and the duration of the fever was significantly shorter for those prayed for. The researcher concluded that this type of intervention was cost effective, probably had no adverse effects and should be considered as a clinical practice.

We can see from these experiments that the physical effects of prayer are not only very mixed but in terms of percentages using any organisation and method approach to evaluating prayer would suggest that it is not worth the effort as the benign results are minimal. That of course is looking at prayer in the narrow sense of material improvement whereas in terms of well-being this will not be a major expectation or result.

There are two initial aspects to prayer which have to be considered. Large numbers of people pray for themselves or who know or suspect that they are being prayed for by people whom they know well. Such situations complicate what might have been the simplicity of prayer and the involvement of divine intervention as there might be placebo effects (White *et al.*, 1985), psychological stress reduction and suggestion (Frank,1961), bio-feedback (Green E. and Green, A., 1977), self-regulation (Locke and Colligan, 1986) and the principles of psycho-neuroimmunology (Ader, 1981). Whatever the connection which it is wished to establish it has to be with this personal relationship, an assessable link involving sight, sound and possibly touch.

Secondly, there are the tests which are carried out under double-blind procedures in which there is deliberately no possible social connection between the prayers and those prayed for. The correlations are necessarily entirely impersonal such as those connected with rheumatic and psychological disease (Joyce and Welldon, 1965), leukaemia (Collipp, 1969) and heart disease (Byrd, 1988).

In Byrd's study (Byrd, 1988) there were 192 in the prayed for group and 201 in the control group. There were no statistical differences between the two groups and both were followed up for ten months. During the prayer period the prayed for group had a significantly lower severity score and under twenty six categories of medical analysis the prayed for not-group did better on twenty. They also spent a shorter period in the intensive care unit and used fewer medications after discharge. In the Collipp study (Collipp, 1969) there was a marked delay in the deaths of the prayed for group in comparisons to the controls. In the Joyce and Welldon study the controls did better and the researchers thought that this might have been due to the praying group's waning interest in the patients.

No difference was found between the directed prayers group and the non-directed impersonal group. The researchers similarly found that this could be attributed to other factors. If it were a placebo effect, prayers could not possibly prove significant and perhaps the prayers did not rigorously follow their assigned method. By design the measures were chosen with the belief that they were God's will and the possibility that there were no differences anyway between the two prayer methods.

Certainly there is evidence that prayer can have benign effects in those who pray or are prayed for. Once this is accepted as the possible consequences of deliberate prayer ethical issues become part of research as the control group by design receives none of the benefits which can be anticipated. So attention has been turned to the effects of thought on other living organisms over which there would be no ethical difficulties (Braud *et al.*, 1989). Similarly it has been found that deliberate thought can have identifiable effects on elements which have no accessible identity such as red blood cells (Braud, 1990).

It has also been found that the laying on of hands is a significant way of getting benign effects (Krieger *et al.*, 1979) suggesting that the form of spirituality in which groups of people hold hands can have these effects. As we have seen this can have effects when there is no actual touching (Quinn, 1984) which raises the possibility of identifiable benign effects coming from the priest blessing the congregation at the end of a religious ceremonial and of course in the case of the Hindu concept of *darshan*.

The Effects of Prayer—Psychological

While the physical consequences of prayer can be calculated by scientific means, the psychological consequences are dependent on those involved being asked questions or completing questionnaires. The answers must be questionable as they depend on relationships with the researcher. Also that those being used in the research have standards of literacy and are used to being asked questions and providing answers on paper connected to cultural strangers. Then there is the factor that most research is related to people who are already ill or dealing with illness rather than those who are anticipating such difficulties. A study of college students showed that their prayer style promoted active solutions rather than avoiding coping which showed both a greater perceived control of anxiety and less anxiety overall (Harris *et al.*, 2005). A study of women who were caring for children with HIV showed that both colloquial and meditative prayer was a frequent daily activity. Prayer was used to shift their attitudes and emotions towards positive perspectives and to regain focus, companionship, collaboration, guidance and mood direction in what must have been a continually stressful situation (Richards *et al.*, 2003).

A further study of distant healing related to people with advanced AIDS (Sicher *et al.*, 1998) showed that those who were prayed for showed significant benefits which went beyond fewer physician visits and days of hospitalisation, lower illness severity scores but most importantly improved mood scores. However a study in the San Francisco area designed to test the effects of distant directed and non-directed intercessory prayer on self-esteem, anxiety and depression (O'Laoire, 1997) in which participants kept a diary of their praying for the twelve weeks of the experiment. As a whole the 400 participants improved significantly in all the subjective and objective measures for which they were assessed and there were no differences between the two methods of prayer. Those praying had pictures of the people for whom they were praying and recorded in what form and when they were praying for them over twelve weeks. Taken as a whole all 406 subjects improved significantly on all subjective and objective measures but no differences were found between the personally directed and impersonal praying for groups. The researchers attributed this to several different explanations; that prayer does not work, may be that just signing up for such a project is in itself a commitment to improvement. The subjects may all have had a very specific expectation of improvement. All those involved signed a consent form which promised that if prayer proved to be a significant intervention, those who were in the control group would be prayed for during a twelve week period following the completion of the study. There was also the possibility that outsiders were also praying and distorting the results. Perhaps no difference exists between prayer and non-prayer methods as there was an overall belief in God predominating and if it were a placebo effect prayer could not possibly prove significant.

In the Redlands experiment which was carried out for nine months with forty-five volunteers with self-admitted problems (Parker and Johns,1957). They were divided into three groups; just plain psychiatry with no mention of religion who had a 65 per cent improvement as assessed by unconnected professional psychologists testing them before and after, the second group composed of faithful Christians who believed in the power of prayer and who prayed each night before sleeping, who showed no improvement. The third group was in a prayer therapy group who met weekly for a two hour long prayer service who showed a 72 per cent improvement. In this experiment there was no way of knowing what may have accounted for these improvements as at least three factors were at work, prayer, group therapy and individual feedback.

Muslim researchers (Yusif and Abduhi, 1988:14) took an entirely different approach perhaps taking the view that all Islamic prayers would have beneficial effects, commenting that orderliness in mind and body proceeds from faith. The orderliness and discipline which is so obvious in the ways that Muslims pray individually or collectively 'will help tranquillity and satisfaction to prevail in all human endeavours'. Similarly in Indonesia local communities, the government and Islamic reform movements also state that the formality and periodicity of Islamic prayer shows an ideal model for society (Bowen, 1989).

Belief in the Effectiveness of Prayer

Does this in practice have to be proved rather than just accepted by the vast majority of people at all intellectual levels and in all cultures who pray or who have prayed. Since survival depends as far as the individual is concerned on pragmatism would they continue to pray if it had no real usefulness and was no more than a rather stupid activity within the concepts of atheism (Dawkins, 2006). An equally effective answer is that people whether highly educated or at the lowest level of economic and political development would not have continued to do so in such multitudes and for so long unless it had been useful. Thus usefulness may not have been any expectations of pragmatic returns but that it contributed to some sense of on-going well-being and order. There was the famous conversation recorded by Livingstone, the early Christian missionary and explorer in central Africa with a rain-maker who enquired if Europeans could be so stupid as to believe that rain could be made in this manner by incantations and potions (Livingstone, 1857:23-5).

A study in Virginia, United States (Johnson *et al.*, 1986) found that 14 per cent had their serious disease or physical condition cured by prayer. The researchers commented that there might have been a higher percentage had the enquiry encouraged the reporting of multiple incidents and non-physical mental healing. A correlation between prayer and cure does not mean that the former caused the latter. It is scientifically a coincidence and such a conclusion is made by someone who is not in any way involved with the problems, yet from the point of view of the sufferer or petitioner it matters immensely (Dossey, 1993).

The high priest of the Hozanji temple near Osaka in Japan which specialises in the provision of earthly benefits (Matsumoto, 1985: 9-10) puts the case for petitionary prayer quite clearly, 'some people say that praying for these worldly benefits such as the healing of sickness or business prosperity is not true religion, but in fact religion has to be something for living human beings. In the end seeking the Pure Land and prayers for its realization are nothing if not a this worldly activity; after all if there were no this worldly benefits there can be no salvation. Is not seeking entry into the Pure Land a request for an extension of this worldly benefits?'

An Overview of Prayer— the Consumer's View

The approach to prayer is dominated by Western preconceptions that if there is a relationship between prayer and the realisation of satisfactory results then there have to be pragmatically accessible reasons for this. If this is not immediately available it will be at some time in the future by future generations of scientists. This is a reasonable preamble to examining any phenomena but when the world of the spirit or the spirit world is universally defined as outside the pragmatic assessments of humans, this is perhaps a self-defeating approach. The data and conclusions from such enquiries are never likely to be successful on these terms. Even if it would seem likely then it would be seen as irrelevant to what they knew all along.

A more reasonable approach would be to look at prayer from the point of view of those that pray and more particularly as not seeing these people as having the general characteristics of credulity, limited intellect and low education and who live under conditions which have not been much affected by modern science. It is always prudent to remember that the effects of science's particularities are soon forgotten. The five million Sukuma of Tanzania no longer suffer from small pox or their livestock from certain mass diseases and it is forgotten that these misfortunes ever existed. The anxieties of those days have been replaced by the contemporary ones of AIDS, drought, locusts, inflation and corruption. The overall burden of anxiety is probably no different to what it may have been a hundred years before. It is frequently remarked that their lives in folk-memory were much better then than now for all the talk of largely only potential development.

Since prayer is overwhelmingly common, the point must be that it is widely believed to work at an individual rather than on the communal level. Prayers for peace and any objective which does not have the essential element of self interest, does not come under this ability to succeed. Of course, if people pray for a narrow objective, the chances of success may be low and to verge on the miraculous. Most prayers are loosely formulated and the results may will be equally loosely evaluated. The results may not be as hoped for but nevertheless personally evaluated as successful. A prayer may in practice be a process of adjustment in which those praying come to terms with their misfortunes rather than relieved of them. How this adjustment takes place can no doubt be explained in social science terms but the fact that many misfortunes cure themselves or become lessened with or without scientific assistance, is irrelevant to those who pray. David Livingstone's discussion with the rain-maker makes this point years before effective science came on the scene. The point of faith was well made in the double blind study of the use of Vitamin E in treating angina pectoris in which an enthusiastic doctor who believed in its effectiveness found it significantly more successful than a placebo while two studies conducted by sceptics showed no effects (Solvin, 1984).

The Conclusions from Experiments in Prayer

We have seen that there have been several double blind studies which have probably gone as far as possible to conform to scientific requirements and their conclusions have provided grounds for thinking that prayer can have physiological effects even if the people do not know that they are being prayed for. There are scientific drawbacks to even these carefully structured researches (Olshansky and Dossey, 2005). The researchers have taken on trust the prayers have fulfilled their commitments at a pronounced level of intensity — whatever that might be — and that those who are prayed for do not have their relatives involved. We do not know the extent to which the control group has been involved in prayers on their own behalf. There is also the possibility that the intentions of the experimenters may have intruded on these processes and that they may have affected the choice of random numbers (Radin and Nelson, 1959). Perhaps we should conclude that the indefinable cannot be experimentally proved or disproved.

Before there can be any conclusions about the weakness of prayers to achieve the results aimed at, we should consider that there are several benefits from using prayer as a form of psychotherapy. It is easy to use, the patients are in charge rather than as some sort of outsider on whom therapy is performed, there are no requirements for specific believing. It is flexible and the patients themselves can test its efficacy (Rossiter-Thornton, 2000).

Experiments as to the effectiveness of prayer are really a denial in terms as to what it achieves and its methods. The evidence of the effectiveness of prayer as they touch events in the material world remains outside the domain of science. The faithful who want to believe can believe in the effectiveness of their prayers and the sceptics who choose not to believe will not be convinced by any experiments. If a deity can meaningfully answer a believer's prayer and if prayer is to remain a spiritual rather than a magical exercise, then surely that same deity would make sure that all empirical studies of the efficacy of prayer will turn out to be inconclusive (Meadow and Kahoe, 1984:120) and that of course is just what happens.

A group of researchers have summarised the difficulties and objections to attempts to prove the actualities of prayer (Chibnal *et al.*, 2001); 'science cannot actualise our spirituality so why do we ask this of it as mixing experimental methods with faith degrades both concepts. We do not need science to validate our spiritual beliefs as we would never use faith to validate our scientific data. The effect is to distract us from the more real and more human interaction of religion and medicine, the acknowledgement that religion and spirituality are often vitally important to our fellow human beings in their experience of illness, disability, suffering, dying and death. Considering ways of bringing medicine closer to a recognition of that importance would be more beneficial than applying the scientific method to prayer'.

The Residue of the Unexplained

There seems little doubt that the applied mind does have an effect with distant healing although little is known about how this activity works so that we are still left with a substantial residue of secular and religious unexplained factors. There is perhaps a tendency to concentrate around spirituality as in the rural Rajasthan Indian study (Gupta *et al.*, 1997) in which more than 3000 adults who participated in regular prayer and yoga were 70 per cent less likely to have coronary health disease. We suspect that this type of study has been replicated many times.

But what can we make of the mental influence of ordinary people from a distant room being able to protect red blood cells from serious stressful influences (Braud, 1990). In a small sample it was found that an individual could influence the rate of hemolysis both of his own blood and that of another person to a degree inexplicable by chance. In another experiment certain individuals from distant rooms in the same building were able to exert a calming or an activation of the physiology of a group of volunteers unaware of these experiments (Braud and Schlitz, 1989). The subjects who might benefit most from such influences appeared to be most susceptible and the authors concluded that this ability to influence the physiological functioning of others appeared to be widespread. But we know that prayers for sons had no observable effect and that in the Redlands Prayer Experiment there were variable results.

Most research into prayer seeks to establish that when people are prayed for they benefit in assessable ways and we know that under controlled conditions this is proportionately possible in a small but statistically verifiable numbers of cases. But we also know that quite a sizable proportion of prayers are malign and are against the well-being of other persons and they are equally likely to be successful. We have to accept that such prayers are outside any possible research procedure as being morally indefensible. It would be prudent to remember this potential malignancy in the context of the almost universal belief in the efficacy of witchcraft in Africa south of the Sahara.

The results of the San Francisco study (O'Laoire, 1997) showed that everyone including the control group improved on all the eleven assessments and that there were no differences between intercessory prayers directed at a particular person and those based on God's will be done. So prayer can have some effect on everyone involved and not just those who were specifically prayed for but then why was there improvement in everyone? It may just be that volunteers generally are more psychologically healthier or that volunteering anyway makes people healthier. We can conclude that it may not be possible to assess the practical consequences of prayer but there does seem to be the possibility that the process of prayer in whatever form it takes lead to some measure of self-improvement or in other words well-being.

8 Spirituality

The Basic Problems in Assessing Spirituality

A young man in Aix-en-Provence, France was wearing a T-shirt which stated in English 'no one knows what a man thinks'. Leaving aside the question as to whether this was a sexist comment or one that refers to human beings in general or at least those who could read and understand English, this surely is the basic difficulty in assessing the relationship between spirituality and well-being. No one can know how another thinks unless he or she chooses to expose this in a public form in conversation or in replying to a questionnaire and if they write or speak about what they admit to thinking. This is subject to conscious and unconscious filtering as to what they consider in those circumstances should be publicized and moreover made more static than would be the case in functional reality.

There may be certain cultural themes which are likely to occur in any population of which the commonest might be the relationship of sexuality to employment roles but these will vary in intensity and consistency for as variety of factors. The youth in the T-shirt may believe in some type of male dominance as he might be a recent Muslim immigrant from Morocco. This is not likely to be put into action with his grandmother who in practice runs the household in the absence of any contributing men, or his sister who has just graduated from a school of pharmacology and his well-educated French girl-friend who has pronounced secular or spiritual beliefs almost inherited from her radical or believing father. He is not likely to be consistent in his beliefs and indeed if he was he would be socially penalised in some of his relationships.

So whatever ideas individuals may have about spirituality whether in Islamabad, Banaras or in the Chittagong Hill Tracts, these will merge with how they consciously or unconsciously decide to use such ideas and practices in particular circumstances. While most people are under the delusion of the consistencies in their own behaviour, should they have ever kept a diary they would find out that they change their basic views with embarrassing regularity.

Thus among the five million Sukuma of Tanzania of whom no more than ten per cent may be Christians or Muslims, the spirits are part of their undefined framework of thinking and explanation. But what spirits are involved is personally defined if at all by reaching agreement with a consultant diviner by a process of mutually profitable negotiation. It is not a take it or leave it diagnosis as might be provided by a medically trained physician. They may propitiate a previously unknown ancestor as a result of the diviner's diagnosis. What will happen then is a ritual which is more or less created rather than one that has been done before because the social and psychological environment will have been different. Even if it had all been written down, this is not the type of situation which could be solved by looking up and following overt procedures when so much covert aspects would still be involved. There is no order of service and there will be hundreds of different propitiation ceremonies even though an outsider researcher will give them the one generic name.

Perhaps it is the function of these ceremonies to put into the concept of propitiation whatever has their attention at that particular time and for a particular purpose. The Roman Catholic Church may have fixed formulas but those that use them will put into their use their own particular needs. Form and function in their practice of spirituality are only loosely integrated so that typicality may be the well-meaning and professional invention of the researcher.

But we do have widely accepted themes of attribution which however much this can be linked to culture will probably end up in entirely personal sub-divisions. It will always come down to personal needs, social environmental factors and personality differences. To what extent are there similarities within a system where its ideas and practices are now as much as it may have been in traditional non-literate practices even if the spirituality system itself is now partially dominated by and administered by literate specialists and bases itself on written documentation. It is indeed open to question whether such written systems are overwhelmingly influential on covert personal interpretations. To what extent are people channelled into particular practices of spirituality by those closest to them, their neighbourhoods and the surrounding culture and what is provided for them in writing as the orthodox requirements of any available major systems to which they may nominally belong.

It seems likely that social science researchers overdo the consistency of systems of spiritual practice. They are dominated in their thinking by what they can clarify in writing. This aims professionally at logical consistency and which they assume will similarly dominate the writings on which spiritual practices are based. At least we can assume this with Thomistic writings but surely this cannot be assumed with Eastern writings on spiritual themes in which there is no required logical consistency. They are perhaps forgetting the fluidity of their own circumstantial thinking.

To what extent are rituals fixed except in terms of their written liturgies. This would certainly appear to be so with the Islamic prayer ritual which has a formal cross-cultural regularity. In terms of its background theological thinking there can be no greater need than the fulfilment of these ritual processes in an appropriate frame of mind in the surrendering of the self to Allah. This supra-cultural regularity is an end in itself. But is this possible when the individual praying has a load of his or her own anxieties and needs. So anything beyond this impressive formalism is likely to show locally developed personal and cultural variations. Sacrifices for rain in the Muslim community in Kilwa Kivinje (Lienhardt,1966) and the wearing of protective amulets by their children made up of Koranic quotations. Similarly with the Roman Catholic Mass which had a uniform expression in Latin until Vatican II. This retains an underlying unity in its spiritual understandings in their current translation into local languages but has in all cultures a great variety of popular para-liturgical rituals and private intentions within this pattern of orthodox thinking.

It seems probable that the approach of the social sciences is a top down one, an inverted pyramid in which more attention is paid to the thinking and practices of the few people in any major religious system that occupy the apex. What they do is written down and authenticated as well as formalised by the institutional deliberations carried out by these few professionals in isolation. The broad foundations at the base of these spirituality pyramids will not receive as much attention or consideration as these practices are usually thought to be of lesser importance and of lesser quality in an official hierarchy of thinking. Why is there this permanent inversion when it must be obvious enough that there are an immense number of individual variations in spirituality behaviour which in their multiplicities must be largely beyond categorization except in terms of the lowest common denominators.

It is not entirely a methodological lapse by researchers as individuals in their spiritual understandings and practices may will have decided nominal allegiances. On the other hand asserting their individuality in their privately composed prayers perhaps unconsciously whether as peasant or professional. It may be that there is in this ideological and practical isolation the sole way in which they see themselves as significantly important.

On the other hand there is considerable psychological and physical safety in being categorized as an actual member of a group. Individuals classify themselves under many headings as is shown in the answers to the question 'I am a ….'. The feeling of insecurity which comes from the projection of individual views without status support and a sharing of viewpoints. Individuals may feel that they are in the right in what they do rather than in the invisibility of thought in which they can maintain their own cognitive isolation.

In accepting some categorization with which they can identify individuals provide themselves with the authority of having a definition as against those with whom they may be in disagreement but their status may still be limited. Such categorizations provide the support of numbers from which they derive some foundation facts, experiences and more importantly comparisons. But above all there is the sheer impracticality of accepting the individual as a research category with its infinite number of factors. This cannot alter the fact that the individuals can be categorized in their individuality only by excluding much of what may constitute this. Overall a perception of the material has framed the thinking about less exact data.

The Diffuse Nature of Spirituality

Even if it was theologically appropriate to think of religious behaviour in monotheistic terms, that there is a final power behind all forms of transcendence. This is almost certainly agreed to by most people in most cultures, this power is rarely the object of direct supplications which are usually made to those lower spiritual forces which are felt to have primary power over what people do or have done to them.

The prevention of misfortune and the righting of wrongs is usually seen to be within the powers of saints whether Muslim or Christian, charismatic men and women who are popularly held to have supra-normal powers. Gods and Goddesses having powers which are refractions of those held by the ultimate supernatural essence of whom they are often somewhat commonplace representations. Ancestors, local historical and mythological figures and nature spirits combine with occupationally related ones.

So it seems that we should conclude that in a personal sense spirituality may be but is unlikely to be restricted to a single focus. It should always be seen as existing functionally in relation to multiple forms of transcendent power related to the varied situations in which individuals find themselves. There is no reason to suppose that any individual from childhood to senescence is going to have a single continuing transcendental focus. While living in a village they will likely to pay attention to local divinity and then when in a town or employed by a particular firm, they will be worshipping whatever is of popular concern there. It will be related to the nature of success in football as much as in business, farming or a general sense of well-being. This might just as much be related to health as the avoidance of ill-health. If there are people who are of a more optimistic than pessimistic nature, then their conceptions of what constitutes well-being are likely to be basically different.

Thus the 'reappraisal of God's power' and similar complicated theological considerations in relation to some personal misfortune would not be questions sensibly asked of someone who has been divined as suffering from the malignity of a particular ancestor which may or may not have been due to their conscious neglect. In fact the list of alternative methods of religious coping (Pargament *et al.*, 1998) could not apply to most people in most cultures particularly Eastern ones. These make no attempt to avoid a multiplicity of divine figures varying between the superhuman beyond human comprehension and others whose powers and frailties differ very little from charismatic humans.

Pargament's list of sixteen models of religious coping may will be methodologically separatable. An individual is likely to manoeuvre between them particularly when the individual's ideas are essentially non-literate rather than being ideologically restricted by institutionalised religious concepts and training. In fact most people in most literate cultures might be able to understand most of the words used without having any understanding of the complex themes listed nor indeed seeing any rational necessity for considering them essential for their personal spirituality.

People use their personal spiritualities to insure their own well-being, so that by definition what they do cannot be compared to any secular methods which are based on existing or potential pragmatism. The difficulty in any attempts to analyse what people do for religious rather than for the spiritual purposes are not only well-known but well observed and often well recorded. There is plenty of data on what pilgrims do on the Hajj or at the *Kumbh Mela* and on what people state to be their frequency of praying and attendance at religious ceremonies and the importance to which they give their religious beliefs (Pargament, 1997). The important point is that we cannot accept the accuracy of such personal statements about their own religious behaviour. We have every reason to believe that these cannot be accurate because of forgetfulness and the tendency to exaggerated behaviour which they feel should be related to the standards set by institutionalised religions. Nevertheless these recorded behaviours in Western societies have been consistently correlated to longer lives and lower rates of morbidity for certain diseases as well as more markedly improved mental health. This establishing of correlations is not the establishment of a necessary chain of causation (Levin *et al.*, 1996; Levin and Vanderpool, 1989). These conclusions relate specifically to Western particularly United States samples and we cannot expect similar conclusions for any future samples from Africa and Asia where death and morbidity rates are depressingly high. In the absence of plentiful data we can only assume that there would be similar effects in African and Asian communities in the relative prolonging of life which would usually be brief according to Western optimum rates.

When we come to establishing parallel correlations for the practices of spirituality, the possibilities are very different. Spirituality practices may be closely or weakly related to the requirement of organised religion but they still remain without corporate requirements. How the individual creates and maintains their own spiritualities remains personal and unsupervisable. The compulsions are personal and the senses of fulfilment and failure are similarly personal. Correlations to well-being once it goes beyond what people say, cannot be based on the same types of quasi-hard data available for observable religious practices; it would in effect be no more than well-intentioned guess-work.

Since the specific coping methods provided by religious beliefs and practices appear to have direct implications for well-being and the resolution of stress, we should surely assume that there are likely to be similar correlations for the practices of individual spirituality. This cannot be done with the same confidence which comes from the consistency in the religious behaviour of large numbers of Christians and Jews. The absence of similar data for Muslims and the almost total absence of data about the corporate consistencies with Buddhists, Hindus, Shintoists and Taoists.

There is also a difference between what outsiders may and can analyse as the reasons for spirituality behaviour and what the individual's behaviour may appear to confirm. A Chinese Taoist who has a religious poster on her wall which contains the images of twenty deities of which only one the Goddess of Mercy is recognisable. The researcher has to decide at which one the distressed individual is directing her needs. Or is it the case that such distinctions do not form part of her spirituality as it is a diffused objectification in a temple full of deities whatever may be the titular occupier of that shrine.

The coping provided by spirituality is certainly going to be multidimensional, not only in its differences with institutionalised religion but in its individualism. A British boy will pray for the success of his favourite football team just as the East African player may bury some transcendentally connected preparation in the goal-mouths at each end of the field before an important home game. It seems likely that Italian and Pakistani national sports teams carry out both private and public actions to invoke spiritual help, just as Roman Catholic ceremonies in Uganda's university are well attended by students on the Sunday prior to their final examinations.

What does the individual Angoni, Hindu, Kachin and Han Chinese get from their personal feelings of transcendency which in respect of the Han Chinese might be as likely to involve the late Chairman Mao as the Green Dragon King and the Goddess of Mercy. It seems likely that personal systems of spirituality may not have the regularity of religious rituals and thus may be more related to the reduction of stress. These private systems provide a sense of meaning and purpose whether it is a Japanese widow discussing day to day affairs before the picture of her deceased husband on the family house altar or an English girl kissing good-night the photograph of her favourite pop-star or boy friend. There may be no other way of giving emotional stability to their social lives.

The emotional comfort coming from something or someone with whom there is a personal although transcendental relationship in which no one else is involved in quite such a one to one closeness. There is also the basic fact that spirituality is always a largely personal creation and that the individual has control over what is being approached, when, where and how. At the same time individuals recognise that what is being approached may be really self-created. They have developed their own evaluation as to how this transcendency can be successfully involved in their lives. It is an intimacy which is individual and independent of any group support. In terms of anyone's personal feelings and appreciations it is quite independent of any physiological, psychological and social preconditioning to which it may be linked by the research of a social scientist. The individual who is mentally or physically handicapped are able to create and maintain in their own spiritualities in which conformities are their own affair. It may be the only independency which they are able to achieve and maintain.

With religious activities the standards and activities are more or less within what is laid down by that faith so we are dealing with degrees of acceptance or rejection. The individuals are not in a situation of being able to create anything personal out of this situation, only interpretations on themes which have already been provided. Anything they do privately will always be a refraction of some hypothetical orthodox perfection and in personal terms there is very little possibility of success.

In order to provide a variety of mechanisms for the solving of personal problems and maintaining well-being religions and the social environments in which they are practised provide the possibility of fulfilment by conformity. The Sukuma of Tanzania have an enduring conception of their own system of spiritualities which has not become institutionalised into what could be classified as a religion. They have been remarkably resistant to conversion to either Christianity or Islam (Tanner, 1985); so they have a satisfactory combination of quasi-religious and personal spiritualities. It is a homogeneity which in its contemporary forms is unlikely to be closely related to what may have happened traditionally but now fits in very well with modern individualistic tendencies and practices. This is perhaps an unusual situation in which widely held questionable traditional memories and ideas fits in by accident with what they are experiencing in the modern world. In the individuality of their spiritualities they are accidentally modern. Other societies such as the Nagas, Xhosa and Yunnanese Yao are not only homogeneous but were too rigidly structured both socially and ideologically to successfully adjust to contemporary global multicultural trends. Modernity will destroy the homogeneity of the Yunnanese Yao if indeed it has not already done so as has happened with the Nagas and Xhosa.

The mechanisms provided by the religions of the book which are set down although in practice ambiguous, have theological difficulties over the extent to which these lead to uncontrollable or controllable popularism. These activities are still under some group control and may not provide the same satisfactions as individually created spiritualities.

In Eastern religions in which beliefs and practices are both multi-facetted and multi-dimensional in part at least because of the absence of definitions and supervisory systems, have both collective and individual characteristics. They are in a better position to produce the systems of spirituality which are as attractive to the subsistence farmer in China and India as it is to the urban-industrial resident in Mumbai or Shanghai. In all of this the success or failure of any particular systems of religious behaviour or spirituality are essentially private evaluations which will fluctuate with the conditions of each person's day-to-day lives. Whatever the social science instruments which are created with great care to assess and make comparable the religious and spiritual status of contributing individuals, they are confrontational measures in which persons are responding to provided questions and provide their answers. These are not evaluated in any relationship to their surrounding psycho-social environments. Even if they provide answers, they would not be necessarily valid for what such individuals may think or do on a subsequent day nor relate much to what they may have been thinking and doing the previous week.

Written statements about the spiritual understandings by people who do not have the intellectual ability to express complex matters in writing, show the shortcomings which come from a limited competence combined with a limited vocabulary. There is no reason to suppose that most people in all cultures are ever able to express verbally their deeply felt emotions particularly over matters of spirituality, an unseen world of shadowy realities. The data on which to base some understandings of spirituality and well-being are no more than feelings of conviction which come from field researcher's knowledge of a few individuals with whom they have achieved a measure of deep personal understandings.

The Fluidity of Spirituality and the Rigidities of Science

From the point of view of the individual's well-being their contacts with social welfare agencies there is usually a statement that they are suffering from a particular malfunction which will either get better or get worse. These are detached statements which have very little to do with the individual concerned as a patient. They will be assessed in terms of the time available and the expenses involved balanced against the anticipated returns on the expenditure. In crude terms there is very little opportunity for holistic treatment. Scientific medicine in social welfare terms cannot afford the luxury of prolonged association with particular patients. In traditional divination consultations as in private rather than public medical practice it pays to give more attention to the person than to consider their misfortunes with scientific detachment. Whatever the policy of holistic treatment may be, it comes up against market demands and economic and institutional realities.

While individuals in their social lives are always negotiating their ways through the complex social situations with which they are inevitably confronted, diagnoses based on scientific facts as presented by professionals are not negotiable except by refusals to conform; it is a take it or leave it situation. On the other hand the quasi-traditional diviner will provide tentative diagnoses of what is wrong with their clients. The possible solutions over which there are negotiations in which the sufferer has some equality with the provider; a pharmaceutical solution may be suggested but it is presented within a social explanation which makes holistic sense. Few doctors are going to say to their patients that they are ill more or less because of the stresses under which they work or with which they conduct their marriages; this would be outside the boundaries of pills and surgery.

Moreover scientific considerations of health are tied tightly to social distance, high standards of literacy and now the hard drives of computers. The name of the person consulting them is no more than an identification label and is not a term for a primary relationship. What has been diagnosed by the doctors makes sense to them on their side of the cultural divide but is rarely an adequate explanation for these sufferers who want an understandable one which puts it into an acceptable social context. The British working class man dying of cancer who asks 'what have I done to deserve this' is no different to the Tamil, Saudi-Arabian or Sukuma in the same situation.

On the other hand the processes of spirituality appear to be at least partially independent of what is unsatisfactory in maintaining good health or identifying ill-health. It represents from the point of view of practitioners to be always an on-going one in which there is constant change. What the individual may have felt yesterday is more or less irrelevant as to what he may feel today. Quasi-traditional practices whatever the overt component of spirituality provide an on-going and adjustable context for what is happening to and by the sufferer; it makes sense of their misfortune. In Egypt the Baladi consultant (Early, 1982) provides explanation for what is happening and these explanations are always subject to revisions and provide a context to integrate illness episodes, not just the illness into that person's social and psychological realities. The priest, rabbi and imam perform these same functions of keeping the sufferers up to date with some assuring interpretations of the contexts of their misfortunes. On both sides of this permeable wall there are always bilateral negotiations to bring these personal sufferings into that day's perspective. It is not so much that this quasi-traditionalism provides multi-levels of covert and overt meaning. The meanings themselves are constantly changing within some loose cultural paradigm in response the temporary and current cognitive anxieties of sufferers. It establishes a reality although the researcher may conclude that this is an illusion.

The Tyranny of Compression in Methodology

The formalisation of human behaviour into categories in order to satisfy the professional requirements of scientific study leaves the material presented in a form of functional limbo with its limited applicability to the people who have been studied or who read these categorized conclusions. They may well feel that it does not apply to them as indeed it cannot since no one can fit into categories which are abstraction from the totalities of behaviour.

Compression constantly occurs because all forms of scientific analysis requires categorization. These are always composed of compressions to ideal types massed in the grey areas between the extremes which are easier to define by the rituals of exclusion. Science and in this context the social sciences require exactness which in practice means a compromise over averages. It is certain that no individual even if studied in isolation, will conform to any such behavioural averages.

Methodology rather than muddling along as opportunity offers in the relationship between the field workers and those they are hoping and attempting to understand, means an imposition of categories onto an almost infinite social and individual variability. This of course is not done with any intention to mislead but is the inevitable consequence of having to compress behaviour into what they hope can be defined as a specific category. Prayer would be an obvious and common category of spirituality but despite the fact that in some of the great religions it has standard overt forms, most of its utility must remain covert within the mind and beyond overt expression. It is not only this that compresses but the reduction of the categories which can be studied to the numbers that can be managed by the methodology itself.

The answers to any open ended question can be as unlimited as the imagination and mental capacities of the answerer chooses to provide. In the answers to a question of 'what is wrong with the Christian Church today in Tanzania' which was answered by five thousand men and women could only be turned into some usable form by at least three hundred categories. Answers varied from too much interested in money to the roof leaks and four men stated that there was too much beating in Church schools (Tanner and Morgan, 1976). If the covert intention of the researchers was to probe the religious and indeed spiritual understandings of Tanzanians then very few thought that the answer to this question should be replied to in terms of abstract religious thinking.

What may have been the reason for both the variability of the answers and seemingly their avoidance of answers which would have involved this religion as a way of relating to the Divine. The survey was carried out through the medium of kiswahili, the national lingua franca and this may not have been the language or rather the linguistic code in which these people had their religious understandings as opposed to the public religious involvements.

Even though the question was asked by fellow Tanzanians the reply would be seen as contextual and make the person liable for the consequences of any reply which was not already common knowledge in that community. It may also have been that the question was asked in a parish by parish basis and most of them would have seen their spirituality as not diffused geographically. Territorially limited by coercive boundaries and priests over whom they had no influence as would not have been the case with their own diviners who remained in business by the popular acceptance of their work.

So this survey carried out with a display of accurate inaccuracies exemplified the basic difficulty of studying religion and spirituality. What people say and think about their relationships with the transcendent will cover every imagined and yet to be imagined aspects of personal and collectivised faiths. Most social scientists start their fieldwork with a limited number of categories with which to work and stick with these making exceptions to the 'rule' a means of formalising these basic categories.

Any attempt to understand the relationships, not correlations which is a far too an exact and harsh word between the practices of spirituality, health and well-being, has to avoid the pitfalls which come from asking questions and getting answers within the 'tyranny of use/no use'. In the relationships of these three factors, it is not possible to ask people to give straightforward yes and no answers to questions which can have no such simplistic answers. Of course at the simplistic level it is possible to ask and get such answers and in doing so both parties are creating a fact. Whether that created fact corresponding to social and psychological realities is another matter altogether. To ask someone if they pray and if so how often, is disingenuous, just as a couple may be married in law but what the relationship may involve is both complex and variable.

But isolating such facts within this rightly called tyranny of exactness tells us nothing about its momentary inclusions and exclusions. What is going on in the minds of those involved in what might be called spirituality, health and well-being and how they relate to other exclusivities and patterns of thinking is not shoun. Each of us carry within us a constantly changing syncretic whole (Adler, 2001). If there cannot be unequivocal answers to relatively simple issues because of social and psychological environmental factors, then this is likely to be much more complex with issues of spirituality in which there can be a very broad range of initiating factors.

The practices of spirituality have to be seen or heard before they can be analysed or discussed but whether the next stage is participants describing what they do or think or social scientists recording what they see and hear. There can rarely be any close coincidence between what may have occurred and what is retained in memory and then written down or reported in interviews, recordings and film. There is also the complication that some forms of spirituality may take up very little social time as in the avoidance of something or someone who might bring bad luck or bad *karma.* Others which take up whole slices of time like going on pilgrimages to Mecca or to the Ganges for the *Kumbh Mela*. Both these dimensions are common enough in all societies and at all social levels.

However, in most cases in which spirituality practices are recorded, what is boxed away into reusable forms is an abbreviation of what has actually occurred. A case in point would be the records of the Vedic ritual of the Fire Altar which occurred in a village in south-west India and carried out by Nambudiri Brahmins (Staal, 1980). This performance covered twelve days which was filmed, photographed, recorded and extensively documented. It is reasonable to suggest that the social scientists involved did their best to record all that they could about this prolonged and complex event which involved hundreds of people in hundreds of different social and spiritual relationships but not a complete record of this complex event. From this mass of data a forty-five minute film was produced as well as two records of selections of chants and two illustrated volumes with a definitive account of the ceremonies. Certainly a formidable and praiseworthy achievement of great value to scholars of Hinduism. Even this extensive coverage is an abbreviation. We are left with the producers word for it that everything of importance has been covered. Important to whom and according to what standards which are probably those of very sophisticated outsider intellectuals; compression has occurred.

Social scientists would certainly start their thinking about this complex and prolonged ceremony by assuming that it is keyed into spirituality. Those involved stated that they performed or participated in this ceremony because their ancestors did it, we are eligible to do it, it is good for society that it should be done, it is just good as it is our duty and because it is said to lead to immortality. One might also add that some of these Brahmins might be bored and tired by the monotonies involved. A Roman Catholic priest might will have a range of similar feelings over celebrating the Mass for the ten thousandth time so that his personal spirituality might be found elsewhere.

It is certainly commonplace for such compressions of the practices of spirituality to occur. No researcher can be everywhere or see everything even if the ceremony only lasts five minutes unless it is a one to one activity for which he or she is the only observer. There are methodological difficulties over this so-called simplicity. The writer was present at a mass circumcision in the coastal village of Kipumbwi, Tanzania which occurred after an all-night reading of the Koran over the children. How much was missed from tiredness, being horrified at the cruelty and dirtiness of the operation and pointing a camera at aspects which interested his European predispositions. An exclusive record but of its religious consequences and preconceptions for those involved was recorded nothing ; it was just a primary performance. Perhaps not in the sense which others have sued the phrase, it was an example of 'ceiling effects' (Bufford *et al.*, 1991) in seeing only within the frame of the dominant activities thus missing its enveloping significances.

Spirituality in Mind and Body

We have established at least for Western societies, more particularly for samples of Christian Protestant believers in the United States, that observing the organisational requirements of a religion by regularly attending their ceremonies and at least nominally conforming to its institutional requirements, has had the effect of lengthening life and reducing the morbidity rates for certain diseases. We have to remember that this has occurred in social and political environments with well established economic structures which has not only contributed to these advantages but may in fact have enabled them.

There is little evidence that the same sort of results have occurred and indeed can occur in other cultures even among the Protestants in India, Botswana and Myanmar carrying out the same religious requirements. The surroundings in which the state is largely successful in guaranteeing certain standards of public health and other commonplace aspects of contemporary Western life do not apply. Of course religious sects and the smaller more exclusive Christian Churches can create their own small autonomous groups which can have comparable health successes. This has happened with the Seventh-day Adventists in the Sukuma region of Tanzania who have combined the prohibition of drinking and dancing with a measure of economic success.

It would seem that these observable behavioural aspects are more related to religious commitments than anything which may be connected with spirituality, a very largely subjective experience. The behavioural aspects of religion to be equally effective in a variety of very different cultures would seem to be unlikely. These institutionalised requirements with their elaborate definitions do not have the capacity to adjust to the needs of individuals in the same comparatively effortless ways that personal spiritualities can. It seems likely that it is the regularity of behaviour religious or secular which has these benign consequences. However, it seems unlikely that religions whether in their behavioural or subjective dimensions can have existed in so many cultural settings over so many known historical settings unless it could have shown to change its behaviour in ways that those involved have assessed consciously or unconsciously as beneficial. These subjective adjustments would always have been more difficult to carry out if they were behaviourally required in set forms, possibly short in form and easy to remember. This is not obviously the case since the Muslim obligations are short and easy enough to perform anywhere while Christian standardised ceremonies are much longer.

While it has been concluded that high levels of involvements in religions are moderately associated with better physical health at least in the Western world (Chatters, 2000). This could just as will be correlated to long-term commitment to any institution with regular requirements such as teaching in a boarding school, the armed forces and middle management in any large industrial concern such as Tata and Mitsubishi. What may be correlated to religion too much depends on factors which are outside the control of both individuals and the religions as institutions.

The picture for mental health is far more positive (Larson *et al.*, 1992; Levin and Chatters, 2000). It is in the subjective practices of spirituality that the individual's mind dominates and creates their own interpretations and the nature of their faith. It is the 'do it yourself' factor which accounts for both the utility and cross-cultural persistence of spirituality. It is in this that there are persistent correlations with well-being. Behaviour can only have a limited number of correlations but how the mind interprets such practices will have many more. It will be within the capacity of individuals to satisfy their own needs with their own interpretations.

The human mind can seek its own salvations and moreover does so in an infinite number of different ways for which individuals have at least the feeling of being in personal control of its nature and ways of fulfilment; they are supervising themselves. Although there may be definitional differences between conformity to the requirements of a religion such as the Islamic one for five sessions of prayer everyday and a commitment in the mind to a particular set of beliefs, it is the latter which appear to have the most significant effects. It is perhaps the unassessability of the latter which may make possible these more significant results. This can only be a form of reductionism avoiding the fact that there are self-imposed regularities in the subjective nature of spirituality.

What are some of the ways in which spirituality contributes to mental health. It contributes to the control of alcohol excesses with a combination of induced behavioural regularities and the attachments to them of spiritual support (Cochran *et al.*, 1992; Koenig *et al.*, 1994). Much the same would apply to the religiously based constraints on tobacco use (Koenig *et al.*, 1998). Both these activities require the observable use of both hands and mouths. Mental distress can of course be related to physical events but it can be much more within the mind and have few voluntary external manifestations such as depression for which spirituality has been used to reduce its symptoms. In this the versatility of spirituality to adapt to personal distress is more useful than physical regularities.

In cross-cultural comparative terms what we have discussed is a specifically Western concept of mental health which may have little in common with some Eastern ideas such as Taoism. The contributions which spirituality makes to well-being depends on how this is seen in the culture and personal contexts of those involved. It is perhaps correct to state that there is more uniformity in the disorderly spiritualities of the Eastern faiths than there might be in the religious and psychological understandings of the West. We have always these contributions to well-being in terms of the variable interpretations by those who seek some return from these ideas and practices. A Ghanian diviner in the opinion of a Western social scientist may show the symptoms of schizophrenia but within that culture it is perfectly acceptable to withdraw into the shadow land of association with the spirit world where such a person has a useful social role. It is not the burden on society which Western schizophrenic inevitably becomes.

Above all we have to recognise that so-called Western spiritualities are quite recent in comparison to Taoism which originated around 500BC and moreover that psychological ones which in comparison came into use virtually yesterday. The works of Lao-Tzu as the most frequently translated work of philosophy with about 200 versions starting with a Latin translation in 1788 AD (Cheng, 1995). We can presuppose that this amount of editions would show that it has some continuing value. In this context we are dealing with very large populations of Han Chinese who have no term for mental health and who refer to happiness, harmony, internal sense of security and relaxity. Taoism is overall a passive approach to coping with personal distress and its practitioners would want to be as little involved as possible in the Western urban-industrial aims of social attainment, self-development, progressive endeavour and personal interpretations. Some Taoist principles (Yip, 2004) clash at virtually every point with Western ideas, transcendence from self and secularity, the relative nature of all standards. Suffering and blessings are both relative and unpredictable, live and attain by inaction, return to natural silence and transcendence from emotion and human limitations summarised as 'the perfect man has no self, the spiritual man has no achievement and the true sage has no name' (Chang, 1990).

The influence of Taoism on contemporary Chinese would depend on the degree that they are involved in modernity. This is likely to be effective and at least the commonest form of spiritual thinking in village life in mainland China and Taiwan. It was certainly resorted to by intellectuals who suffered from the personal persecutions of the Cultural Revolution. Even in cities the Taoist approach may be the primary spiritual one but in multi-cultural cities such as San Francisco, Brisbane and London where the Chinese are an ethnic minority and where there is considerable pressure to conform to the predominant surrounding Western culture, it may only appeal to some. In such communities there are degrees of absorption according to the situational demands on people of different ages, interests and experience (Hong *et al.*, 2000). In these varying mental and social environments individual Chinese may find in Taoism an easier way to cope with their difficulties because it has no statutory form by which spirituality can be assessed even if it is acceptable as a goal.

The Methods of Spirituality

How do the systems of personal spirituality rather than religious ones contribute to the creation and sustaining of well-being whether they are quasi-traditional persons or possibly rather reluctant livers in Calcutta, Lima or Cairo as well as those who have achieved a measure of self-assessed success; the hinge being between the need to achieve well-being and maintaining it. There is a difference here between religions which have institutionalised themselves in literacy and which cope with the problems of their constituents according to formulae evolved from the theological study of the basic tenets committed to writing. Rabbis and imans are in practice no more than interpreters of canon law whatever their private spirituality may be. Systems also in which individuals are largely left to themselves to develop their forms of spirituality with or without the help of spiritual advisors and their enveloping culture. So religions provide their adherents with a variety of approved mechanisms and channels for assistance with what they want in their lives and for coping with their distresses (Pargament, 1996).

These advisors in institutionalised religions with their own professional and indeed commercial needs will be dealing with immediate personal problems within the broad understandings of the culture in which they live. On the other hand the advisors in religions which are not institutionalised and committed to writing, find it much easier and indeed profitable to provide help certainly within cultural paradigms. These are closely linked to the needs and personal understandings of those who consult them. In such situations we can be certain there are few solutions which can be imposed and what does occur will be self-imposed ones which have certain similarities within varied social situations.

What in contemporary terms are the differences between these two seemingly different ways of relating to the transcendent. There are few if any societies today which have a dominant way of doing this such as the Wahabi interpretations of Islamic doctrines in Saudi Arabia and Shia ones in Iran. We do not know the extent to which there are small scale alternative cults and individual forms of spirituality which do not conform to these politically dominated systems. They must exist such as the Zar cults among women in the Sudan and Somalia from which men are excluded.

Elsewhere the governments will be in practice secular with political and economic ways of coping with large scale distress. There will be innumerable variations in the extent and degree to which individuals will conform to the doctrines and practices which will be on offer in multi-facetted and mass media flooded societies. These may be different to the monotheistic political dominances in Islamic states as Indonesia with its Muslim majority recognising other faiths as having equal political validity. These other religious affiliations are recorded on personal identity cards.

The modern urban industrial situation whether in London, Calcutta or Djarkarta in their social and religious diversities may only be different in degree to the India, Chinese or Sudanese village community with their television sets and transistor radios. The dominance of personal choice over denominational and cultural requirements not much different in effect to the situation among the Sukuma of Tanzania with their individualism and long-standing cultural diversities (Tanner, 2007).

In cross-cultural terms of comparative population sizes and the diversities of their individual and communal spiritualities, it seems rare for God or whatever the supreme force is called, to be involved beyond the theological acceptance. There is a primal force but too far off to be considered of any immediate significance for their day-to-day lives. The temple in contemporary China dedicated to the Green Dragon King has this transcendent entity as the focus of the people's religious interests. From where and how he gets his power to help petitioners is not a matter of any interest to the day-to-day isolated visitor there and certainly not to the thousands who drop to the temple as part of their coming to its annual celebrations, the yearly religious fair with its sideshows, market and opera.

A Sukuma subsistence farmer with one or more problems goes to a diviner who works on the clues provided by him or her and then produces a series of tentative solutions which he tests out on his clients as what are in opinion the causes of thee problems and possible solutions. There is no set menu in the whole process except that the 'what' and the 'how' will be considered within some vaguely understood cultural paradigm. This is an opportunity for the diviner to test out his or her quasi-traditional and indeed innovative ideas against the understandings of their clients and their agreement that what they say may be a solution to their problems. We cannot be certain from where diviners get their new ideas such as using Coca Cola bottle tops for divination instead of stones and bones, particularly the Bukumbi diviner who told some of his clients to walk on a pit of hot stones in order to propitiate their ancestors (Tanner, 1997). Whether this ceremony came from this diviner's imagination or from seeing a poster with such a ceremony being performed in a Hindu setting is irrelevant. The structures of Sukuma spirituality allowed the insertion of such innovations without any changes in theological thinking or institutional readjustments.

Faced with such a range of potential alternatives as solutions to their difficulties, what would a contemporary Sukuma consider to be possibly appropriate. If they are living in a predominantly static social environment the usual diagnosis might be ancestor malevolence for neglect or for behaviour which would disrupt the continuity of the family patriline but if connected with Christianity the devil and sin and if Muslim then evil spirits '*shetani*', an Arabic word which has become commonplace in Swahili. If the individual is urbanised or working in some institutional setting then the attribution of witchcraft or the malevolence of non-ancestral spirits become commonplace. There are always the possibility of sibling rivalry over the inheritance of land and livestock and trouble with in-laws over bride-wealth and legal parenthood have giving rise to persistent discontents. In any patrilineal society a joke about mother-in-laws is always appreciated even if translated directly from an English setting. There are always a wide ranging but culturally restricted menu of possible options including the resort to the arbitration of the civil administration, the local church or mosque leader and a political party as well to scientific medicine.

A Hindu man or woman would similarly have a range of alternative options for the solution of their problems. This variety is woven into a much tighter cultural setting and much more specific than the paradigm within which any African subsistence farmer would be operating; caste. Religious pollution, social climbing up the sub-caste levels through getting a daughter married to a person of a higher caste than herself thus insuring the improvement of their grandchildren's position. Mother-in-law and dowry problems as well as the need for male children combined with some certainty of combining Western scientific with Ayurvedic medicine.

These lists of available methods of coping through religiosity and spirituality which are possible in the cases quoted come out of the socio-religious environments in which they live. They are not as it were on offer and then selected but choices which come out of the situations in which people find themselves. There is no overt process of selection from the ideas listed by Pargament's team (Pargament *et al.*, 1998). It is highly unlikely that any but a very small highly educated intellectual minority would see their own situations as one in which they could choose from such a list of possible options. As for example 'redefining the stressor through religion as benevolent and potentially beneficial' might be the case with propitiating an ancestor. Redefining the stressor as punishment from God for the individual's sins is a situation which is confined to the Judaeo/Christian paradigm and would have no relevance at all in Buddhism, Hinduism and Shintoism. So the methods of spirituality will always be a complex amalgam of cultural predispositions, dominant religious requirements, individual psychology and social environments. However there will be a basic and lingering split between the thinking patterns of Eastern and

Western societies around a one life escheatology and the *karma* of multiple lives.

Literacy as a Minor Factor in Spirituality

It is obvious that the social sciences can only function analytically through the use of literacy and literacy of a very high standard which is probably beyond the comprehension of nearly all of the people in their own societies and certainly in the social universes which they research. These researchers are dominated by the demands of their own professional literacy without which they cannot work and the data which they collect in their fieldwork is overwhelmingly written by the people being researched in. It is usually doubtful that the writers and the researchers are working on the same wavelength or that of the researchers' own abbreviated descriptions of what has being going on in front of them. The utility of writing always seems to overlook the fact that except for the few words which have real meaning, it is always a symbolic compression of what a word or phrase may or may not mean in its social and psychological environment.

The social sciences are not happy with speech as it can have none of the fixity of writing and so whenever possible they convert it as soon as they can into writing; 'I mean what I write' has an implied reality which can never be applied to 'I mean what I say'. Social scientists have difficulty in accepting that most of life gets on easily enough without the use of writing. In practice most of the world's population literacy is no more than the basic ability to send and read a simple message. The standard required to accompany institutionalised systems of spirituality is almost certainly beyond the literacy abilities of most of those involved and indeed may not be a necessary part of their use. Even if the language is simplified, the meanings are complex although in most cases the linguistic code used is beyond commonplace understandings. It is a time consuming activity in which it is not always clear that there is a proportionate social and psychological return on the effort. We always prefer to talk if we can rather than write. The enormous popularity of mobile phones shows this clearly enough when we see people walking the streets and talking animatedly into their phones; a quarter of the current adult population of Kenya have mobile phones and just as with television, the uses of this device have hopped over the need for even basic literacy.

The ability to record and make an idea into a independent fact is a recent event and widespread literacy of certain groups of people making it a general feature of Westernised societies is even more recent. It would seem that only Christians go to worship holding prayer books and sing religious songs in specially printed collections. In other religions such as Islam there is only one necessary text, the divinely written *Koran* of which personal copies are not a required part of worship. In Eastern religions worship in the popular sense is not related to literacy nor indeed is literacy part of the ways in which millions of all faiths participate in pilgrimages.

It is likely that literacy can only be related to spirituality in a number of restricted senses. As a mnemonic to aid memory and then discarded, as statements of the spiritual understandings of the great and the good and its use as a means of gaining status by the acquisition of special knowledge through the learning of languages which are no longer spoken such as Pali and Sanskrit.

It seems reasonable to conclude that printed religious requirements have obtained institutional legitimacy possibly more as an object which has achieved a mantra like quality. Their repetition of what is printed allows for the accumulation of benefits contributing to a sense of well-being. It can only be a small part of what individual's create as their personal spirituality system.

The principal difficulty in the analyses of religious activities is the Western practice of separating it out as an isolatable type of behaviour almost in the same category as a disease with symptoms. This cannot be so and a traditional minded Sukuma if asked what is his or her religion and they have to use the Swahili word 'dini' based on the Arabic word used for the Islamic religion, will probably reply that they are Sukumas particularly as only a small number have converted to either Christianity or Islam. So right from the start Christian missionaries in both Africa, Asia and Latin America have always missed the point. The Sukuma, Gujaratis, Nagas or Cantonese cannot separate out their relationships with the spirit world. They are always part of their political, economic and social environments world which similarly cannot be divided into any such three major categories except by the process of excluding or diminishing the importance of factors which do not fit into such preconceptions.

From the Sukuma point of view Christianity and Islam are systems of ritual activities which have to be carried out at specific days and times. We must not forget that time is a very new concept coming into their culture from the Western world. This is now being enforced by their central government through the time signals of the government controlled radio programmes. The imposition of time was one of the basic changes in the Manus islands when the community decided to go modern and it has thus become a feature of conversion to their forms of Christianity (Mead, 1975).

The Chinese could be described as having a highly literate culture with its thousands of separate ideograms rather than an alphabetically based system enabling widespread literacy. This means that few can read the writing associated with spirituality and religion. Literacy is in effect confined at the most to the thousand or so ideograms connected with the necessities of daily living. Much of the need for emotional literacy achieved by Western societies has been circumvented by the successful arrival of television rather than wireless. Literacy and spirituality coincide but not in a way that suggests that it is a dominating and necessary element.

The Consequences of Electronics

When religions become irreversibly linked to writing, governments have always attempted and to some extent successfully, to control what is printed and circulated. This was made possible by the limits of cost, education and public interest. Communist states have always acted to control religion and if possible to eliminate it as an ideological rival to their own policies based on the belief in the inevitability of a specific form of economic and political progress. Electricity has continually simplified the passage of what can be seen and heard culminating in increasingly small and powerful computers, hand held telephones and televisions. Thus individuals of limited literacy but who are numerically competent enough to read numbers can bring into their perceptions an almost infinite range of culturally potentially usable images and ideas. They could never have got these through their day-to-day lives and the limited range of 'normal' social relationships (Buruma, 2001:112).

There are handicaps to this incoming flood of information and its circulation apart from the attempts at control by the government. The Chinese authorities reaction to the use of mobile phones by the Falun Gong to organise protest meetings. One suspects that Christian groups are using the same channels for organising their ceremonies in McDonald fast food outlets (Yang, 2005). There are differences in physical access to these machines; it seems likely that the purchase of a television set and a mobile phone have now become priorities for people on very low incomes indeed as their use brings almost instant gratification which is quite independent of intellect and the status discriminations coming from literacy. Television starts as a group watching event as it is in India where there are crowds watching programmes on public screens. Then with the spread in the numbers of machines the watching groups become smaller and smaller and ultimately single viewers. In the earlier days of broadcasting there were few channels and people might have listened to anything because of its novelty but listening and viewing becomes increasingly discriminatory. At the moment this access to information through the electronic air has been a top-down one. This is already being changed by the cheapness of machines and the measure of control which they give to individuals to access what they want from the enormous range of available sources and its potential freedom from government controls, paralleling the increasing individualism of most people in urban and industrial environments.

Mass Media and Spirituality

There can be little doubt that the passing of messages and pictures electronically through space has revolutionalised what is potentially available to those who have access to cheap transistor radios and television sets. It is not so much that this exists but that the many and various wave lengths provide multiple messages. It is increasingly not so much what is available relating to religion and spirituality but what individuals have the felt need to access particular programmes as well as the time and means to do so. So what is seen or listened to is a combination of variable social and psychological factors with the basically important one that it requires less effort to receive them into the mind than it would to open and read a religious book or poster. There are also the factors that cheap receivers breakdown and at low levels of income the purchase of batteries can often not be afforded for television, electricity may not be connected or it is intermittently available. However machines may become more reliable, batteries cheaper and longer lasting and electricity more reliable and provided by wind powered generators.

There are many programmes on the air provided by governments particularly in countries with dominating Muslim populations or Islamic constitutions. An agency external to any particular country such as Vatican Radio broadcasting from Rome or the Voice of Prophecy which used to come from Addis Ababa or more local religious institutions. Since there is obviously a gap between what is heard and seen and any institutional involvements, it would seen that what is received into the mind may relate more to personal spiritual needs than to the requirements of institutional religion.

In Egypt the state radio broadcasts Islamic sermons on Friday and it was obvious in a crowded Assuan coffee shop that no one was listening even though it was inescapably loud. In West Africa there are rival Protestant and Roman Catholic broadcasting stations on the air competing with at least half a dozen secular ones with some topicality and popular music programmes. It seems likely that as an influence broadcasting on religious themes unless carefully packaged to appeal to particular sections of a community will have limited audiences. A sermon is unlikely to attract large numbers of listeners however worthy the speaker and topical the subject may be.

In Japan the national broadcasting company ran a religious series which mentioned without intending to promote certain temples which specialised in providing hope for the elderly that they would have easy deaths without the prolonged indignities of terminal care. This sets off a new and still on-going popularity with the growing number of aged with small families (Woss, 1993). The broadcast in Egypt of a serial obliquely related to the life of the Prophet Muhammad was certainly listened to with interest. Listening to the radio never provides the immediate emotional return provided by television which is harder to avoid once sets have been turned on. Television provides instant gratification without the effort required for reading as it combines the two senses of sight and sound. The broadcasting in India in many episodes of the Hindu mythological epic the *Mahabharata*, was immensely popular and parallels that of coloured religious pictures available in all markets and in most homes to a greater extent that Christian pictures in southern Europe and Ethiopia.

An important development is the use of personal computers to log on to programmes of spirituality which are becoming more and more common with the cheapening of their price and their reduction in size. The Society of Jesus has developed a personal spirituality programme in twenty languages. Although such programmes are developed for their mass appeal, they are received and appreciated individually and channels are provided for answering back. We are talking here of many millions who log on to such programmes. Their numbers are sure to increase as computers become more available and the appeal of what seems to be assessed as personal spiritualities perhaps growing as at least in Western Europe there continues to be a decline in the collective use of religious institutions. There is also the availability of privately made and circulated tapes and videos. These are reported to have been influential in extending the appeal of Islamic extremism to Muslims living in Western societies. These have enabled people to evade official and quasi-official frameworks of belief and practice and their various forms of censorship and of course to cross international borders with relative ease.

It is difficult to evaluate the extent to which the mass media has influenced individual spiritualities. It seems likely that it will enlarge the appeal of any topical theme as it has done with the anxieties of the elderly in Japan and that of anti-Americanism to the culturally discontented younger Muslims everywhere reacting to the failure of their secular governments to provide expected overall development of their societies to the comparable standard of living of those in the Western world.

In all of this it is competition for the use of time which dominates the use of the mass media to extend channels of spirituality to individuals. It may be that the well-to-do elderly will predominate along with the unemployed whose livelihoods are supported by welfare systems and families as well as those outside subsistence agriculture who have spare-time created by the limitation of hours of work in factories and offices.

Mental Trafficking Across Cultural Boundaries

It has always been difficult to keep an idea confined to or out of a particular place, area or country and as far back in history and disclosed by archaeology, there has always been trading in objects and this must have been accompanied by a movement of ideas. The Melanesians sailed great distances to and fro across the Pacific and Chinese monks came round the Himalayas to India and took back Buddhism with them to China. The Al Jazeera independent television broadcasting from the Gulf spreads versions of the news which are not available in states in which the news is either controlled by the government or the editors self-censor themselves for fear of hostile government reactions.

Only in very rare circumstances such as the inhabitants of Easter Island who immobilised themselves by the destruction of the trees from which they could have made boats. Even there we cannot be sure that there were no accidental incomers during their centuries of isolation. We have to accept that men and indeed women have always drifted off from their natal groups. The distribution of blood groups shows that this has always been happening except for the general genetic isolation of the pre-Columbian Americas, and in doing so passed and received new ideas. We do not know what ideas have moved around the world but when they are unattached to writing, we can be sure that those connected with personal spirituality have always been in the processes of catching new ways of coping in new social environments. Traders must have seen things with new interpretations and their simple presence must similarly have given rise to new thoughts; the arrival of iron has to be seen as a social dialectic in the running of societies. We have to accept that mental trading over cultural boundaries has always been a part of the human condition (Howell, 1995:165), but we can only guess at the extent to which this is trading as the commodity is intangible. Diffusion is possibly a more reasonable explanation for the spread of ideas and their dependent practices rather than spontaneous mutations however attractive the idea of inspiration may be rather than rearrangements of ideas within cultures (Tanner, 1997).

The Digitalisation of Spirituality Thinking

There can be little opposition to the global process by which the storage, development and publication of information is being progressively digitalised with an accumulation of knowledge modules constructed with the technique of binary oppositions. The same process of development is occurring in the mechanisation of spirituality in which what is passed through the air electronically is no longer one way and becomes a dialogue. Large numbers of people develop the simpler digital techniques for business and more personal relationships dominated by their commercial needs and the convenience and stimulus of talking to strangers. The needs of spirituality fit easily enough into this process. Large numbers of those who log-on to the meditation and prayer channel provided by the Society of Jesus respond with appreciative comments relating to their own personal spirituality. It is likely of course that self-help courses such as Dale Carnegie's 'How to win friends and influence people' will be digitalised into many languages as will be those offered by Alcoholics Anonymous. There will be still be the questions of expense so that the simplicity and relative brevity of material related to spirituality will be attractive.

There will always be the differences in the thinking between the designer and sender and the receiver. The systems of prayer and meditation available through the internet may appeal to the same range of people as the over-ritualising *mantra* users but which has none of its attractive simplicity and readiness to hand. On the other hand binary systems are made up by combining two value units, simple one-off switches where extraordinary complex sequences are generated. The mainstream of cognitive science has extended this crisp approach to knowledge and has tended to produce computerised models for human thought. Models that treat human understandings as a kind of prepositional logic where programmes in the form of manipulative symbols can be run on a computer (Shore, 1996:152, 167).

This technological frame of mind represents a convergence of the logic inherent in industrial production. The commodification of all forms of experience and the methodologies of empirical science. Human understandings become equated with taxonomic knowledge which in turn are equated with classical categories which are straightforward and neat rather than fuzzy. Not unsurprisingly this approach fits in neatly with Westernised thinking. Thomas Aquinas's Summa Theologica in its written layout is ready for digital computerisation as no doubt is the case with Jewish law and Islamic regulations for inheritance. When it comes to Eastern thinking which in contrast is fuzzy with its pronounced dislike of firm boundaries, and indeed the virtual absence of taxonomies of spirituality, then their future is much less likely to be dominated by digitalisation. Overall it seems likely that however exact the translation of matters connected with spirituality may be digitalised, the listeners will always be interpreting what they hear in terms of their own personal understandings. It may be received in ways that are seen as personal rather than within the more collective understandings of religions.

Social Distancing and the Understanding of Spirituality

Social distancing is perhaps the basic fact in all social science field-work as the researchers are never 'one' of those on whom they are working except in some occasional ideological senses. This distancing enables the researchers to be detached and to see the wider world in which people are involved. At the same time it misses the petty realities which govern most behaviour; it looks for true spiritualities in this distancing and yet when it gets nearer it records the grubbiness of short-term self-interests.

The practices of spirituality once it goes beyond the brain and takes on some physical form is always handicapped by relationships between researchers and the researched who have different conscious and unconscious ideas as to what is reasonable and appropriate. Few social science researchers would consider the 'extreme' Tantric activities as reasonable and some Jain practices such as sweeping the seat before they sit down or veils over their mouths to prevent the killing of insects might be seen as slightly absurd. The practices of spirituality can antagonise as much as unify and the systems which may be more successful are perhaps those which restrict social contacts and minimize the possibilities of social tensions. If a priest, pastor or imam is married then it is likely that their partners see and are much more influenced by their secular behaviour than the spirituality which is supposed to be their primary motivation. In any close relationship behaviour is perhaps more likely to be patterned and judged by orthodoxy and factors related to social distance necessities than by factors intrinsic to spirituality.

On the other hand certain forms of monastic life which restrict inter-relationships, seem to enable spirituality to emerge and continue and yet may seem to provide an unattractive form of social living. The Benedictine system of monastic life which has survived for nearly a thousand years without much ostensible modification, has combined a form of dedicated life limiting inter-relationships by restricting association and talking between fellow monks within a structure of calendrical almost monotonous ritualism. The researcher is able to see in such a system the distancing which they would encounter anyway in seeking for evidence of spirituality without getting entangled in primary more social considerations. The Lord Buddha ruled that arguments over the finer points of doctrine for which almost by definition there can be no agreement, would be best dealt with by dividing the community rather than compromising to retain unity between divergent personalities. So both for the carriers of spirituality and researchers there are benefits from social distancing; the glass is still dark but not clouded by social immediacies.

There is also a pattern of social distancing among the Sukuma of Tanzania when they are in personal difficulties but they are unlikely to consult any local diviner even though he or she may have a good reputation according to the number of clients which they have attracted. This social distancing is shown by the diviners themselves who when possessed 'speak with tongues' which is said to be the language of the Nyaturu, a less developed tribe with a reputation among the Sukuma for their successful forms of spirituality. So it would seem overall that assessing spirituality and its utilisation is best done at a distance when the major issues are not too entangled in personal relationships.

The Boundaries of Tradition and Modernity; Reflective Spirituality

It is perhaps a truism to describe modernity as being typified by logical thought but not to recognise the limited extent of rational thinking. Any factory manufacturing articles to exact specifications and within financial limitations has to do this with the management of their employees which is not an exact science. A laboratory and a bank will both be always having to deal with the limitations of rationality. For those who are seemingly part of the urban-industrial culture, the way that they conduct their personal relationships in free choice or arranged marriages involve emotion even though the latter have an implied rationality about them.

The dividing line or more appropriately the boundary between the supposed rationality of modernity and the supposed irrationality of more traditional thinking, may be theoretically exact. There can be no irrationality only mistakes in the conclusions drawn from the analyses of inorganic matter but the study of any traditional community shows that these people are remarkably pragmatic in all that they do. What we have here is a theoretical but varying boundary between two forms of cognition. While the sheer quantity of pragmatically based data has certainly increased and is inevitably increasing. There is no consistency in this division and so-called traditional thinking is independent of the observations and conclusions of educated outsiders, and is constantly moving backwards and forwards over any such boundary. Similarly in modernised society traditional ideas about the functions of magical rituals are as universally visible in Cambridge and Calcutta.

Sometimes issues of spirituality have national prominence and as such receive international attention which look at such matters in political terms without understanding the metaphysical background. The Yasukuni shrine in Tokyo involves the deification of the Japanese war dead from all the conflicts in which they have been involved and not just in World War Two and their invasion of China. This is an active shrine in comparison to the national war memorial not far away which is deserted and shows no sign of ongoing memorial rituals.

The idea behind this wholesale deification is only different in degree from he domestic deification of the family dead kept active in household shrines (R.J. Smith, 1974), but war dead are in a special category. In 1969 the government passed a law stating that the shrine was in memory of those who had sacrificed themselves for the sake of their country. This left in place the rationality of bowing to the deities there and only in the wording would we find any differences to the ceremonies that are carried out annually in the Western world for the dead of two World Wars.

It is widely understood not only in Japan (Antoni, 1993) but also in other south-east Asian societies (Sell, 1955; Lebra, 1966) that premature death in war as by abortion leads to wandering spirits who have to be appeased to prevent their evil influences over the living. In contemporary Japan there is little reason to suppose that the range of these rituals are any different to those carried out by business concerns. A synthetic fibre factory employing 4000 people carries out a wide range of religious rituals involving the management (D.C. Lewis, 1993). There are seven rituals at the beginning and end of the year with Shinto prayers for safety and Buddhist ones for feeding the souls of hungry ghosts, company vehicles have annually renewed religious charms attached to them for safety. When a new building was started, there was a ground breaking ceremony to appease the local deity. In addition there were ceremonies specific to that firm such as the festival for the God of the hillside behind the factory, the annual Shinto blessing of the company's martial arts hail and for the anniversary of the founding of the company dedicated to the fox God Inari, the patron of merchants and traders. There were as well Buddhist ceremonies relating to fires one of which in 1973 was attributed to the spirits of warriors killed in a battle nearby eleven hundred years previously on a site near to that of the factory.

In particular the film department which had a series of accidents held monthly petitions for safety at the Inari shrine.

Thus we find concern over what the spirits of the dead may do to the living to be a matter of current concern in societies which range from the very modern to the more isolated and traditional ones in Indonesian islands. If we take that there are four theoretical distinctions between the so-called 'savage' and the traditional mind and modern patterns of thinking (E. Gellner, 1974:149-167) it seems likely that these distinctions are heavily weighted in favour of the few in the contemporary world who think logically according to scientific criteria in at least some parts of their lives. Much importance has to be given to the overlap in which the thinking patterns of the subsistence farming Sukuma of Tanzania and the factory owning Japanese coincide.

The Limitations of Factual Thinking

If the ability to create hard and fast categories is characteristic of the thinking of men and women in modern societies, we have to accept that there is a weak dividing line between modern and traditional thought. How far in practice do modern men and women think logically as opposed to thinking that they do. The very general use of modern medicine based on the scientific analysis of symptoms by specially trained technicians is only the beginning of an assumed process. If it is left to the patients we know that large amounts of these expensive medicaments remain unused. These people are using the peripheries of science and their thinking is as much on belief in what is being applied to them than any scientific thought on their part.

It seems likely that the only narrowly accurate calculations in their lives will have been in their use of currency, dog's teeth or cowries which have a constant assessable reality. For someone to have a hundred head of cattle is not parallel to this as each animal will have a different religious, social and economic value. Modern men and women use scientific accuracy in accountancy but not in other aspects of their lives. Specialised thinking by specialising people for specialised circumstances but beyond this it should not be classified as a universal cognitive process.

A Sukuma subsistence farmer or a Xhosa cattle keeper just as a housekeeper in Osaka or a small trader in Kohlapur make very accurate calculations of any of their activities whether it is agriculture, trading, foods purchasing and their rituals involving spirituality. Their processes of assessment will be more or less the same for all that they do. There is nothing particularly modern or traditional about these calculations or indeed classifying them as benign, ambiguous or malign.

All societies have ideas as to how their own community should work and the public and private offences which hinder this. These do not always coincide with the law and their ideas are interrelated to the practices of spirituality. These categories are abstract and they are always tested against particular social situations and whether these solutions are acceptable to public or personal gods, goddesses, ancestors and spirits.

There is nothing particularly contemporary about these calculations except that literacy enables some of them to be recorded and become facts detached from the situations in which they were created and which usually have moved on into equally important new ones. There is always a cost-benefit calculation involving social knowledge, the relationships with the spirit world and material consequences. It seems likely that most people calculate to their own satisfactions what they get out of their spirituality commitments. Modern commitment to the ostensible accuracy of records may make people more committed to practices which do not involve writing.

There may be a social as much as cognitive boundary between what is new and what is old which is much studied by the social sciences. The distinction is likely to be between pre-defined aspects of what may be considered to be traditional and what is modern. In between these two extremes there are many individuals who come and go between these two dimensions and that this is particularly likely in the practices of spirituality. A recent Gallup survey of Christian church members in the United States (Wuthnow, 1998:137) found that 22 per cent believed in astrology, 24 per cent read their own horoscopes in newspapers at least once a week, 20 per cent believed in reincarnation, 12 per cent had consulted a fortune teller and 11 per cent believed in the trance channelling of spirits into living individuals. Wuthnow's book is entitled *After Heaven. Spirituality in America* and is thus not a study of American religion.

It is not realistically possible to conduct similar surveys into the beliefs and practices of contemporary quasi-traditional peoples. If we take this United States survey as relating just to the more orthodox Americans since they admit to belonging to a Christian Church, it is a restricted sample. Add to this the beliefs and practices of those outside these church-goers, there would almost certainly be higher percentages for these quasi-traditional behaviours. It would not be reasonable to parallel the beliefs of just subsistence farmers in Africa, Asia and Latin America but we can expect rather similar figures for those who live in Nairobi, Mumbai, Lima and Kuala Lumpur where such behaviour would be considered quite normal. In Western societies it would be classed as certainly irrational and as fringe symptoms of abnormality. Perhaps the distinction is between reflective and unreflective forms of spirituality.

It is usually assumed without proof and within the safety of social science speculation that there must be some definitive differences between the cognitive patterns of those socialised within so-called traditional and modern social environments, this has proved an illusory theory grounded in ethnic biases in comparative data. The assumptions that there must be a difference because they are so obviously not like 'us', has led to a lot of effort being spent in trying to prove just that. Most social scientists in their fieldwork have met men and women of limited literacy who in their understandings and explanations of their own forms of spirituality and religion are certainly the intellectual equal of their interrogators. David Livingstone's conversation with the rainmaker on one of his missionary journey in Central Africa, recorded that man's remark that he hoped he was not credulous enough to believe that he actually made rain. The Sukuma Chief Lupembe of Massanza, a man of limited education was able to discuss quite dispassionately the fraudulent nature of many but not all diviner/herbalists in his chiefdom.

An alternative approach would be to assume that in any society at whatever level of social and economic complexity since in personal terms all societies may be experienced as complex, there will be a proportion of reflective individuals who think about what they experience in terms of their personal spiritualities. The Chinese have always made a distinction in their approaches to popular religion between the reflective nature of the upper classes who adopt an attitude somewhat similar to that of the social secular theorist and the thinking of the common people who just carry on performing their rituals without any conscious reflection on what they might or might not mean (Teiser, 1996:24).

The ability to reflect and indeed to create must start with those who have above average intelligence but this has to be combined with the opportunity to do so as subsistence farmers would not be able to think much in the cultivating seasons but shepherds and herdsmen have always had unlimited time. It is not that modern man thinks more but that in modern economically developed societies there are more people detached from the immediacies of organising their own survival and some indeed who are provided with the time to think as the multitudes of priests and academics show.

The Unreflective Ascriptive Forms of Spirituality

For subsistence farmers, hand-to-mouth workers on the fringes of urban-industrial centres as well as the average time-worker in office and factories combined as it is to time consuming commuting to and from work which considerably lengthens the working day in Tokyo, Mumbai and London, do not have the time for reflection. When they are not in fact working, they may will be dozing on their feet. Often tired, tied up in primary relationships and provided with television; they are committed to knee jerk behaviour unrelieved by any need to think much beyond the current month.

For those born into one of the major religions there may be little opportunities for choice as to the religious and cultural overload which they receive by birth. It will consciously or unconsciously remain as the background for whatever more personal forms of spirituality they may develop. Most people in their private personal spiritualities whether they can be classed as traditionally or modern minded are unlikely to be reflective in these matters. It is always going to be within existing paradigms dictated by the societies in which they live with shrines provided as well as the talismans sold in markets whether at Katagarama, Lourdes or Banaras.

The so-called 'religions of the book' have set forms of prayer written into their books of ceremonies and canonical works. Their more orthodox practitioners are likely to keep repetitively to these set form of spirituality. Roman Catholics are more likely to repeat the 'Hail Mary' than the 'Our Father', but these two prayers ascriptively dominate their public and indeed probably their private religious as much as their spirituality practices; it is an unthinking heritage. Much the same would apply to the Muslim prayer processes which are repeated in exactly the same form five times per day by the orthodox. In both these cases their users could be said in general to more or less understand what they are saying aloud or in their heads.

What are we to make of the repetitive mantras of some Eastern religions and their use of prayer forms in languages which require special scholarship to be able to read much less understand. Northern Buddhists repeat '*om mane padme hum*' and its frequency is augmented by the use of prayer wheels moved by hand, wind, or heat and is even printed on water with wooden blocks and is used by porters on Himalayan climbing expeditions where it is often heard as a background hum. Whereas the Christian and Muslim standard prayers have understandable meanings, this Buddhist mantra has no meaning at all in the commonplace understandings of the words.

When these people are asked why they are carrying out their spiritualities in processes which are to all intents and purposes as repetitive and identical as factory produced biscuits, they usually have no answer beyond that this is what they or their group have always done. It would undercut their proven validity by trying something new. Some might suggest that such questions should be addressed to specialists in the understandings of spirituality who would know the answers. In terms of Merton's typology of adaptation most people in all societies and in systems of belief are conformists to what their age-cohort is doing within a caste, class or occupational groupings. Within this classification there will always be a majority whose behaviour is classifiable as ritualistic or retreatist by the repetitive use of what are functionally the equivalent of Buddhist and Hindu *mantras*.

It is wrong to see the ascriptive use of basic prayers as necessarily restrictive which might be the case with any form of spiritual devotionalism as it would be the framework of thinking that will keep the individual within certain boundaries of thought. It is correct that the majority may for most of the time keep to these prayers as a form of cumulative devotionalism as an end in itself. Beyond this it is certain that these commonplace prayers often learnt in childhood are the point of entry into transcendence for a variety of individual reasons arising from their personal lives. It would be wrong to write off these forms of spirituality as only used by those of limited intellectual understandings. The use of prayers must vary in their acceptable value within the varying mental, abilities and spiritual requirements of those who use them. They cannot be assessed only according to the standards laid down by the intellectuals of each particular system.

Karmic Thinking and Spirituality

Between Western pragmatic thinking within the 'religions of the book' and Eastern ways of thought, there are ascriptive cognitive patterns which separate the former with its single life and death reality and the latter with their seemingly endless sequence of lives. Both can be equally disturbing with their oppositions and restrictions between single and successive lives. Thus in karmic thought there is the explanation for present misfortunes lying in previous lives. This goes in part to explain the institutionalised discrimination in current Japanese Buddhism towards outcastes and the disabled whether this comes from historical Tokugawa legislation and foundation documents, are still part of the thinking and practices of believers there. Buddhist doctrines of karmic retribution suggest that disadvantaged people deserve their miserable fates. In the often quoted 'Ten fates preached by the Buddha' come from butchering animals and injuries and sickness comes from ritual impurities just as poverty and desperation come from miserly thoughts, crippling and blindness from violating the Buddhist precepts. They cannot possibly attain awakening as the blind cannot read the scriptures, the deaf cannot hear sermons, the mute cannot chant and cripples cannot sit in the proper postures for meditation (Bodiford, 1996).

This way of thinking fits in well enough with a variety of discriminations in Japanese and in all societies with entrenched spirituality thinking and practices. This system does provide ways out of this seemingly inevitable continuing miseries. Soto Zen Buddhism has responded to this inevitability by developing rituals to block off these karmic connections between such people and their descendents and by the provision of talismans and charms against pollution as well as to prevent the vengeance of aborted foetus' denied life (LaFleur, 1992).

The Overall Nature of Spirituality

Any human activity such as spirituality at the point of action must involve an enormous concentration of predisposing factors. Some will have been of major importance such as age, sex and psycho-social capacity as well as some of minor influence such as seeing an omen on the way to work which activates some socialised memories. To all intents and purposes the supposed reasons for what is happening will not only be causally multiple but become explicable by any number of theories which may be proportionately influential. The door through which the researchers enter their fieldwork experiences may well dictate the door through which they exit.

Thus we find that the theoretical approaches of the individuals involved in particular events disclosed by their field work is likely to be a series of sequential elaborations starting with some aspects of functional explanations and then going on to a further series of possibilities. The choice of these approaches and their order of priority lies with these researchers and one can presuppose that these sequences have some connection with how their importance is assessed. These explanations lie in the minds of the researchers and not necessarily in that of the person(s) who are the object of these enquiries. This sequential approach automatically misses the fact that whatever has happened is ego-centred and linear explanations miss this unity. Whatever its antecedents may have been personal spirituality has a constant overallness.

The linear framework of explanation is the simplest approach to the so-called understanding of any event. It seems unlikely that this is the route down which humans make their decisions or the frame within which they formulate the background to any decision-making. In fact spirituality may be a process or pattern which cannot be examined in the same way as an event might be. Going to pray probably cannot be analysed by the same procedures as going to plant or purchase. About what can an individual be so certain that they can base their subsequent actions on any such singularities. Of course in the primary sense there are numerous clear cut acts such as the fact of death, the legal event of divorce and a variety of finite disasters from fire, flood and devaluation. The overall predispositions which are entailed in spirituality may or may not be initiated by such wide-ranging possibilities in which the linkage may be no nearer than a correlation such as would connect tea drinking with almost any type of subsequent activity.

Social and psychological factors can push towards one decision rather than another is a permanent cause of unconscious or conscious anxiety as much as some narrow finite form of reality. It is into this vacuum surrounding causation that spirituality becomes both the medium if not the method of putting events into place.

The Nature of the Practices of Religion and Spirituality

While religious practices may be standardised in some religions which have become institutionalised by the creation of official doctrines and the social importance of personal as well as institutional charisma, what people actually do in their personal privacies is always going to be variants of this because of the basic personality of each individual and their personal experiences. Indigenous concepts of personality are as important as Western based psychological ones as can be seen in the Ghanian Akan ideas (Danquah, 1944). The spirit of a dead relative through the intermediation of god or a spirit enters a child influencing and shaping its disposition so that there is the need for propitiation and in addition the appearance and individuality of a person can wander about while they are asleep.

Secondly, the basic visible demographic facts which divide up any community according to age, sex and ethnicity. Then there are the created social factors related to education and socialisation and finally, environmental immediacies. In view of these basic divisions and the immense variability of how they must affect every individual's ways of looking at themselves and the world around them, it is fundamentally incorrect to think of any religious and spirituality behaviour as being consistent. Even the carrying out of the simplest and repetitive ritual, the reasons for doing it and what is mentally put into such performances make them inevitably variable and varying on even a day-to-day basis.

The Hindu orthodox daily domestic prayers *puja* contains nineteen stages but it seems unlikely that each stage will be performed in a standardised manner accompanied by standardised thinking. A Roman Catholic priest with a highly developed form of personal spirituality took so long to complete his daily carrying out of the Mass, that he was quietly persuaded to carry out this daily obligation in a private chapel rather than one which the public could attend. At the other extreme regular Christian monastic devotions taught the novices how to sleep while kneeling (Drobin, 1999).

Any attempts at standardising this behaviour by religious authorities or by social scientists are created by the terms in which such behaviour is approached but almost by definition it cannot have any such permanency. There are cultural boundaries which make it more likely that certain types of spirituality may or may not happen. Spirit possession is more likely to happen in Bali and Bamako but that does not mean that it will not happen in different forms in Birmingham and Berlin. Populations are more on the move now than ever before in history, both physically and mentally through the mass media. This makes the creation of effective cultural boundaries an illusion, if indeed it ever existed in anything approaching social science exactnesses. Thus we are likely to find that although there are always going to be cultural dimensions that may make certain spiritual behaviour more likely, it will not have any social or mental fixity. So spirituality is always going to be highly variable as people cannot remain the same in their behaviour even if they think that they do.

Now behaviour which is physically observable can be recorded quite accurately, where, when and indeed what they do and that in practice is the beginning and end of definable accuracies in which facts can be verified and agreed on by a variety of observers. But there are always going to be 'grey' areas which are not quite this or that. How are we going to classify the behaviour of a mentally handicapped or semi-conscious person at Lourdes. If bathing in the Ganges at the *Kumbh Mela* is supposed to be auspicious at a particular moment so to what extent does being late by half an hour constitute attendance and loss of auspiciousness.

It is in the interpretation of these acts that the spirituality of the individual has to be understood and interpreted. Crossing oneself or performing *puja* can be carried out for a multitude of reasons and these can be changing by the minute. Since spirituality is a personal activity to presuppose any consistency would be to ignore the basic factor of human variability and its dialectic function as a factor in human survival as species.

The Prevalence of Traditional Forms of Spirituality

The persistence of traditional beliefs and practices involving aspects of spirituality can be accounted for on two levels, the psycho-social and the professional-*cum*-economic. The idea of a culture into which individuals are socialised as much by accident as by deliberate teaching, comes from nowhere that is accessible to evaluation. It is usually worked backward from events which have already happened for which there must be explanations waiting to be created rather than forwards in anticipation that certain patterns will continue.

It seems possible that traditional ideas remain in the conscious and unconscious thinking of individuals particularly in Eastern and traditional cultures because they provide broad based explanations for well-being and misfortune. Since these explanations are without definitions their very ambiguity makes them far more successful than the so-called pragmatic answers which cannot have a similar range of usefulness. God's will or whatever are far more useful explanations in human terms than that disastrous events whether earthquakes or tsunami occur because of the movement of tectonic plates beneath the earth's surface.

The enduring popularity of quasi-traditional healers with their divinations and homeopathy are not just evidence of the persistence of such beliefs attributable to wide-ranging backwardness that misfortune has been caused by bad *karma,* ancestor irritation, witchcraft and malignant spirits in the same way as unorthodox cults have their explanations in New York, Berlin and Birmingham.

A social scientist (Swantz, 1974) stated that on any one day in Dar-es-Salaam, the capital of Tanzania, the number consulting traditional healers however defined, at least equalled the number going to all governmental and non-governmental social welfare institutions together. In South Africa it has been estimated that there are 300,000 traditional healers, fifteen times the number of medical practitioners and there is no reason to suppose that this proportion is likely to be any different in Yangon, Mumbai, Shanghai and Tokyo (Rogerson, 2000).

This may have been principally because the latter all operate along the lines of Western pragmatic understandings and even if successful only deal with proximate causes. They may cure a physical symptom but such assessments of causation if given at all requires belief in the trustworthiness of an alien and incomprehensible system. Few have seen a virus or bacteria except under conditions which most would describe as magical even if alleged to be based on scientific pragmatism. These quasi-traditional healers are market-oriented and proliferate where their services are needed and do not operate from social interactions in which petitioners and patients are defined as inferior in an intimidating environment by people wearing culturally upsetting costumes. In China white is the colour of mourning and so red the colour of happiness might be the more appropriate one for the uniforms of doctors. and nurses. Much medical information is passed on to patients by nurses rather than by infrequently seen doctors. There are cultural problems here apart from those over age, sex and communal background.

These men and women healers live round the corner from those in difficulties, know their shared background and speak in their linguistic code and even if the diagnosis comes in the form of glossolalia, the sounds are socially acceptable whereas most medical language in terms of those to whom it is applied might just as will be talking in tongues (Yih-Yuan, 1976; Youngsook, 1976). It is only officially that government and non-government services are only officially that government and non-government services are free. It may be necessary to give bribes to get treatment and medicines while with the traditional healer, the sufferers get what is paid for in face-to-face consultations. Culturally acceptable standards of payment as the traditional healers reputation, their street credibility is at stake.

However well trained bio-medical staff may be, it is based on scientifically assessable facts. On the other hand 'popular or rather known by their reputations traditional healers are priests, religious ritual specialists, family and communal therapists, moral and social philosophers, teachers, missionaries, empirical scientists and perhaps political leaders in addition to being healers in the more restricted Western sense' (E.C. Green, 1994). In modern Western terminology they have always been holistic in their approach which has not yet received anything like a similar functional utility in Western societies. There is not the financial incentive nor the time to assess patients in their social and psychological holistic environments.

It is certain that these quasi-traditional healers spend more time per patient as perhaps Western doctors may do in private practice. They provide medicines which they themselves mix rather than providing substances manufactured elsewhere. They are adaptable because in a crude sense it pays them to react to market needs. Medical personnel have no such incentives except for the need to rise in their professional hierarchy and the humane one of wanting to reduce human suffering. The rewards for an holistic approach are not material or immediate.

Since the belief in the existence of widespread malevolence in all societies regardless of their level of social, political and economic development, not just in traditionally backward ones, the disruptions of modernity appear to have made these malevolent potentialities even more prevalent and indeed shown to be so in the popular press. Individuals may believe that they are already vulnerable because of their *karma* whether thought of as the sins committed in their previous existences through the upsetting of ancestors and a sense of fatalism.

The Persistence of Syncretism

We must accept that globally people have spiritual needs and practices, their form and the boundaries between one system and another can only be nominally kept intact. While non-Muslims can be excluded from entering the boundaries of the holy city of Mecca, the separation of personal systems of spirituality is extremely inexact. Certainly within the major Western religions of the book which have their rules and regulations committed to paper, there are nominal conformities. Elsewhere and for the majority of people, there are immense variations in what is believed in and how it is practised.

If we take the festivals which occur at the pilgrimage centre of Katagarama in southern Sri Lanka as an example which has its season around the full moon of July/August currently attracting some half a million pilgrims in comparison to a tenth of that number a century ago. This festival as a centre of pilgrimage seems to have had its origins in the spiritualities of the early forest hunters but the current large area is dominated by a Buddhist stupa, a Hindu temple and a Muslim mosque all with their supporting buildings. Every pilgrim is doing their own thing but what that is can never be clear since the crowds contain Tamil Hindus from the north, Sinhala Buddhist from the south and even Muslim groups of Sufi ascetics and almost certainly some Roman Catholics (Younger, 2002).

We can be certain that few are there because of any knowledge of or wish to read the classics of their faiths and its tenuous connections with this site or indeed pay much attention to their professionals. On a recent visit about half of a large gathering of white clad Buddhist women listening to a senior monks were asleep. It is not at all certain who or what is the Lord Katagarama but those coming there in specially decorated buses are in pleasurable ignorance of such niceties while remaining certain that they know all they need to as he is active in their lives. There is the usual reality of dispersed indefinable devotion which must be the key to any appreciation what such festivals mean to the pilgrims attending. 'It is really the portrayal of the stubborn search of the human heart for contact with the divine which is the creative genius of the drama' (Younger, 2002:50).

There can be little doubt that the major contemporary religions had their origins in dispersed different cults with their own theologies which can only be called syncretic because social scientists work backwards starting from the viewpoints of the major religions. But somewhere in history Western religions of the book became nominally monotheistic in their institutionalised and written forms without being able to eliminate the syncretic practices of the groups and individuals adhering to these faiths. We cannot be certain how this may have occurred but it may have been related to the alphabetical simplicity of their languages, easy to learn and easy to read which allowed some control over the practices of at least corporate spirituality. Latin and Arabic had wider uses than simply to maintain a religion.

In the Eastern religions this did not happen and the languages used for religion either did not have any secular uses such as Sanskrit and Pali or their ideograms became so specialised as to be beyond the capacity of most people either to learn or to use. It is not just a question of learning just a few more than two dozen symbols which can be combined for innumerable meanings and related definitions. To become literate in a religiously acceptable sense becomes a massive learning exercise which can have had little popular appeal. This has resulted in the practices of spirituality remaining not so much syncretic, as only related into larger religious groupings by the use of imaginative mythology. The reasons for the Eastern faiths flourishing in such immense variability and the West driving syncreticism into its current second-class discouraged status must be related to these linguistic differences.

The Individuality of Spirituality

However much we search for and anticipate homogeneity in the societies which we are researching, this is not likely to be found in any society however simple their social and economic structure may be as forms of spirituality are shared between mental and physical processes. All contemporary systems of spirituality have syncretic elements within them no matter what has been theologically defined as the basis of any particular pattern.

In some cases it may be reasonable to state that there are a number of different systems of spirituality available in any culturally distinct environment as among the Navaho American Indians (Csordas, 1999) just as may be the case in the complex urban environments of Banaras and Birmingham. There is the traditional system based on a philosophy of obstacles which their medicine men and diagnosticians can identify, making sense of misfortune and reaffirming the personal identity of those that come to them for help. Then there is the Native American Church based on a philosophy of self-esteem with its sacramental use of the peyote cactus and the whole night sweat lodge sessions. Thirdly, there is the independent Native Pentecostal preacher with his revival meetings and the laying on of hands by Roman Catholic prayer groups which both integrate communally. Finally, those solutions for those Navaho who have lived outside their legally exclusive Reservations in the south-western United States, for whom the systems of spirituality and religion would be the same as those of other Americans regardless of their ethnic background. Everywhere there is a substantial amount of cultural cross-pollination.

If we look at any gathering of Christians, Hindus or Muslims which involves thousands of people whether at Lourdes, Banaras or Mecca, the numbers are so large that it is almost inevitable that the social scientists have to group these participants so that the numbers become more manageable for research needs. They are seen as pilgrims and not as a number of individuals who at that particular time happen to be pilgrims in their own personal ways.

the religious organisation to which they belong as well to the Deity which it represents. This is easiest for Islam in which the Five Pillars of Faith are clear and from which within both Shia and Sunni forms there are no deviations. With Christianity there is no such clarity even within a major denomination such as the Roman Catholic Church. We have also to accept that in South Africa alone there are some four thousand known Independent Christian Churches (Barrett, 1968) and probably an equal number in the United States. So the formulations of a denomination or sect are at best going to be limited to the small numbers of conformist practitioners of a particular form of Christianity.

When it comes to Hinduism such uniformity as might exist is even smaller since there are no centralising institutions, supervising authorities or authoritative texts. If we accept that the 'orthodox' *puja*, regular worship of Hindus has around twenty components and that the average popular religious picture contains very large numbers of symbols, the possibility of analytically provable group conformities is negligible. In all these three major religions people are Christian, Hindu or Muslim because they say they are and not because they actively follow the precepts of their faith.

Then there are the non-literate religious systems of quasi-traditional communities which are based on the popular devotions of family and neighbourhood systems involving their ancestors and local spirits with village temples. Collective understanding and practices becomes more a creation of social science than social realities.

If we then consider the religions or rather the spiritualities of these people which are in practice non-literate. The majority of Buddhists, Hindus or Taoists cannot read Sanskrit or Pali or the specialised ideograms of Mandarin Chinese. In addition these systems of religion are not based on any literate compilations and are no more than practices based along undefined and indefinable cultural themes, then we have overwhelmingly individual spiritualities.

The Bricolage Nature of Spirituality

If ever there were assessable differences in mentality it is unlikely to be between what has been called the 'primitive' and 'non-primitive' without communities or individuals sufficiently isolated or sufficiently less developed to have identified forms of thinking which could be called 'primitive' in the senses meant by Levi-Strauss. It is doubtful whether the small populations of a few isolated Pacific communities such as existed on Easter Island could make a case for so-called primitiveness when they are distinguished by a yet to be deciphered written language and sophisticated religious practices at least paralleling the megalith building societies of Western Europe still to be seen at Stonehenge, Carnac and Callanish. From the similarities between the language and culture of the isolated Easter Island and elsewhere in Melanesia it would seem that they all form of a single cultural system (Diamond, 2005) whose western fringe would have had contacts with the Asian mainland.

If differences do exist they are likely to be between individual variations in intelligence within a population rather than between aggregates of populations and these differences in intelligence probably have no relationship to any overall levels of literacy. It may will be that a thousand non-literate Tanzanian Sukuma contain the same number of people with above average intelligence as a comparable number of Indians in Banaras and Belgaum. There will always be some individuals who put together their symbolic world in a startlingly different way to that which is done by others in their community.

There is the entirely personal way in which individuals put their symbolic lives together in ways that are likely to be as varied as human dispositions and experiences can envisage. In the mind there is a constantly changing input of images of which the individual is likely to be largely unaware. A turnover while the individual always assumes that there is a consistency in what they interpret. This turnover in what is taken into the mind and retained there may be no more than what the individuals feel fits into their current lives. The creation of a personalised correspondence of symbols with personal needs and what is retained and expressed as treasured pictures on the walls of their minds, memorabilia of varying importance. Many of these images keep their ability to sustain their host's interests and others become worn out and fade away.

So the construction of various forms of spirituality cannot be tied in some cultures to so-called savage or indeed modern mentalities which after all may have been the creation of Western intelligentsia dealing with people whose ways of living and understanding would have been unintelligible to them in these forms of explanation. In order to learn about other people's ways of behaving and thinking it is perhaps unwise to start with Amazonian Indian groups whose languages are intellectually incomprehensible and are interpreted through a natal understandings of major European languages passed through the processes of higher education. Let us look at the possible ingredients which may go to make up the spiritual understandings of any individual whether from Mumbai, Bandung or Bamako.

1. There are possibly intellectual mutations in the same way that there are genetic ones; some things may have no assessable origins and we can only assume that some symbolic ideas come out of nowhere as in some poetry.
2. The new combinations of existing symbols by intellectuals which are the inevitable result of their permutations which must reach infinity.
3. Inputs from the conscious socialisation to which individuals are continuously subjected from what they see and hear.
4. Inputs from unconscious experiences; the endless pictures which enter the mind of which only some are retained long enough to be remembered.
5. The inputs from genetic factors about which we cannot

be certain but which must certainly have existed firmly enough to contribute to the survival of the human species such as the need to reproduce and the differences between men and women.

6. Inputs provided by existing social practices which do more than suggest to their members that the currently understood ways to attempt some control over matters which are beyond direct human abilities; that there are spirits, ghosts, pre-incarnations of which every culture and society has a number.
7. The inputs provided by written systems of spirituality provided by institutions.
8. The inputs from accidental readings which may or may not have any deliberate connection with spirituality which may be interpreted as having some transcendent elements.
9. The inputs from human contacts in which an individual may meet people who are seen as either charismatic or provide an entrance to some aspect of the transcendent.
10. Input from the current lives of individuals involving remembrances of 'loved ones', family graves, photographs, objects from the past which are in some cases placed in household shrines or graves.

Thus there are innumerable inputs into the minds of those who have spiritual needs and it seems unlikely there can ever be any straightforward transfer of an idea in some sort of identifiable linear progression since it is always going to be mixed in with each person's symbolic complexities. Even if the person is in an institutionalised environment in which only one model is provided as in the Muslim prayer procedures for which there are no cultural variations, the mental framework in which the individual performs these will be individualised. A Buddhist monk and his abbot may have public agreement over the goals at which their meditation is directed even if the word 'goal' is outside the pattern of their orthodox thinking. It is no more than an assumption that they are in fact meditating along parallel lines.

The extent to which bricolage occurs tends to be avoided by researchers into spirituality because firstly the initial impossibility of getting enough factors under control and possibly because of the reluctance to recognise the scattered nature of what makes up their own symbolic system. The extent of bricolage is often disguised by the almost universal influence of written liturgies and the inevitable passing influence of charismatic personalities. These may formalise certain patterns and thus make themselves more readily available but they do not necessarily confine either behaviour or thought within these printed orthodoxies.

The extent to which bricolage is inevitable may be in some cases due to the simplicity of what is written. A fundamentalist Christian meeting hall may have no religious decorations at all with the minister in a business suit. Avoiding a crucifix on the wall as a form of idolatry which must make it inevitable that worshippers will create their own college of symbols, just as the absence of decoration in a mosque may make calligraphy more important. On the other hand a Tibetan Buddhist 'tanka', Hindu popular religious art and a Mexican Roman Catholic church provide enormous numbers of images from which individuals will compose their individual symbolic systems. The bricolage nature of these faiths channel partly what the composition of the individual whole may be.

In the distinctions which are often made between literate and non-literate social and religious systems, the differences are made more absolute than they may exist in reality since literacy will involve a very small proportion of daily lives. It is more held in reserve than existing in the forefront of sensuous spiritualities. The Sukuma of Tanzania who do not have any figurative art except for a limited range of stylised linear forms for their woven baskets which may no longer be made, may rely on their tonal language for the constructions of their individual spiritualities.

The symbols which individuals receive are part of the on-going socialisation which occurs throughout life. Whatever the original understandings of these symbols may be, individuals will attach to them their own interpretations to provide a personal on-going network of significances. These interpretations may not be conscious and at best it seems likely that there will only be partial coincidences with what is externally offered and what is internally accepted. Since it is virtually impossible to define the meanings of symbols beyond argument it seems likely that their main function by which they survive lies in their ambiguity. The more ambiguous the image, the wider the number of individuals who can see it as something of personal importance.

While the form which the practices of spirituality take will be within the paradigms of thought which are broadly current in the societies in which individuals have been socialised or in which they have lived for some time. Few will be interested in going too far beyond the boundaries of social acceptability which they sense are currently in order in that social environment. That is not the end of how we should examine these activities.

It is never a question of a set menu of what can or cannot be used as even in the socially simplest of societies, communities or households have a variety of objects and words which can be connected with spirituality. It is how they are put together, the sequences and their bricolage nature and of course the personal meanings attributed to each word or object and their changing collectivity. Each individual is putting together in their own minds, their own form of spirituality in entirely original ways to which they attach a continuing validity. A constant process of picking and choosing which the individual always experiences a whole.

Levi Strauss has suggested that bricolage is the foundation of any practice and in the context in which he formulated his ideas this as related to 'simpler' Amazonian Indians and more specifically to the ways in which their shamans came to work out their understandings and practices. Only recently in human history with the laying down of regulations for the rituals of particularly Christian denominations; has there been any attempt to confine committed believers to a single set of ceremonies. This has always failed because of the presence of personally attractive alternatives on the fringes of moral acceptance but too far over this borderline to become more than part of a ceremonial limbo, the popular religion which theologians have been unable to fit into religiously acceptable thinking.

The incantations of the witches in Macbeth cannot have been just the working of Shakespeare's imagination, but what he may have heard in the gossip of people with whom he associated when he was 'off-duty' from working as a writer. Most contemporary social scientists will know of the many and varied ways in which people create relationships with their personal transcendentencies. The bricolage way in which they put together the solutions to the problems confronting them in their consultations. This is a too narrow conception of how ideas become connected to action. The concept should be widened to include most formulations which are not narrowly connected to but not necessarily resolved by scientifically establishable facts. Causation may be established to the satisfactions of science but it is rarely the end of how the sufferers see what has been happening to them; it is too immediate to satisfy personal emotional understandings.

Within the individual mind there is a mass of vaguely interconnected ideas put there and retained from any number of sources which come from on-going socialisation.These are pulled into consciousness and sorted out to fit the situations in which individuals feel themselves to be involved. Although individuals may feel sure that their ideas have some permanency, there is little evidence for this and within each mind there is a constantly changing bricolage.

The Historical Nature of Shopping Around

Abstract thought has the particular quality of being sustained by abstract impracticalities rather than being closely related to the practicalities of the thinkers' own lives. What most people do when faced with the need to do something rather than nothing about the situations in which they find themselves choose from the cultural menu of what is already available. These menus in even the most materially limited society contain many elements of which only some can be described as particular to that culture. At some stage virtually everything that humans do has originated from outside the social circle in which they live. The traditional ritual paraphernalia of Sukuma chiefs contain sea-shells from the coast five hundred miles away and possibly a brass bangle traded into that area in the 19th century. Their core ceremonies are pervaded with ideas and objects which have no essentially Sukuma element in them but yet are thought to be just that.

A Tibetan 'tanka' wall hanging cannot have its symbolism confined to Tibet anymore than a contemporary Chinese religious poster can be seen as exclusively Chinese, just as the Gandharan Buddhist sculptures found in Afghanistan are visibly linked to the Greek ideas left over from Alexander's occupation in the third century before the Christian era. One can imagine the new ideas coming into Western Europe as a result of the series of Crusades involving the Christian occupations of Palestine from the comparable influences from the British far longer one in India where there are thought to have been over two million buried.

Consumer Pressure for Spirituality

Even if we concede the cruder aspects of spirituality in whatever form it takes as a response to human difficulties, scientific medicine has been remarkably successful in prolonging life but less successful in coping with this lengthening. The publicity given to its failures to cope with the extremes of biological failure and its limited success in dealing with the constant appearances of new diseases, AIDS, bird flue, SARS and others. So at least in the Western world spirituality has come into the medical field because of its perceived shortcomings and the customers' felt need to augment its accredited practices with the shadowy area of complementary and alternative medicine allied to personal spiritualities.

There are two aspects to the relationship of those who practice some form of spirituality which will always have commercial connections. Even the smallest of personal ceremonials will use up materials either in something which is actually used or in the using up of time as alternatives to its use in secular activities. In their enormous numbers pilgrims collect souvenirs and their movement to and from pilgrimage centres uses up fuel and food.

The first of these aspects is when a commercial interest promotes a trend in religious and spirituality practices which brings them a profit as will answering the spiritual needs of their customers. A Japanese manufacturer of temple fittings had the idea of coordinating the needs of the elderly. Their need to visit temples which had reputations for answering the widespread wish for a painless death without any long period of shaming dependency on the resources of their now small size families. Their pleasure in tours which combined these needs with shopping and sightseeing which filled up their loneliness (Traphagan, 2000; Young and Ikeuchi, 1997). Much the same could be said for the growth of pilgrimage centres such as Lourdes and Medugorje which have turned small villages into towns ostensibly dedicated entirely to the practice of this form of spirituality but in fact are centres of economies based on religion.

Then there is the enticement of the consumers in the spirituality market place by commercial developments in anticipation of religious trends. There are monopoly games for adults and children using places in the Holy Land as property to be competed for (Joselit, 1994:82) as well as a range of statues, pictures, posters, prayer books, manuals, pamphlets, rosaries selling in what is largely a captive market. The growth in the quantity of published Islamic material in Iran (Najafi, 1976) reaching a total of over a quarter of all published material there and indeed throughout Islamic societies following the resurgence of interest in that faith.

The Individualised Spirituality

The coming together of people for religious ceremonies are the ends of a process which is entirely individual. We assume its pre-eminence because we have the convenient evidence of our own eyes, religious documentation and innumerable photographs. In fact the arrival of each individual at a religious ceremony is the end of a process which in its origins must be in that person. There are firstly the physiological ability to get there and the degrees of participation which this imposes which allows for these attempts which would include circadian rhythms and hormonal necessities. Then there is the psychological individuality of each person which is a combination of their genetic predispositions, their psychological aptitudes and the circumstances in which they develop to be what they are at a particular time.

Each particular time will have its particular social environment composed of many different factors which will have their own degrees of urgency. A Japanese praying at a temple along with others who have come by bus as a way of filling up time in the loneliness of retirement in a small family and getting companionship, might be praying for an early death without the indignities of infirmity, the forgiveness of an aborted foetus of many years before (Lafleur, 1992) and so on. They are classified as a group at a temple because they came as a group but their names are all different; they are not a busload of cloned sheep.

Only recently in human history with the laying down of regulations for the rituals of particularly Christian denominations, has there been any attempt to confine committed believers to a single set of ceremonies. It seems likely that contemporary spirituality is even more in a market place for those in need in which to choose ideas and practices than it was in the past. An expanding bricolage enabled by the printing of pictures, television and what has been enabled by electronics generally. But the individual has always had to choose however much these choices may be channelled by the cultures in which they live. The orthodox and the unorthodox may be running parallel systems, but it is more likely to be a multiplicity of personalised ones in which what is done moves in and out of personal immediate needs.

There is absolutely no way that the practices of spirituality can be considered as uniform except in the narrowest and simplistic senses. There are congregations of people at a particular time and place who are alleged to be doing the same religious things which can only be seen as correct in a limited primary sense. Beyond this all so-called specialities are individualised mixtures suited to the individuals and situations in which they are involved.

The Personal Nature of Spiritual Commitments

Spirituality in its beliefs and practices will always be a personal interpretation of the transcendent power's relationship to themselves. Parts will have come from the high-cultural literary traditions of the great religions and parts from local popular and personal sources. The former is always too impersonal to satisfy individuals who have narrower less abstract and more specific personal needs. Thus it is that most of the practices of spirituality which we know to be practised globally are way outside the orthodoxies which the major faiths lay down. They are more personal even idiosyncratic in the form of personal devotional practices everywhere and totally so in cultures which have their spiritualities uncoordinated by writing.

A study of village Buddhism in Burma (Spiro, 1971) which shows a basic deviation from the original teachings of the Lord Buddha which is no more than a philosophical system aiming at the abolition of self. He divides what he found into Nibbanic Buddhism, a religion of radical salvation, Kammatic Buddhism, a religion of proximate salvation with its central concepts of merit and *karma*, Apotropaic Buddhism, a religion of magical protection and finally Esoteric Buddhism, a religion of chiliastic expectations. We can see that in Spiro's division of Burmese Buddhism into four groups which indeed he classifies as four different religions only the Nibbanic form in world-renouncing monks could be said to follow the teachings of the Lord Buddha. In addition the Burmese follow cults to the Thirty Six 'nats' spirits centring on such places as Mount Popa but in most places there. In nearly Thailand it is possible to see innumerable shrines in compounds of offices, factories and houses, the verandahs of apartments in the cities, and in the countryside on the edges of fields, at the foot of large trees and in isolated forest clearings. So we have to conclude that these Burmese and Thais who carry the title of being Buddhists as do Christians, Hindus and Muslims, are following their own personal interpretations of their faiths which have little relationship to the requirements of orthodoxy.

It was the discovery of modern American sociologists (Bellah *et al.*, 1985) that many people at least in the United States would classify themselves as religious without any affiliations to any identifiable large or small religion. The so-called Sheila from whom the theory took its name, stated that she was religious and had a set of beliefs and practices which as far as she knew, were entirely personal to her since she had not discussed them with anyone else. We can assume that in oblique ways she will have absorbed what was available in her culture and that she had personalised some aspects of what she had read, seen, heard or been told, picking up some items and neglecting rather than rejecting others. Moreover as a modern American woman she would know something about many religious systems if not from reading then from television documentaries and magazine pictures.

What is perhaps unusual about this theory is that it has come as a surprise presumably because Westerners have for centuries become accustomed to consider themselves monotheists. Without going into theological arguments about the Christian dogma of the Trinity, it is debatable whether Christians have ever been monotheistic in the ways that the doctrine requires. To whom in fact do Christians pray and expect results from as certainly the Virgin Mary predominates followed by large numbers of local Saints who in terms of their historical authenticity may be no more than locally created mythical spirits. From the pictures in the homes of Christians it would seem that there are personal pantheons of spirituality including luck to which prayers are directed.

Muslims have the shrines of innumerable Saints to whom they pray for intervention and the Eastern religions have innumerable

Gods and Goddesses to whom prayers are directed. Indeed it is difficult to attach the concept of belief to the religious ideas of Chinese, Indians and Japanese when their spirituality seems to be related to practices based on proximate needs rather than on distant abstractions. It is reported that a Japanese on being asked whether he believed in God replied 'what God had you in mind'.

The popular religion of the average contemporary Chinese (Chau, 2005) do not speak of belief explicitly. They engage in activities that imply belief and their spirituality is largely based on a practical dependence on their lower ranking deities. The average Chinese does not own any religious text, does not become part of a congregation at regular intervals, does not pray to any particular deity with any frequency. His or her religiosity is normally diffused but intensified from time-to-time by personal and familial crises.

The single most important concept in the understanding of the Shaanbei deity worshipper is 'ling' magical potency and their basic postulates are that there are Gods or that it does not hurt to assume that there are Gods. People should respect the Gods and do whatever pleases rather than displeases them. The Gods can bless and help people, and people should show their gratitude for the Gods' blessings with plaques, paper money and flags publicizing the Gods' names. Some Gods possess more power than others and have specializations. One is allowed even encouraged to seek help from a number of different Gods provided that one does not forget to thank them all when the problem is solved. Leaving aside that this is a description of contemporary Chinese mainland religiousness, it might will be a description of the religious behaviour and beliefs of individuals in Minnesotta, Manchester and Marseilles. What they do rather that what they think they ought to do and believe as a socially pervasive individualized pluralism.

The Limited Extent of Any Form of Spirituality

Even if we accept that there is a certain obvious uniformity in the performance of some forms of religion and spirituality. Kneeling is always the same physiological movement as there are no local variations in how Muslims go through their prayer procedures. Pilgrims change their position geographically whether they are going to Lourdes or Banaras, this is looking at spirituality within a narrow framework. The social sciences delight in the confirmable presence of uniformities in cultural and social situations which are alien to their own. A devout Muslim academic will not interpret his or her own practice of the standard prayer processes in terms of conformity to what others may be doing in the same mosque at the same time. The man on his right may be a street market seller and on his left a waiter in a secular restaurant across the road which does not serve ritually slaughtered meat. He will accept that before Allah they are doing the same thing in theological conformity to the understandings of Islam. The workings of the minds of these three men will be inevitably different because they are psychologically and socially dissimilar.

So even in faiths which have an obvious titular similarity the purposes for which it is used will always be different. There is also the factor that outside the carrying out of such core rituals whether Islamic prayer, Hindu *puja* or ringing the bell or hitting the drum in Shinto temples to make the spirits aware that they are being addressed, there are personal combinations of the orthodox and unorthodox in what these people do. They might have a personalised sequence in their spirituality practices of which no one else is aware which they carry out when they have any special needs and go through before planting their seeds, going out fishing, sitting an examination or taking part in a cricket or football match. Many forms of decision making are tied to transcendent links and are varied and varying with the situations in which they are environmentally tied.

Merton's typology of adaptation (Merton, 1957) suggest the ways in which individuals whether working in a university or restaurant are likely to adapt in their spiritual and religious practices in thought and performance to the situations in which they find themselves. Orthodox as they may think they are and indeed may be in their more obvious public religious activities, conscious or perhaps more frequently subconscious adaptation will always be taking place. Conformity is probably the main form of assessable and primary adaptation. There will always be some forms of spirituality which are culturally available and it is easier to conform than to react in ways which are not so easily available. Hindus will not usually react in ways that are available to Shintoists or Roman Catholics. This conformity can be at several levels varying with fitting into an institutional process or to that of a cult or sect tied to particular personalities. There is always the problem of whether there is any necessary coincidence between institutional exactness and the states of mind in which exactness is performed. Gertrude Stein the surrealist poet may have written 'a rose is a rose is a rose', but that is surely a somewhat naïve assumption. There is also the probability that there are different conformities paralleling the roles which individuals perform. There may will be different forms of conformity in the family, neighbourhood, work place as well as private personal conformities.

Then there is adaptation by ritualism in which conformity is entirely without conscious thought. Certainly ritualism is not well thought of as a form of acceptable intellectualism as it may be thought of as having parallels to Pavlov and his dog. What is the dividing line between conscious intellectual conformity to some type of institutional or personal regime and the accompanying thinking that it has automatic consequences in the enhancement of virtue by just doing it because it is the accepted thing to do. What is the difference between the repetition of a form of spirituality assessed as a mental defect, the pathological extreme of ritualism and going through these religious motions in the cultural and religious certainty of getting a spiritual reward from this accumulation of ritual. The carrying out of the Islamic five prayers daily and monastic prayer periods for years on end would appear on the surface to be forms of behaviour which have no ostensible realisable objective unless there are private conscious injections of individuality.

Thirdly, retreatism which covers an outsider's interpretation of the spirituality of those who choose a non-activist approach to their religious thinking and the solution to their problems, but these are two different approaches to transcendence. The first is taking time out of active life to achieve a spiritual goal through meditation and a contemplative style of living, a positive approach and retiring into a form of religious life which is in fact the avoidance of life. There are issues of definition such as the taking of mind changing drugs which have been part of Tantric cults and the Assassin form of Shiism. Such forms of retreating from the strains of social life which have become intolerable may be a form of religious therapy which is more successful than its secular equivalents.

Fourthly, there is innovation which may be extremely common as individuals develop their own personalised forms of spirituality. There is a constant process of conscious or unconscious change in which even if the individual does not change the external form of their spirituality, they change the meanings. This must have happened to most Roman Catholics after the liturgical changes initiated by the Vatican II Conference in which the expression of devotion was change from being in Latin to being in vernaculars. There will always be people in any society who are quite able to work out according to their own standards of pragmatism what they want out of their spiritualities and devise the ways of carrying it out. The Japanese before abortion was legalised in 1948 would go to a Shinto shrine for fertility and instead of placing their placatory offerings before the altar would drop it down the temple lavatory, thus changing the hope for fertility into one for its termination (LaFleur, 1992:130).

Finally, there are revolutionary changes in which individuals either publicly or privately change their whole system of spirituality by either conversion from one existing system to another or by initiating some radically new approach. Alice Lakwena an Acholi woman in northern Uganda who became possessed by a spirit who communicated with wild animals and who told her that all evil there was caused by two legged beings and that she had be sent to purify Uganda. She formed the Holy Spirit Mobile Forces in which thousands thought they were protected from bullets by following her Twenty Holy Spirit Safety Precautions. She shared her body with a loud mouthed American, several Korean and Arab spirits. Her revolt against the Ugandan government was initially successful before it was eventually destroyed. Such radical and violent movements have occurred elsewhere in part at least as a result of cumulative disruptive changes.

There is also the possibility that all five types of adaptation may occur more or less at the same time according to the different role situations in which individuals are involved and without these people being aware that this is happening. Lineal conformity to a scientific concept may have little relationship to how individuals behave in particular situations which do not have any such simplicity.

Spirituality and Its Consonance with Personal Feelings

Most of the time people are comfortable with their own beliefs and practices even if they do not go through the processes of working them out in any coherent way which could be defended in argument. Any definition of coherence is unnecessary for our purposes as most individuals live in a constantly changing self-satisfying coherence of their own beliefs. All that they experience in their daily lives is constantly adjusted to within these personal belief systems even if they themselves may be unaware of these processes of adjustment. Some of their problems may resolve themselves or go through processes of adjustment within the spirituality and secular activities of the societies in which they live.

Those people with unresolved conflicts in Western societies do not in general have access to independent traditional ways of resolving their difficulties. They are referred to specialists who find it difficult to see such problems in the holistic terms of traditionalism. Perhaps because of this there are seemingly an increase in people with psychological problems and a sense of dissatisfaction which is not necessarily related to anything particularly modern in their surroundings. Life has always been uncertain if not from floods, famine and disorder, then from fluctuations in international commodity prices and health concerns. If there are increases in degenerative diseases, it is no more than a replacement for mass ones whose morbidity rates are always catching up in public concerns. Relatives, partners and neighbourhoods are just as likely to bring discontent and disaster now as they may have done in previous eras of almost mythological stability. In China the recent policies of Chairman Mao probably killed as many people as the horrendous Taiping revolt of the early 19th century.

On the other hand those people who do not have access to modernised social services and they are clearly a majority of the global population, have access to independent sources of relief which are both cheap and convenient. They provide what the Western world would clearly define as psychotherapy which the people in such societies appreciate as being within their understandings of spirituality. A study in contemporary China (Buruma, 2001:253) concluded that 'in Shenzhen there are as many cults and religious groups as discos. Personal belief is an escape from the group thinking imposed by religious dogma'. Attributing ill-health and good living to the activities of transcendent entities may be a more satisfactory and understandable explanation along with their ideas of spirituality than psychotherapy attributing mental distress to some aspects of personal inadequacy which the individual has to correct. Thus spirituality may provide a range of ways in which there can be adjustment between personal needs and personal realities within which individuals can come to terms with their own lives. In this there is no clear division between the indefinable auras of modernity and traditionalism.

While there can be no denying that people in modern societies may have a range of factual data on which they can if they so wish base their anxieties and which indeed they have to know about. This is not the same thing as asserting that they see their beliefs and understandings as having any firmer foundations than those of a Sukuma subsistence farmer. These millions in Tanzania have characteristics (Wijsen and Tanner, 2002) which are as much modern and Western as traditional. They live in widely separated nuclear families and have resisted conversion to both Christianity and Islam. They believe in the influence of ancestors and unrelated spirits and the potential malevolence of those with whom they live and work combined with a vague background of monotheism. These characteristics could to some degree be applied to those living in the suburbs of Amsterdam or in the slums of Mumbai and Beijing. They have similar metaphysical ideas about the persistence of good and bad luck and the expectation of misfortune. One has only to observe the approach of the English to examinations, horse racing and football and indeed marriage to see that little is related to rationality.

If there are firm metaphysical foundations in any type of society, they are the mental property of serious thinkers who try and rationalise their personal worlds and they are few indeed. It is reasonable to remember the views of both contemporary and historical Chinese thinkers (Teiser, 1996:24) who divide the religious ideas between the unreflective common people's belief in rituals while the upper classes had the attributes of secular social theorists.

The Limitations to Spiritual Understandings

There may be a scale of religious understandings which relate to the intellectual capacities of the believer and the form of information provided by the denomination or religious group to which they belong almost always thought up and formulated by intellectuals of high institutional status. The difficulties here come from the fact that outsiders seeking to understand the spirituality of any society, community or culture look for the books written for and about these people and work from this top-down data. It is only in rare cases that there is anything written about the spin-offs from these productions as what believers actually think and practice.

It seems likely that spirituality in its individuality has to be seen as a wholly separate pattern of thinking and behaviour which need not and probably is not related to any intellectual capacities to be personally effective. Leaving aside such complexities as the religious understandings of the schizophrenic, we should accept that the Down's Syndrome man or woman just as any person who is mentally handicapped will have some personal ideas of spirituality even if it is no more than affection for a favourite dog or doll. Individuals will always to some extent create their own standards of spiritual concern whereas in religion these are much more specifically set by the groups to which they are affiliated. In practice personal spiritualities have no Ten Commandments or Five Pillars of the Faith. It is not quite a free for all but something very like the self-created nature of its bricolage. A bricolage in the mind which must come in the Eastern mind from the simple viewing of the images displayed in temples and in the popular religious art in China, India and Japan.

Thus there are other limitations on understanding the religious and spiritual ideas and practices which come from the inability of outsiders to access details of these cultures because it needs something far more than competence in other languages. Westerners or Western trained social scientists shy away from this because if they wish to study Chinese and Japanese spiritualities for which there are libraries full of detailed works. It is not so much a foreign language in the sense that French, German, Arabic and Russian languages can be learnt easily enough with reasonable application. Chinese and Japanese are written in ideograms which require not only enormous feats of memory beyond the capacities of most people to learn in adulthood. It also requires calligraphic skills which most Chinese and Japanese cannot read for furthering transcendental understandings. Two-thirds of the bibliographies of recent studies of Chinese (Mu-Chou, 1998) and Japanese religion (LaFleur, 1992) were printed in ideograms; in both cases the references written in English were of a more general nature. So those seeking an initial understanding of what may be foundations of the very diverse spiritualities of these cultures have to rely on the interpretations of outsiders (Hearn, 1894; Xavier, 1973-82).

We are better off for understanding the background to Indian religious thinking as there have been numerous works of outstanding intellectual quality published in English (Radhakrishnan, 1923). So for foreigners the way in can be through the intellects of nationals and it is perhaps only in Arabic, that there has been a comparative shortage of writers addressing a wider intellectual audience outside their own culture.

This is beside what must be a basic issue in the under-standings of religion and spirituality in cultures and sub-cultures other than their own and that is the over-dependency on written and thus limited sources written by intellectuals for an audience of intellectuals. The majority of people in all cultures whether classifiable as literate or non-literate do not feature much in these sources except perhaps in their realisation that these outsiders whether nationals or non-nationals do not equate them with the realities of their own beliefs and practices. It seems likely that social scientists starting from the foundations of book knowledge see the spiritual practices of the majority of any society in terms of predefined inferiority and thus outside serious intellectual consideration.

9 Well-being

The Nature of Well-being

A health professional can tell an individual with some certainty that as far as can be assessed, he or she has no diagnosable disease and discharge them from any further medical attention until they come again to this professional with some self-assessed symptoms. The state of well-being is totally different and no one can tell another person that they are in a state of well-being. They might suspect it but there can be no data to support any such conclusion. It is an entirely personal feeling.

So well-being may coincide with clinical good health but there can be no automatic assumption that there is any correlation. The Peruvian Matsigenka are clinically in much better health than they were twenty or thirty years previously but they consider that their well-being has altered for the worse (Izquierdo, 2005). These Amazonian people state that they feel sickness and suffer more because their traditional way of family social organization has changed to communities that have integrated themselves with the outside world and outsider knowledge. Apart from the fact that along with many other cultures, there is no word that translates into English as health, well-being or wellness. Illness may be a factor but it is basically a feeling of being in good interpersonal relationships with those around them. Cross-culturally there is often a very general feeling that the past was a better time to have lived in than the present which has so many apparently insoluble problems despite some improvements in standards of living.

On the other hand the contemporary Aborigines of Australia were found to have relatively poor health but reported better subjective well-being than would have been expected from the clinical data (Wiseman, 1999). The self-reported well-being of Israeli Arabs and Jews appeared to have some correlations with the absence of diabetes and cancer (Baron-Epel *et al.*, 2005) but different cultures and backgrounds may perceive factors in different ways; Arabs do not see obesity as a serious health hazard. So-called superstitions may have different evaluations such. The effects of the evil eye are not just negative as they understand how to deal with that problem. In the Jewish population it may be more common to share personal feelings with strangers than would be the case among Arabs (Kaplan & Baron-Epel, 2003). Tiredness in one community was associated with ill-health but in the other it was connected with hard-work and success and thus would be self-assessed as a sign of well-being.

So we have to accept that well-being will always be self-assessed in terms of different cultural norms and even within cultures according to different reference groups and situations. Even in the situations of war and extreme deprivation as among British soldiers involved in the long 1942 retreat in Burma, these men may have felt a sense of well-being just from still being alive and in a continuing sense of brotherhood among them as survivors. By any clinical assessment they should have been hospitalised; for them it was a simple issue of 'march or die'.

Well-being unless it is predetermined by standards set by institutions outside the control of individuals, is a personal assessment which may or may not correlate with widely accepted Western concepts of health. In a community with an obviously low standard of nutrition, well-being may be set below levels of what developed societies would consider reasonable and only reach these adequate levels on the occasion of religious feasts. This is the case among Ethiopean Copts who overeat after fasting and this has caused 'injera' gastritis a recognised clinical condition (Knutsson & Selinus, 1970) and thus associated with well-being.

What are some of the typical situations in which individuals may have a sense of well-being. The terminally ill under medication and at peace within their own spiritualities; tubercular patients are known for their optimism (Mann, 1996). Persons with chronic disabilities who have come to terms with their conditions, seasons in which there is a sense of communal well-being such as Christmas for Christians, the end of Ramadhan for Muslims and Holi for Hindus. The particular days in which village communities celebrate their own protective saints and gods, the seasons in subsistence communities in which there have been successful harvests, the birth of a male child particularly and the rites of passage which celebrate status change or enhancement. The occasions in which an individual may experience feelings of well-being in which spirituality is a contributing element would be almost endless and in many cases the unforeseen consequences of unpredictable events. At one extreme well-being is the state of not being physically and psychologically incapacitated and at the other the temporary condition of being able to get by marked off by extremes of happiness and misery. In all circumstances well-being is a very temporary condition and its temporary nature has an intermittent connection with spirituality in the individual's attempts to reach and maintain such a state.

In order to begin to assess well-being in its cross-cultural contexts rather than having to rely on particular national studies such as the study of life satisfaction taken from an American sample which ended up in some statistically based conclusions (Medley, 1980), let us assume that there are some general factors. Individual assessments that are always present according to some hierarchy of needs to which personal spiritualities may be contributing. It would seem likely that attempts to standardise reactions of individuals to their own situations is likely to have the same methodological shortcomings as occur with tying any such assessments to blocks of people of similar ages, sex and occupations.

At any one time an individual may will feel that they are more or less happy with their lives at that moment, in a state of well-being. This will always be tied to short and long-term factors; it seems unlikely that that there would be much stability in any such feelings. An individual's economic situation is personally assessed and even subsistence farmers at harvest and daily workers on being paid will have a feeling of well-being even if they know that it is transitory. Many subsistence farmers as the year goes on will face their futures with increasing anxieties as their food stocks diminish and the rains may not come onto their particular fields.

Then their satisfaction with their known health may have little to do with the absence of disease or its effects. Well-being may be related to their ability to carry out the roles appropriate to their own requirements as sibling, son, daughter, father, mother and grandparent. The totally blind Tanzanian Zigua woman splitting firewood with an axe with her child on her back may will have had a feeling of well-being that her ancestors had been good to her in that she had been able to become a mother and wife despite this handicap. Similarly Abuje Mattaka, the Yao chief in Tundure although paralysed and carried about on chair must have felt equally blessed as he was well able to carryout his duties as a local leader even though he could not walk.

Feelings of well-being may be related to standards of living which for subsistence farmers might will have been seen as satisfactory enough a hundred years ago, but is no longer considered so. They have been given the disease of the wants. This was expressed by one West African intellectual as the presence of Europeans with visibly higher standards of living augmented by the subsequent invasion of mass media advertising and soap operas has made most people in the developing societies of Africa, Asia and Latin America dissatisfied with whatever well-being they might be able to achieve on their own.

How individuals assess their own well-being will always be basically divided between men and women and even in the more effectively egalitarian society these aims are not likely to be similar. In most cultures men are more biologically free and women more explicitly tied to their physiological status as has been shown for men (Hacker, 1957) and for women (Friedan, 1963).

It is safe to assume that individuals pass through a series of stages only defined by specific age related rites of passage in some societies and binding legal definitions of adulthood and retirement in others, which carry with them some culturally specific but only vaguely defined ideas of what should be their individual well-being as biological and social ages may be different. Certainly we can assume that adolescents in Western societies will have conceptions of well-being as adults since their biological maturity has occurred several years before their legal one. In subsistence societies social maturity coincides with biological abilities and thus starts with the menarche and indeed before that. In such societies children achieve status by contributing work to the family at a very early age so they may have a sense of well-being just from that involvement. The general dissatisfaction of Western youth and the absence of any sense of well-being may come from their legally prolonged adolescence.

In most societies there is early adulthood with marriage either without family responsibilities or remaining as a working member of their extended family, a period of some personal optimism (Gould, 1972). Then early middle age with family growth and segmentation from the natal group in which both sexes are expected to perform adult roles, followed by late middle age when the family diminishes in size and responsibilities when there would be some sense of well-being from achievement, followed by old age (Riley and Foner, 1968; Maas and Kuypers, 1974). Even in the best of organised families and societies, this is an uneven progression through life in which well-being is by no means assured.

There are significant trends in the proportional sizes of age groups in particular societies which have had influences on well-being and spirituality. The gradual growth in the numbers of the elderly in Western societies and the accelerated rise in Japan combined with the decline in the birth rates and the emergence of women having roles independent of their physiology, has led to a correlation of well-being with spirituality. In China the enforced birth control policy is leading to a shortage of women available for marriage and in many developing societies there are majorities of the young because of the control of many mass diseases well-being in such societies has spirituality involved in fertility and the sex of babies and in the reducing the fears of as well as the control of AIDS.

Well-being is Egoistic

In our assessments of well-being Western researchers are perhaps tied up in considering moral and religious obligations to others as fundamental to what we consider to be the right life and selfishness as a sin. We forget that people's concern about their own lives and their relationship with others has been made ideologically second to this. It is surely self-evident that the individual in their eschatological thinking will only be considering themselves particularly in the Eastern doctrines of *karma* and the transmigration of souls. Concern for others may augment the personal chances of the individual but self interests whether it is based on the selfish gene or not, must be the dominant motive.

Whether the practices are religious or related to private spiritualities their relationship to well-being is inevitably personal however complex the conscious or unconscious reasoning may be. These may be extreme cases but the contemporary Muslim suicide bombers and the Japanese kamikazi pilots attempting to hit enemy ships with their bomb laden aircraft certainly believed that they were ensuring their survival in post-mortem benign states. That such acts were morally unacceptable is an evaluation external to their own thinking. Similarly suicide may will be the terminal part of an individual's idea of their personal well-being, a solution within this thinking upsetting as it may be to others.

Thus on the one hand each individual is as selfish as their social and psychological circumstances allow. On the other hand Western studies of well-being take the individual as far as possible in isolation as if in fact it would be possible to separate any individual from his or her social environment. No man is an island and these attempts to isolate factors are almost certainly fruitless.

It is a feature of political and social science in Western cultures that the pronoun 'I' predominates. Those who think accidentally in quasi-traditional terms use 'we' more frequently.

In quasi-traditional social environments the village environments of Asia and Africa and indeed in the Western world as well, the individual whether man or woman spends most of their time with people in primary and secondary relationships. A circle of associations in which people are known by name; it is difficult to separate any individual from these continuing named associations with most of the people with whom they will have dealings, so they will be thinking and doing in terms of 'we', corporate thinking.

When individuals move into the urban-industrial environment the situation changes radically and the number of people whom they know by name is reduced. Most of their associations are with people in 'touch and go' relationships. In the street and at work they will in any day meet thousands of people with whom they will do no more than avoid them. This is an 'I' social environment which is used and indeed people avoided in a much more crudely personal sense and in which well-being is turned inwards to isolated personal evaluations.

In the former situation relationships with the transcendent in ceremonies are likely to be more religious in the ways that they are corporately expressed. The Sukuma will have some personal perhaps even perfunctory rituals, throwing some left-over food into the spirit house in the family compound, spitting into the water before going fishing or putting a bunch of grass or a pebble in some spot with spirit associations. Anything that they consider important brings the group together even if most do not pay much attention to what is actually going on.

However in the urban-industrial environment the individual is much more alone in their difficulties. The ensuing relationships with the transcendent world and 'I' becomes the dominating social unit and predominates in spirituality. Watching the burning of candles and incense whether in a Roman Catholic church or Hindu temple and indeed cigarettes in a Taiwanese shrine, it seems that these are individual acts. These are 'come and go' relationships with the spirit world which mimic the relationships which these petitioners have in the outside social world. Even accepting this individualism it seems likely that these practices of personal spirituality are in loose but semi-permanent relationships if not with God who is too anonymous and impersonal to attract much close personal attention, then with lesser manifestations of divinity or transcendence whether the Virgin Mary, localised Muslim saints, family ancestors or village gods or goddesses.

There is also the fact that many people who may not go to shrines except in extreme emergencies, nevertheless have objects in their possession which have spiritual significance and certainly contribute to their sense of very personal well-being. They carry about with them amulets containing a personal mantra or passage from a sacred book or some protective creation of their own making. Enormous quantities of religious literature are bought and remain unread but which contribute to the purchasers sense of well-being.

Well-Being and Personal Satisfaction

When we look at the workings of political and economic systems in terms of their selling products to potential customers. Those who are confronted with these choices, will by and large choose what in their opinion is to their advantage in a situation in which they are confronted directly or indirectly with a range of alternatives even if one of them is to do nothing. Success of any system is usually seen in the proportionate numbers appearing to be satisfied more or less in their level of participation. How many choose this product rather than that one.

However, this is easier to assess with religion which is usually thought to be more of a grouped relationship with the transcendent than spirituality which is individual although there is substantial overlap in these classifications. Those who provide religious service whether they are charismatic figures or administrators of religious institutions, may admit in private that there is a marketing factor in religious practices which share some of the characteristics of commerce, they do not accept any such patterning in their public and theological thinking. The whole institutional process of religious practice whether in temple, synagogue, church or mosque is one defined as a matter of divine concerns which cannot be paralleled to the marketing of toothpaste, bananas and clothing. There is an almost instinctive reluctance to apply the methods of social science secular rationalism to religion and spirituality.

Christian theology from the time of the Reformation has consistently told their potential customers what they should do. The Vatican II Council was for Roman Catholics a pivotal event instituting radical change in their ceremonial practices which were carried through without consulting their 'customers' (Wills, 1972:71). Any multi-national corporation deciding on a radical change in policy which resulted in the resignation of large numbers of branch managers and in the loss in some markets of over half their customers, would have sacked their board of directors and apologised to their remaining share holders for gross mismanagement. It is almost as if there was a management slogan which stated that the purpose in employing theologians to advise on change was to engineer the emptying of churches of believers.

This is not the first case in which Christian customers of a Church have been ignored. Since the Reformation in England was part of political process but its result was that the faithful attending services came to be lectured about what they should do and think rather than have their largely unexpressed and perhaps inexpressible spiritual needs provided for by the abstractions inherent in the ambiguities of ritual (Duffy, 1992). Ignoring the laity or perhaps more explicitly arranging policies and practices based on the abstractions of theological thinking, often appear to have had a disastrous effect on or at least a contributory one on public religious practices. Leaving people to drift into agnosticism or create their own systems of spirituality which they feel contribute more effectively to their own well-being.

It is no doubt theologically right that the Christian churches should acknowledge the realities of religious pluralism perhaps rather more than their rightness since its denominational divisions following on the Reformation. There are thousands of institutionally different Christian churches probably over four thousand in South Africa alone and even more in then United States as part of freedom of belief in its democratic environment. Also to get away from the anti-Semitism in the Christian story of Christ's crucifixion. But these are high level considerations of little interest to the laity kneeling at the altar who may want and indeed need the exclusivities of theologically stated faith. They are really only interested in their personal well-being and at most their immediate families. When this acceptance of pluralism goes further into the acceptance rather more than the tolerance of non-Christian faiths, then the laity are not interested in promoting such an obvious handicap to their own religious and spiritual stabilities.

The Eastern religions with their absence of institutionally supported definition of what should be believed in and practiced have an almost built-in pluralism. This means popular support on which their institutions depend. They do not have any need to assess their practices in economic terms and agnostic evaluations. They are permanently adjusting to the market. The contemporary black Dragon Temple in northern China (Chau,2006) and the widespread adjustment of Japanese temples to the religious needs and economic opportunities connected with a suddenly aging population show that in these faiths there is no need for such detached deliberate assessment of what is religiously needed and how it should be fulfilled.

The Language in which Well-being is Expressed

In English this word is only known from literature since 1613 AD with parallels in French '*bien etre*' and Latin '*bene esse*' and it is defined as 'the state of being or doing well in life, happy, healthy, prosperous condition....the moral and physical welfare of a person or community'. There is no mention of spirituality. All the nouns used are abstract and their definitions would result in further abstractions. From the start we are entangled in personal interpretations not only on the side of the researcher but also on the side of the person being questioned. The tone of enquiry from an acknowledged agnostic or one who has the professional standing of attempted detachment are likely to get different responses from those who have a more sympathetic approach if not understanding of what the former group would regard as superstitions.

The identification of well-being as an individual assessment of their present situation is particularly difficult for any view has to be expressed in linguistic codes which are not likely to be shared by people of different intellect, social status and spiritual understandings. It might be difficult to get agreement on well-being within a single closely knit family or even partners of long association. Well-being is a personal term for a state of mind rather than a material at least partially accessible and assessable condition. Surveys of well-being carried out in Western societies list the matters about which degrees of satisfaction have to be expressed; income, known health, leisure, neighbourhood, transportation and relations with other people (Andrews and Inglehart, 1979).

Any form of direct questioning would exclude those interviewed from developing their own ideas as to what may or may not constitute well-being. This at best is a vague abstract term and to relate it in a question to something specific does not fit easily into some personal feelings. These may or may not include spirituality and that person's relationship with the transcendent; it would seem virtually impossible for anyone not to have some connections with ideals rather than material factors. There is the plain fact that no one has ever scaled their own feelings of satisfaction or dissatisfaction numerically or adjectivally. If such an approach is detached from social science methodologies it would seem almost ridiculous to think that any man or woman has ever on their own recorded their relationships with the spirit world or each other on such scales. If well-being is to be assessed at all in the hope of reducing opinions to numbers and has the theological and philosophical implications of such numeracy and open ended questions on the lines of "how's your life going on" been considered; and then sorting out the answers according to the linguistic code in which they were answered, followed up by 'what do you mean by that word'. Even then it is doubtful whether respondents would think that such a question however toned would provide any answers relating to spirituality. This is such a personal matter that opinions about relationships with the transcendent might only emerge in the course of prolonged inter-relationships. Common sense and the barriers of linguistic understandings would do more than suggest that turning spirituality into something that can be reduced to statistics is not a reasonable way into any understandings except possibly for a small if not minuscule number of people who think in this way which anyway would exclude all believers in Eastern faiths.

The Multi-dimensional Nature of Well-being

Unlike health which has its formal scientific base and is related to medication, insurance assessments and as a condition for certain types of employment and indeed as a classification which can be tested in the courts, it may or may not be related to well-being. Although considerations of health and ill-health have important personal and often dominant aspects, well-being is a more personal self-evaluation which will be the result of concentrations of many long and short-term social environmental factors which are often filtered through each individual's ideas of spirituality.

Every individual has some transcendental beliefs however tenuous in a wide range of their lives. They are moved by poetry, some aspect of nature, the beauty of their wives or husbands or their new-born child, various forms of reincarnation and memories of their dead apart from the ways in which they endeavour to reduce the statistical inevitability of misfortune and success. A passing interest in female cleavage shows that there as many amulets being worn in Manchester and Mumbai as in any so-called traditional society. So this sense of well-being may be related to transcendental as much as material realities. Individuals may have this despite physical handicaps and problems which might overwhelm those with entirely secular beliefs although total extinction and materialism is probably the approach of a very small Western intellectual minority.

Apart from the more direct contributions of spirituality to any sense of well-being, it is often the background to other aspects of personal life. Spirituality whether as a defined part of some organised faith or whether it is a more personal construct, it is likely to set the requirements which are also the background of social living. Well-being cannot exist if it consciously or unconsciously contradicts some tenet which an individual holds to be necessary. There are inevitable clashes between what an individual is compelled to do by the circumstances in which they live and the requirements of the own form of spirituality. The commonest may be the requirement to care for parents, conformity to marriage legitimacies and transcendent obligations.

So well-being and the easy ways in which it correlates with any system of spirituality is always going to be multi-dimensional, fluctuating in and out of modules of influence which themselves will always be varying. It will also have to be accepted that the individual and their senses of well-being will always be to some degree dependent upon patterns over which they have no personal control; biological factors, psychological predispositions, cultural constraints and its channelling of behaviour as well as social and physical; environmental realities.

Well-being and Swings of Mood

It seems a questionable assumption that an individual's sense of well-being can be anything more than a fluctuating predisposition which in some people may be more prevalent than in others but still modifiable by the circumstances in which they find themselves. There are still hormonal swings, circadian rhythms (Aschoff, 1965; Dunlap *et al.*, 2003) in which there will be daily, weekly, seasonal and annual rhythms of which the commonest are the menstrual cycle and jet lag. The effects of these changes in time are not well understood but they are certainly not confined to women. There are also biological correlations to the feeling of well-being related to being well fed and the completion of sexual activity.

So these mood swings may be either of biological origins or occasioned by social circumstances and of course in combination or occasioned by outside stimuli triggered off by some sight or sound linked to past pleasures or miseries. Feelings of well-being are also likely to be brought on by formal religious and secular situations such as celebratory parades and installation ceremonies, Easter, Holi and Id-ul-Fitr as well as lowered states occasioned by Good Friday or the Shia remembrance of the martyrdom of Ali. So mood swings have these alternative or indeed connected sources in which the collective ambience of a popular celebration is shared and surrounding the individual.

Is it correct to associated well-being with happiness as there are forms of spirituality and religiosity that would not fit into any such definition. Demonstrations in support of Hamas in the Gaza Strip and in the Israeli occupied West Bank or in attending a funeral of a Palestinian killed in what they see as Israeli violence are certainly not totally secular and political but they involve a sense of well being which is certainly not similar to that experienced at a wedding or coming of age ceremony. We know that the Muslim suicide bombers of the World Trade Centre and elsewhere went through detailed spiritual preparations and apparently prayed as they went to their deaths. So well-being can be defined to include the suicide of Muslims in anticipation of entering Paradise or Buddhist monks in hope of nihilism rather than rebirth and this is only strange when seen from the point of view of contemporary secularism since it has been common enough in many cultures in the past.

Well-being and Social Discrimination

The sense of well-being besides being individually experienced may also come from being socially and psychologically at home in a group enjoying the results of its exclusivities either because of their religious involvements or because they have done better materially and socially because of these beliefs and practices. This has occurred with Jains and Parsees in India and the Seventh-day Adventists in parts of Tanzania.

While discrimination on combinations of religious, political and economic grounds may provide a measure of well-being from the experienced unity of the dispossessed. American Indians, Afro-Americans and Hindu Untouchables may prefer the social and psychological safety of associations within their own communities. This has become the focus of a new sense of well-being from the creation of pride in the isolation of their own identities quite independent of any active concessions from the surrounding societies forced on them by legal changes.

Discrimination in Hinduism against the Untouchables or *dalits* as they are now known, is an extreme example. Despite the outlawing of such practices under the Constitution of India, this is a continuing example of religious extremism. The discrimination against black Africans in South Africa under Apartheid and against Afro-Americans in the United States while having some basis in Protestant interpretations of the Old Testament, has never had the close integration with religion which has still backed the overall degradation which persists in some Hindu communities.

The end of legal discrimination has not had the automatic effects hoped for and anticipated despite considerable legal and political activism. The *dalits* have initiated the creation of their own communal identity independent of any recognition or acceptance by the caste Hindus with whom they are in daily contact and conflict (Arun, 2001: 284-90). In order to do this the *dalits* 'are now trying to use the same discursive formulation which had defined them as low and polluted, to deconstruct the identity given to them and construct their own. Instead of mobilising themselves to move up in the hierarchy by what is called Sanskritisation… they stay where they are in the caste hierarchy but make it the true level of themselves and community. They reverse the meaning of the symbols and repossess the transformed symbols and re-identify with them.' They consider their drumming at festivals, beef eating and land ownership as symbols of their identity and culture as caste but not in the sense of purity and impurity. The sense of a separate and distinctive community that has an identity of its own (Jaffrelot, 2003). This whole process involves religiosity and spirituality in a much clearer way than the Afro-American movement for recognition in their own right with slogans such as 'black is beautiful, say it aloud, I am black and I am proud' (Perez-Sarduy and Stubbs, 1995).

The American Indians after several centuries of attempted physical and cultural genocide by the invading white Europeans, have retained and accentuated their own cultural perspectives (D.L. Hill, 2006), of a universal connectedness between the individual and others as holistic beings (Lowe, 2002); thinking as 'we' rather than as 'I'. This can be interpreted as a circle containing the equal and connected mental, physical, emotional and spiritual components (Struthers *et al.*, 2003). Whether conscious or unconscious this is a turning inwards as a survival skill and away from the surrounding American culture which has failed to provide any adequate support for their well-being.

Well-being, Spirituality and Materialism

It is a well-known assumption that many people in communities with uncertain as well as low standards of living have become Christians for the material benefits which would come to them as members of missionary supported Churches, the so-called 'rice Christians'. This was said to be the bases for the membership of Christian Churches in China. This may will be true not only in developing societies but for Church membership in the Western world as well as for retaining membership of Shia communities such as the Ithnashiris and Bohoras and of course for belonging to occupational sub-castes in Hinduism. Although there may be material advantages accounting for the increase in Christian numbers in China today, it can no longer be in anticipation of or hope for help from foreign missionaries which no longer exist there but from such factors as the reliability of their self-help groups.

But is there anything in getting material and social benefits from belonging to a religious group which prevents such people gaining less obvious but just as personally rewarding benefits from attached beliefs and practices. It is doubtful that anyone is likely to see their own spirituality in such clear cut terms paralleling accountancy. Certainly the Chinese Communist government in gaining power in 1949 and expelling foreign missionaries of every nationality, may have thought that Christianity as a foreign imported faith would fade away from lack of material support. It would then cease to be seen as a possible challenge to their ideological suzerainty. However, this has not happened and there have been substantial increases in the numbers of open Christians after the relaxations following the death of Mao-tse-Dong over politically supported and legally enforced atheism.

Many Tanzanian Sukuma give material reasons for their conversion to Christianity and indeed their failure to do so despite over a century of missionary efforts. These reasons are grossly material only if taken out of context; finding a place in Christian schools for their children which have better reputations than secular ones and wanting to become a member of the Legion of Mary with its efficient self-help groups (Tanner, 1957). Many of the current Roman Catholics in Tamil Nadu were Untouchables and in Pappanallur village south-west of Chennai, they had converted because the Indian parish priest had intervened with the police who had arrested demonstrators, arranged for a roads to the village to be built and a school started. Certainly there were material elements there but the whole process was in an Indian social and religious context. All these material factors do not necessarily imply or much less prove that new personal religiosity and spiritualities were not involved. Now in India as among the Sukuma membership of a particular Church comes from infant baptism as much as from adult conversions which are usually the result of long considerations rather than overwhelming emotion.

Well-being and the Spirituality of Kinship

While well-being may be individually assessed and evaluated, its major constituents are usually ascripted rather than achieved. There is a pattern which individuals are expected to follow and indeed do follow and that in itself should lead substantially towards a form of socially and psychologically acceptable well-being; an expected hoped for pattern but not an inevitable one.

Thus for a Chinese peasant there is a culturally ideal path to pass from birth, childhood, through adulthood and to death. The path is obviously different for men and women because there is a persistent patrilineal ideology and patrilineal practices with matrilineality only occurring in some cultural minorities. In China 'a peasant man should get married, have sons or at least one son and may be some daughters, to bury his parents properly, to get wives for his sons and to marry off his daughters into good families. (A wife) is equally implicated in the success and failure of these household events. A man and his wife's status within the community gradually increases as he fulfils these obligations one by one and his sense of identity also consolidates' (Chau, 2006: 127). This means that under this ideal life-scheme an individual has to complete certain obligations to others as a condition for cultural well-being. Only then can the more individual aspects of well-being be considered.

This pattern is certainly becoming more difficult to fulfil within or without any Chinese system of spirituality because of state pressure to stop the expansion of the population which has doubled since the Communists came to power in 1949. With state pressure for single child families and the ability to find out the sex of the child early in pregnancy and to abort female foetuses, there is going to be a shortage of women. This will also cause the cost of dowries to rise which will also hold down the possibility of marriage for many men.

Also the move to the cities for factory employment is certainly likely to increase and with a rise in self-evaluated well-being along with individualised systems of spirituality. If we look at the reasons for which contemporary worshippers consult the divination at the Black Dragon King temple (Chau, 2006:101-2), we can see that the majority have little or nothing to do with household well-being. Business and examination success, law-suits, desirable jobs have priority. We can presuppose that in the use of oracles before the Communist revolution, the use of divination in the lineage shrines in most localities would have been more family related. We know that there have been a substantial number of temples built or restored but that this has not occurred for lineage shrines which previously had predominated.

Individualism and well-being may become more closely connected where people are more socially isolated and where the government provides comprehensive welfare provisions which make them less dependent on close relationships. Most people in societies without these wide-ranging and efficient systems of anonymous support, experience well-being in terms of very necessary family support. In such situations spirituality is a practical way of providing the background for holding families together when they would rather split up for more personal successes.

Oriya Hindus (Menon and Shweder, 1998) have the term 'hitu' for well-being and it refers to the state of being satisfied with the way one's world has turned out. A woman's access to and achievement of well-being systematically varies across the life cycle and no woman's life is uniformly a success or uniformly a failure. These women have a well understood perception of a life satisfaction trajectory which can be altered to some degree by personal behaviour, but is largely preordained within lives which are always changing. Before marriage living in her father's house she will be aware of the next phase when she marries. In the first years of her marriage she will be better off than previously but will be much better off as a mature woman taking over family management, she was worse off than in the last phase but better off than in the next phase and much worse off in the final phase. What is significant is that well-being is first considered in the context of family life and this research found no mention of well-being as related to economic success or failure, illness and accidents. So their well-being is based on the assumption of inevitable overriding change and not the attainment of a state of well-being which is both individual and permanent.

Spirituality and the Restoration of Well-being

If well-being is related at all to the practices of spirituality then it can be assessed as to the ways in which it maintains or restores them to what their practitioners accept as a reasonable life for social purposes and in this there is usually a connection with health. As far as women are concerned this is closely connected with fecundity which for most is a state correlated to well-being. Usually more important than her ability to work in the fields, factory or as a clerical worker so that the maintenance of fecundity is often closely connected with spirituality. Infections of the reproductive tract are often the cause of infertility and in the absence of adequate medical services, the dominance of society by men and their creation of hostile social environments for infertile women, then forms of spirituality come into play. Such women in Sukuma, Tanzania make up a substantial proportion of those consulting diviners and repetitively criss-cross the area looking and hoping for cures.

Everyone is a rationalist about their own health and the ways that it can be maintained or restored even though this pattern of thinking will not necessarily coincide with the patterns of biomedicine. Whether an individual consults a biomedical facility or a mixture of this, formal religion, quasi-traditional channels or entirely personal spirituality is a combination of these people's age, sex, education, family and extended kinship commitments, gossip networks, personal psychological make-up and the ideas and practices into which they have been socialised as well as the severity of the problem and the geographical nearness to various options. We know that the major cities everywhere have a wider range of social welfare and health facilities but in Dar-es-Salaam the capital of Tanzania the numbers of people who consult so-called traditional healers exceed those who go to government and non-governmental agencies. It may be that many cities have greater tensions than rural areas perhaps reflected in the higher proportion there of those with mental as well as diagnosed physical distress.

Shopping around for a more successful healer or doctor is common to all social systems and societies which attempt to cope with misfortune and illness and it certainly cannot be seen as only likely to occur among the less educated rural populations. It seems clear that virtually everyone in the modern world is aware of the potential rather more than the actuality of biomedicine as it concerns them (Aikins, 2005). The reality facing the infertile Sukuma woman is that the local dispensary will not have the ability nor the facilities to help her and the town hospital is a long, unfriendly and expensive way away. The local diviners provide inexpensive hope in an acceptable social environment.

To give mental priority to biomedicine is one thing but to rely on it to the exclusion of other possible means of alleviating suffering is rare in all cultures, is to give judgement on their actual behaviour and to ignore the realities of the social and economic environments in which suffering actually occurs. Even in the most developed societies, hospitals, clinics and their personnel vary in their efficiency and their access to equipment, drugs, knowledge and expertise. It is an uneven spread of which the public are well aware. For most of the world biomedicine is not an option because either it does not exist at all or is limited in what it can provide because of their limited budgets. Even if medicine does exist it is too costly to be used for chronic conditions or its use is terminated when the symptoms subside rather than such a course should be completed as prescribed.

There are many bizarre forms of spirituality according to contemporary Western thinking which can be seen as the ways available for obtaining and retaining well-being. It is salutary to remember the numerous Western biomedical processes which were highly regarded at one time which are now assessed as ridiculous according to modern understandings. In the circumstances in which Ghanaians and many other peoples not necessarily just in the developing world, biomedicine is accepted as best for some conditions. When it fails with chronic conditions and conditions which biomedicine defines as terminal, it is entirely logical to turn to the various forms of faith and healing available. It is a plain fact that under modern conditions individuals are just as likely to go shopping for forms of spirituality in which they hope to find personal well-being rather than to keep within a particular faith tradition into which they have been socialised (Roof, 1999:82). It would seem that the contributions of spirituality to individual well-being lies in various even ephemeral combinations of belief and practice and it is the latter which we now examine.

10 Some Conclusions Relating Well-being to Spirituality

The History of Religions

What we know about the history of religious understandings shows that their ideas and practices must surely have antedated any scientific knowledge of the nature of disease. Current epidemiological understandings only cover a proportion of known diseases. A high amount of current biomedical activity is palliative rather than curative. It is in fact having to deal with an enormous increase in degenerative diseases created by medical successes in controlling some mass diseases and the rising standards of living. This has occurred without much change in behaviour other than attendance for inoculations and in the Western world by political stability and economic success.

The major religions are based on sacred documents which in their various ways show orthodox methods for relating to the transcendent. Even accepting the existence of these documents for more than a thousand years, the vast majority of religious activity whether regularly performed or in reactions to distress and anxiety have been carried out independently of any direct dependence on this sophisticated literacy and its linguistic code. Any relationship with health which correlates to these written religious requirements must be seen as accidental rather than a matter of design.

We have seen that some public religious activities have been accidentally benign or hostile to the short and/or long-term survival of individuals and communities but this cannot be evaluated in purely biomedical terms. Assessed pragmatically suicide bombers whether modern Muslims in anticipation of paradise or Shinto

Japanese kamikazi pilots expecting to become spirits to be worshipped in Tokyo's Yasukuni shrine, are terminating their lives and their breeding potential. Nevertheless these men got exactly what they wanted according to the pragmatics of their eschatologies. The pragmatism of faith and that of science can have similar consequences.

There are many cases of self-sacrifice according to religious principles in which people suffer in order to save others. In 1665 in Eyam, England following an outbreak of plague which was known to be carried by personal contacts, the two priests of rival Christian denominations decided to stay rather than flee as an example to their followers not to spread the plague. They and their families died of the plague along with a high proportion of villagers (Daniel, 1966). Much the same moral rationality would apply to the killing of girl babies by the Netsilik Eskimos as an adult hunter could only keep about two non-hunters in his family alive during the winter. Their mothers were sacrificing their maternal instincts in order for their families to survive in latter years (Rasmussen, 1931). A Hindu husband during the flight from Burma in 1942 across the mountains into India stayed with his family and they all died together whereas he and one child might have survived if they had gone on alone.

So clearly the evaluation of the connections between religious behaviour and health cannot be simply in terms of biological consequences. Religious practices cannot be looked at solely in economic and political terms unless the study has been predefined in these limited exclusive terms. Some contemporary theologians and indeed politicians with some idea of harnessing religious understandings and fervour into what they see as more practical and modern benefits, modernise their thinking and in atheist China see the advantages of a limited tolerance for religion.

It may will be that in some states ostensibly based on Islamic principles which were laid down in medieval times with mediaeval understandings, have had to work their way round these possibly outdated theological proscriptions. Their politicians might will think it somewhat ludicrous to see their women legally defined as inferior. The contemporary outside world has seen numerous women in both professional positions and in political power and to see that religions define bodily functions as ritual pollution. So in Egypt the government in order to counterbalance Islamic fundamentalism has produced religious textbooks for schools which state that Islamic prayer procedures teach valuable lessons for discipline and orderliness. Reinterpreting ritual ablutions prior to prayer in terms of personal hygiene without apparently referring to their primary religious functions (Yusif & Abduh, 1988).

This is of course a possible course of action when the religion has laid down specific requirements of a rather obvious material nature and are well documented. This is not possible with polytheistic popular Hinduism, Taoism and Shintoism with their thousands of Gods and Goddesses of varying applicability and innumerable connected local and personal ritualisms. It would be virtually impossible to take the activities required to complete a Hindu *puja* prayer process and to even suggest that they teach some practical aspects of ordinary life.

We are perhaps partially mesmerised intellectually and theologically by the great religions. We should always recognise that human needs for well-being are in contrast somewhat petty and immediate. The Tanzanian Sukuma accept that a High God exists but yet this concept is outside their everyday needs and so they pay religious attention to ancestors, spirits and neighbourly malevolence. Wherever we are it is probable that we are not much different to the people of Rajasthan who for everyday needs pray to less remote, less awesome figures of their local lesser gods and heroes. The almost numberless pantheon of sprites and godlings, tree spirits and water nymphs that are worshipped and propitiated in every village who are thought know about these local and personal difficulties about which the great Gods are disinterested (Dalrymple, 2006).

If religious and spiritual ideas and practices are aimed at relationships with any aspect of the Divine or transcendent anything that they do which materially benefits them must be secondary accidental spin-offs from these activities. How can we know this as it might be the other way round with material success getting a religious connection because of its success. We can never know the origin of behaviour which antedates anything which we can only know about academically and imaginatively Indeed it may rather be that practices and ideas develop in tandem with no linear causalities.

The theme of millennial earthly paradise is common enough and depends on some eternal reward but the degree that it can be achieved must always be by the accidents of history. Jonestown failed catastrophically. The Latter Day Saints who moved into virtually empty Utah were able to set up their own settlements based on agricultural practices which benefitted them all and led to their survival in an otherwise hostile environment. Others such as Alice Lenshina's attempts for the religious and political separation of her followers in Zambia failed because it could not be fitted into the existing state structure. The Canadian Doukhobours failed in their desire for separation because of their destruction of state property and their nudity whenever they were prosecuted.

The American Amish have been more successful in their attempts to lead godly farming lives because their satisfactory religious lives fitted into high material and social returns for individuals and communities. They have had a long and abrasive relationships with State authorities over wanting to educated their children for the lives that they were likely to lead rather than for a general purpose future and their refusal to be conscripted for military service. But then this success may also lead to their destruction from the effects of over-breeding, in-breeding and unavailability of land within the geographical circle of communalism. On the other hand the Hutterites moving into the emptier areas of Canada split into dispersed communities where over-breeding and in-breeding were no problem. In all these cases it was not millennial achievement in the sense of achieving 'heaven on earth' but parallel channels of material, religious and spiritual practices which for them had eschatological consequences.

The Loss of Conviction in Western Theology

There has been a sharp division between Western theological thinking and the thinking of other religions which have not been tied to the restrictive logic coming from the Enlightenment. This thinking is perhaps only now beginning to realise the short-term nature of proximate arid theology in pluralistic social and not only religious but spiritual environments.

Eastern and Third World thinking that has not overwhelmingly benefited from either the Enlightenment or competitive capitalism, has always had pluralistic understandings and no particular leanings towards the creation and maintenance of unitary ones. No society appears to have tied its well-being to systems based on definitions acceptable to Western thinking and science. They have always found exclusivities in the end self-limiting and temporary; perhaps a little too human for eschatological comfort.

Ecumenism for Christian theologians may be a social and political necessity or the occasion for low level tolerance in mixed religious communities. It is not shared by the members of other faiths who believe in their own exclusivities. Well-being may come from exclusive faith that all will be well in the end and along the way to those ends. Once going beyond commonsense tolerance to those with whom believers are often socially in touch, any form of ideological unity requiring more than this, deprives any group of believers with the principal social as well as religious benefits of shared exclusivities. As public religion and private spirituality provide well-being for the individual well beyond their range, to be told that everyone else is believing in more or less the same thing will not be seen as helpful for getting through the difficulties of life.

There is also the fact that Western theological thinking is top-down and elitist. It does not pay much serious intellectual attention to what more ordinary people want from their transcendent relationships if only because they are institutionally independent of their support. Few Western thinkers about religious and spiritual issues have taken in that the decline in orthodoxy religious behaviour in the Western European world has been paralleled by an enormous growth in pilgrimages in which simple performance brings satisfaction to pilgrims. Whether Western theologians are prepared to recognise it or not, the split is between the belief in the efficacy of ritual even for rituals sake dominates Eastern and Third World religious thinking and practices. The need to prove worthy of divine concern has progressively emptied many orthodox churches since the Reformation. The United States mega-churches appear to operate a modernised form of efficacious rituals in which minimal religious ceremonial is associated with secular special interested groupings.

There is possibly a process of stages by which individual well-being is catered for by religious participation and spirituality according to global trends rather than related to particular religious systems of spirituality. Firstly, pluralistic familial individualism and then a short lived attempt to institutionalise religious practices through elitism and literacy and finally, the stage of urban industrialism of pluralistic individualised familialism.

The Secular Basis of All Social Systems

Although we have to accept that forms of spirituality are present in huge amounts of visible practices in all societies, it may not have dominated their day-to-day lives in the longer term for two reasons. Firstly, these practices which are often tied to natural processes such as the annual rains and the flooding of fields cannot have interfered too much with what happened. Secondly, if these practices did handicap the long term survival not so much of the individual but their societies, they would have contributed to their extinction. Easter Island may be a case in point with their involvement in carving enormous statues, the castration of the Russian Skopsi and the institutionalised segregation in the Shaker communities. All these communities virtually extinguished themselves because of their corporate religious practices rather than individual spiritualities.

We may be safe to conclude that all peoples and all individuals have religious and spiritual ideas and practices which dovetail unobtrusively or not into the pragmatics of ordinary subsistence. We do not know and cannot find out which started first in adapting but adaptation is a constant process as most people sooner rather than latter see the futility of non-adaptive practices. The Sukuma, Sioux, Samba or Seventh-day Adventists have their particular spiritual practices which are not so onerous or exclusive as to repetitively hinder their survival as individuals, primary groups, neighbourhoods or societies. Processes and practices which appear to be leading to extinction are not going to attract recruits. But this may be a too personal humanistic view of these processes. Historically the barbarism of the Aztecs held the population at sustainable levels just as the Tikopia did by more humane methods. It may be that we should always look at the longer or wider view. The ostentatious quasi-religious feasts of pork in Papua New Guinea would appear to strain the resources of both individuals and families perhaps even impoverishing them for a time. This is a system which provides for peaceful competition for status and relieves these communities of a surplus of pigs which the women cannot control and which are menacing the community by destroying crops. We can conclude that overall the practices of spirituality do not actively handicap the pragmatics of living.

While it might seem obvious that some individuals and communities have higher levels of spiritual involvement when assessed in work-study terms such as the Amish, those living in a Hindu ashram, students of Islamic law in Cairo or monks in Buddhist and Benedictine monasteries. For most of the world's population it is a secular environment in which there are occasional and fluctuating uses of spirituality. Those planting rice, fitting parts in a factory assembly line, making up medicine for a hospital patient or paying out money in a bank are not and never have been thinking of their spiritual needs. However, at times of crisis and at peaks of emotion the balance of thinking and practice turns decisively towards the ideas and practices of spirituality. But what is the social environment in which this resource is used.

Surely we can conclude that the focus of these uses of spirituality has steadily moved from a social environment in which the individual was enveloped by the primary groups in which they spent most of their lives. Their individuality had to be predominantly submerged in the needs of others into a social world in which the individual is socially alone within a social world predominantly made up of social strangers in 'touch and go' contacts.

The difficulty here is that the practices of spirituality used to be more observable in a group context from which social science could infer underlying themes. Now for the individual the groupings are so ephemeral that it is much more difficult to reach any conclusions outside the results of close personal understandings with a few persons accidentally created by social situations which are not randomly initiated.

Contemporary lives in Beijing, Beira or Birmingham are underlined with aspects of spirituality about which little is known such as the thinking surrounding luck, *karma* and the almost universal use of protective amulets and tattooing. Some Western groups and individuals just as much as the Burmese have their private beliefs in 'nat' spirits. Are there not private repetitive 'mantras' which so-called secular individuals use in their thinking and behaviour which may have the same function of contributing to well-being as those of the major religions.

The Search for Regularities

The absence of long-standing and identifiable regularities in the understandings of and the carrying out of spirituality is a constant difficulty for the researcher. There is not only the problem of viewpoints from which any analyses are taken but the fact that spirituality will always have a variety of origins and meanings according to the situations in which individuals as distinct persons find themselves. This is beyond the possibility of finding definitions which can go beyond the broadest of generalities.

Contemporary spirituality in Japan is a case in point in which there is a conventional text book view that there is a division of labour between Buddhism being used for death and Shintoism for life seen as a series of oppositions. However the Shinto ritual by which a child is turned into an adult is paralleled almost exactly in the Buddhist rituals by which a dead person is turned into an ancestor (Ooms, 1976). Explanations for this vary from the normal term for ancestor 'hotoke' being written with the same Chinese ideogram as 'busu' meaning Buddha, and the split between temples 'dandedera' supported by donors or parishioners and the large and famous ones 'shinjadera' supported by believers (D.W. Gellner, 2001:340). Then there is in Japan the problem of secularity in which public opinion polls regularly show that 65 per cent regularly claim to be without religious beliefs, whereas 75 per cent pray to 'kami' Shinto Gods at New Year although only 21 per cent affirm that they believe in their existence (Reader, 1991:5). To try and order this spirituality into some sort of pragmatically understandable structure is an impossibility.

The research situation into spirituality may be so deeply at variance with other types of social relationships that one can even be tempted to set the results aside as being so alien to normal interrelationships as to vitiate the results. How different to the realities of commonplace relationships is the description of an anthropologist of his work with the Tạbwa of Zaire (Davis, 2000: 7) 'one of my deepest pleasures in Zaire, a shared play with words and ideas in a situation where everyone talks at once and no one gives the appearance of listening to anyone else and of course no conclusions are drawn because everybody already knew everything in the first place and had no intention of changing their minds'.

Unless one is going to tie interrelationships of any type to written communications, there is little in any relationships which can be exact beyond the moment of exchange. The Ayatollah Khomeini of Iran is said to have remarked that there could be no expectation that what he said yesterday would be the same as what he might say today. Certainly hard science demands and can be expected to get exactness but human relations in day to day circumstances are inherently variable and the connection in the contexts of spirituality even more so. The individual relationships with the spirit world will always be variable. Those involved can bring it into play at any time and in any form and in circumstances which will vary not so much from day-to-day but from minute to minute. In the context of misfortune and illness 'everyday routines and relationships, hitherto taken for granted, are disrupted and explanations can no longer be met. Sometimes these changes require a fundamental reconstruction of one's sense of self and identity. Narrative is the means by which such changes can be brought about, since personally constructed stories about the self provide as space in which values can be reasserted and new ideas described' (Skultans, 2000:232).

In so far as it relates to memory there is even more inexactness. Foster expresses this built-in variability within a personal assumption of stability (E.M. Foster, 1974:288) stating that 'to study Hinduism for years with the best of teachers and when you raise your head, nothing that they have told you quite fits'. Another wrote 'whenever the uninitiated outsider is surprised, embarrassed or repulsed by the exuberant paraphernalia of materialistic display in Hindu cults, he must keep in mind that, side by side with these stands the utmost abstraction in religious feeling and thought, the search for the Neti-neti Brahman 'not this not that' which denies itself to all representations', higher or lower' (Heimann, 1964:33).

So in considering spirituality social scientists seek to find the regularities of systems and so it is not altogether surprising that this is what they find. Researchers know that the Sukuma pay attention to their ancestors who are still involved in their lives so they look for evidence of this and turn their data into evidence of a system. However every ceremony of propitiation is different and a prototype is laid down from which every occasion will vary. Look at this data from another angle and we find that each event is a special creation to fit the current circumstances which will have certain aspects in common. The dominances of individualism rather than that of an overall system. This leads to a paradox that the individual does not like to have it assumed that they are conforming to a system or just reacting to the contingencies of the moment. It is obvious enough that they conform at least in part to the ideas and practices of ten of assumed to be of great antiquity which are part of the culture into which they have been socialised.

To study the individual as an object in motion has to be different to studying that person as if he or she had static constituent molecules. There can be no doubt at all that every individual and their societies are in constant social and demographic motion. There is the constant creation of static categories which are easy to find and easy to record but to turn such categorisations into models round which a wide range of behaviour is then found to cling is unwise. 'My own discomfort with flattened accounts of cultural models. They also squeeze the life out of the reality of a people by treating human action as if it proceeded from a single activation of unrelated cultural models. Real life often involves the problematic and always partial resolution of dilemmas... that are a function of a particular individual's prior experiences and expectations. Salience normally changes over time and as context or circumstances vary. These kinds of changes are sometimes culturally standardised. The mental models are dynamic' (Shore, 1996:343-4).

Of course the five million Sukuma in Tanzania just as the hundred million Hindus in the Ganges valley have cultural paradigms. These are always and inevitably treated differently in how individuals, families and communities put these pieces together in ways that are essentially individual and transitory. It is unwise to think that any form of spirituality however well organised and well intentioned is other than idiosyncratic in practice. This may will be the importance of contemporary spirituality.

The procedure of creating models from categorised behaviour will always fail to give recognition to the fact that each individual's interpretation of these models whether they are highly educated intellectuals or mentally handicapped people with Down's Syndrome will always be idiosyncratic as it will have combined their personalities with their social experiences. The saying of standardised prayers whether by Buddhists, Christians, Hindus or Muslims will not have the same cognitive responses from one day to another. Whatever changes may be made institutionally into the practices of spirituality there must be a close connection between the individual's creativity according to the alternatives provided by Maslow's Hierarchy of Needs and Merton's Typology of Adaptation, and the sense of conscious or unconscious well-being that these create.

In a social world most of what is thought about spirituality and theology is committed to writing. Researchers into the practices of spirituality start with the systems that have been committed to writing such as the spiritual exercises of St. Ignatius, the writings of Al-Ghazali on spiritual formation and the *Bhagavad Gita* Hindu classic. It is correct that such classics of spirituality provide the more authoritative guidelines within which a reading elite feel that they should follow in their own spiritual development, but what happens in the individual mind of that elite. The vast majority of people who have never heard of these writers much less read them. To follow one of these systems requires the setting aside of time which is not impossible for people dedicated to spirituality in an almost professional capacity and marginally possible with people who do repetitive work in factories or are shepherds which have not much decision-making to do beyond stop and go.

But to follow such authoritative guidelines does require not only literacy but literacy of a high standing rather than the UNESCO definition of literacy which is the ability to write and read a simple message. Most literates probably have this ability and usually read no more than large print headlines in newspapers and some simplistic novels. The recent translation into kiswahili of the Spiritual Exercises of St. Ignatius by a Tanzanian Jesuit (Mkenda, 2005) is extremely hard to read. So is the work of any linguistically specialised theologian writing in effect for the benefit of other similarly inclined specialists.

It seems more likely that most people in their spiritual aspirations will theoretically follow the vague guidelines of the systems thought to be appropriate in their contemporary culture and regardless of their level of intellectual understandings. They carry out in practical terms the interpretations which suit their individual and very variable circumstances. This means that the practices of spirituality will always be largely an individual interpretation within the paradigms of their culture and these in almost all societies will be very varied indeed. Even those Westerners who assert that they are actively aligning themselves with Eastern counter-cultures in Western cities are probably aligning their spiritual allegiances somewhere between their natal culture and its mainstream spiritualities and their interpretations of newly acquired and partially understood foreign systems. We have described the problems of Westerners requiring silence for their spiritual needs and to them the 'hideous' noises of Hindu public worship. It may be that the attraction of spirituality systems is that however systematic they may be in their written form, there are no ways in which uniformity can be imposed or supervised. It is always the individualised interpretations which provide this attraction and self-assessed fulfilment.

Individualism and Spirituality

If too much attention is paid to structuralism this may make us less aware than we ought to be that all social activity probably pivots around the urge of individuals to better themselves in whatever situation they find themselves. It verges on nonsense to suggest that traditional and modern societies are able even theoretically to obliterate this constant self-aggrandisement in both the practicalities of day-to-day living and in their practices of spirituality. In fact in every society the individual is consciously or unconsciously looking for ways to better themselves. This is not a situation in which assets can be enlarged to provide everyone with what they want. We can surmise that much of what is involved in spirituality may be towards enlarging a personal share at the expense of the shares of others. The amorality of spirituality practices of which witchcraft is the commonest example rather than their moral bases. It was amongst the Sukuma that the many disturbing effects of modernity created a wave of witch killing through aggressive divination which resulted in the lynching of over two thousand women and a thousand men between 1970 and 1984 (Mesaki, 1994).

The majority of people in so-called traditional societies live in villages and neighbourhood communities in close proximity to the same people from the same families often over generations. They are face-to-face on a daily basis with the people on whom they depend and yet with whom they are in competition. To keep this rivalry within reasonable bounds requires a careful balance in social behaviour with overt friendliness and covert manipulation of opportunities. It seems likely that the tonal Mandarin and Sukuma languages aid this social duplicity.

What keeps such people from overstepping this reasonably competitive pattern of living into more openly aggressive avenues must be at least in part the restraints of public religion and private spiritualities. In many societies ill-health and misfortune can be attributed by diviners to the displeasure of distant rather than immediate ancestors over the behaviour of their descendents. In terms of descent there may be hundreds of people who are in competition for whom this form of spirituality is a restraint. In addition there are the spirits — the 'nats' of the Burmese, Gods and Goddesses of which there are many thousands in both China and Japan who may react against those who overstep reasonable behaviour and in their ill-discipline upset the social and material environment. Thus for these varying forms of spirituality that the phrase 'quiet individualism' (Moskowitz, 2005) was coined to describe the way that the Taiwanese managed their close and continuing social relationships. People whose ideas do not change all that quickly with modernity are socialised to recognise the boundaries of acceptable behaviour and changing forms of spirituality adjust to those who break these limitations.

In contrast to the quiet individualism of quasi-traditional societies and their forms of spirituality which effectively masks and indeed controls the efforts of individuals to succeed at the too obvious expense of the people with whom they spend their lives, modern societies and their political systems base their policies and their forms of spirituality on individual rights. This loud individualism and the predominance of 'I' in thinking results in part on personal conduct being controlled and indeed relying on their own spiritualities and on the impersonal controls of state institutions and organisations which have in practice replaced the communal controls over personal behaviour.

Self-control is not a dominant or indeed prominent human characteristic and that individuals will always push outwards to further their own interests. Societies with high percentages of social and geographical mobility may be difficult to control because of their multi-functional nature. While there may be a range of moral paradigms as the background to all societies which are generally agreed to be valid, they are always interpreted in terms of the situations in which they occur. All societies do not tolerate theft but this comes down to borrowing and not returning from relatives and taking whatever has no obvious owners so this crime is interpreted in terms of social distance. In Cuba crime against the property of persons has declined but from the property owning state the rate of theft is high. It may be that the communal controls of the past, have been in part replaced by that of privately created systems of spirituality running parallel to the relatively uncontrolled dominances of self-interest.

The Limitations of Science and the Necessities of Hope

Do we not overdo the influence of science over the thinking of modern men and women. There is recognition that science has had some practical effects in its ability to cure certain diseases and increase crop yields, but how this occurs is as much a subject of belief as any religious precepts. Delaying death may be a mixed or at best a short-term blessing. Science has had no effect at all in preventing the arrival of new diseases tsunamis, earthquakes and the continuing ability of humans to kill one another for ideological reasons on the fringes of spirituality. Even when modern medicine is available it is both widely ineffective and replete with ritualism.

'All the evidence of the 16th and 17th centuries suggests that the common people never formulated a distinction between magic and medicine.... The modern working class woman who remarks that she doesn't 'believe' in doctors is acknowledging the fact that the patient (has a) human essentially unformed allegiance. Usually he knows no more of the underlying rational for his treatment than did the client of a cunning man. In such circumstances it is hard to say where 'science' stops and 'magic' begins...If magic is to be defined as the employment of ineffective techniques to delay anxieties when effective ones are not available, then we must recognise that no society will ever be free from it' (Thomas, 1971:800).

Thus to assess spirituality and its connections to well-being in terms of scientific understandings would seem to approach its effectiveness from a viewpoint of its inadequacy and there seems to be very little evidence for this. A more rational assessment would be to see its prevalence as a reaction to the inevitable helplessness of the human passage through life. To accept the extent to which its beliefs and practices whether consciously designed or unconsciously absorbed are successful in this respect.

Spirituality as a Need rather than an Option

There seems little doubt that the practices and ideas of spirituality are so commonplace and universal that they are a basic element in all societies if not always, ostentatiously visible. Moreover they are just as much a part of all individualism at whatever levels of intellect and understandings are considered. It is perhaps unwise to seek any division between modern or traditional understandings and practices except in the contexts of new difficulties to which it may be a reaction.

It is certainly a mistake in any consideration of spirituality to assess its ideas and practices as some specialised if not esoteric activity which requires learning and training. There can be little doubt that relating to the non-pragmatic is a periodic feature of all social and personal life. Those who claim to have no aspect of their lives which is not based on pragmatism are making statements which cannot be supported by current methodologies.

Almost all personal relationships have non-rational elements not so much on the periphery of their practice but as core factors. As far as we know personal attraction to others, art and the transcendent are not entirely explicable in psychological and physiological factors but as symbols which are essential to well-being. Nevertheless these factors are important as being based at least in part on the five senses. Any symbolic activity which involves the five senses is likely to be more used and indeed usable than one that does not. Fasting and asceticism excludes that of touch. Public communal ceremonies and pilgrimages and family feasting involve all five in some detail. It would seem useful to look at these commonplace religious and spirituality practices in terms of their involvement with the senses even to the extent to which they involve low, medium or high experiences. Clearly some forms of spirituality such as some of the *tantric* activities are so sensual as to exclude those with more particular and individual perceptions.

The Process of Recognising Individualism

Since all human beings are different in their social behaviour, social experiences as well as in their biological characteristics, the process of fitting them into categories is more theoretical than real in order to explain what people do and why they do it. It ends up in diminishing the versatility of the individual. In this the researchers are looking at behaviour in as detached a way as they are capable. This detachment is a dehumanising one, diminishing people with their passions to no more than digits. However much it may be part of the methodologies of the social sciences; they apply to others what they would never apply to themselves. Thus the group becomes theoretically more significant because it is more numerous. This would appear to exclude the very real possibility that the smaller groupings and indeed the individual are more important in considering the relationships between spirituality and well-being.

This process of research is reducing observed behaviour to pyramidal concentrations, ignoring the possibility that the peak may be less socially significant than the bases on which is it reliant but not necessarily dominant. The fact that any individual whether grouped as Mishmi cultivators or Chennai office workers may share more or less common characteristics such as age, sex, location and the less exact categories of marriage, religion and education. These may indeed be influential but whatever that may be, it may diminish the individuality of each and every combination of factors which relate to spirituality, well-being and health.

All in all perhaps the best evaluation of the well-being of individuals and how it relates to spirituality, is to stand back and consider the issue at the simplest level. The vast majority of human beings practice physically and mentally some form of spirituality and that they consider or show that they have benefited from what they have chosen to believe in or do. It is easy enough to get data from the obscure fringes of social behaviour and to show that there these particular behaviours are destructive. There are numerous small scale studies that show just this such as the handling of poisonous snakes as a test of faith, extreme diets, Jonestown mass suicides, Amish closed breeding pools and the refusal of available biomedical treatments by Christian Scientists or Jehovah's Witnesses. This is looking at these people from the restrictive outlooks of the pragmatic outsider and ignores the fact that these same people in possibly destroying themselves are satisfied that they are doing the 'right thing' according to their standards.

It is a misjudgement of this basic simplicity that most researchers into such practices either do not accept the possibility of spirituality as a pragmatic fact. They are primarily hostile as part of their socialisation into an agnostic profession to such activities as deluded and coming from a fundamental failing of intelligence of which there are perhaps numerous examples. A comment on this approach has been that 'if a deity can meaningfully answer a believer's prayer and if prayer is to remain a spiritual rather than a magic exercise then surely that same deity would make sure that all empirical studies of the efficacy of prayer will turn out inconclusive. The evidence of the effectiveness of prayer as they touch events in the material world remains outside the domain of science. The faithful who want to believe can believe and the sceptic who chooses not to believe could not be convinced' (Meadow and Kahoe, 1984:120). Alternatively some researchers accept its reality as they are professional believers but maintain that popular forms of spirituality are low down on the scale of belief at which they should be aiming (Molinari, 1965). Others explain spirituality practices as psychologically understandable but that they should be worked into more theologically acceptable forms (Meissner, 1984). Both these writers were Roman Catholic priests and yet just as much as secular intellectuals, they do not see that they are pushing the vast majority of believers, the practitioners of spirituality, into the limbo of theological unacceptability. It would seem that the majority of those investigating spirituality are not prepared to accept its realities which they would extend as a matter of course to the generalities of art whether in painting, poetry, literature or stage performances and to their own emotional relationships.

The individuals kneeling before a Christian altar, prostrating themselves in a mosque, burning incense at a Hindu shrine or ringing a bell before Buddhist, Shinto or Taoist statues just as the long queue in St. Petersburg waiting to view an icon are there because of some personal idea of well-being. Except for a very small minority of specialist thinkers all the billions of people practising public and private forms of spirituality are not the best of subjects for research by hyper-intelligent, articulate, literate and opinionated social scientists. In whatever cultures these ordinary people are situated, they are behaving in the complex ways dictated by socialisation and the packaging of their own personal understandings. They are no more able to describe and discuss what they are doing in bathing in the Ganges at the *Kumbh Mela*, circulating the Kaaba at Mecca and a temple in Nepal or attending the evening ritual at Lourdes, then they are able to explain why they like particular foods, partners or places.

It is not that social scientists falsify but they are researching and reporting on what is not there to be described and discussed. They can give refractions of light from what may be behind their calculations as in describing the forms of prayer. To go further than this to produce suspect conclusions sometimes in a statistical form as if spiritual practices and well-being could ever under ideal research conditions be reduced to such exactnesses (Poloma and Pendleton, 1991). We must start and remain with the facts that people who are carrying out public and private religious and spiritual practices believe that they are better-off and that this contributes to their understandings of personal well-being.

It is understandable that social scientists whether psychologists, sociologists or anthropologists should be professionally sceptical and indeed as a group are usually agnostic. But what is perhaps strange is that those who are by profession believers even if their vocation has called them to study the behaviour of believers rather than to deal with the realities of spirituality in pastoral work in parishes, are similarly disinclined to accept the popular forms as important and valuable theological realities. To conclude that the majorities of Buddhists, Christians, Hindus and Muslims fall short of what is required of them by their faiths while seemingly fulfilling it to their own personal satisfactions.

The Cultural Understandings of Well-being

The dimensions of well-being cannot be confined to the success or failure of spirituality and it may be that religious and other issues relating to the transcendent do not come into personal understandings. The Danes are unrivalled in their satisfaction with their lives (Christensen *et al.*, 2006). For more than thirty years this country has ranked first with more than two thirds of their five million population stating that they are 'very satisfied' with their lives. These authors considered a range of factors to account for this; hair colour, genes, food, climate, native language, alcohol and smoking, marriage and children, general health, welfare state provisions, exercise, prowess in sport and expectations. 'The causes of the stolid depths of Danish well-being are undoubtedly multifactorial' and their conclusions were that the football win in 1992 which gave an enormous boost to the national psyche and a key factor 'seems to be that Danes have consistently shown (an indubitably realistic) expectation for the year to come, year after year they are pleasantly surprised that everything is not getting worse'.

The importance of this summary of the Danish national character underlies the possibility that forms of spirituality which stress a mild but noticeable pessimism will possibly provide for people the realisation that their lives have not turned out all that badly despite their expectations to the contrary. They have had a reasonable harvest, they have remained in employment, their children have done reasonably well in school and grandchildren have survived. A rational pessimism allows for more satisfaction than seemingly unrealisable optimism.

The Definition of Health

Whereas doctors would look on health as the presence or absence of clinical conditions which denote the absence of health, they would have no reason or the ability to define it in abstract terms. Many if not most people have clinical conditions for which they have not gone to a doctor about and for which they receive no treatment. There are of course many reasons for this including the absence of doctors with the necessary clinical expertise and the facilities for treatment so the question cannot be answered in bio-medical terms. Others are frightened by doctors working from different cultural systems and many more who see such misfortunes as outside the curative powers of alien techniques. An American dictionary (*American Heritage Dictionary*, 1995) is equally evasive of anything more than generalisations; the average condition of an organism at a given time, soundness especially of body or mind and the condition of optimal well-being.

So we can perhaps agree that the relationship of well-being to health is likely to be no more than an individual state which depends on how particular persons view their social situation at anyone time. Anxiety about AIDS in Africa as much as the number known to be infected would both affect any sense of well-being. Large populations affected by near famine or their status as refugees from civil war, would have very few people definable as healthy. The fact that they are alive would make them think that they are as well as can be expected in the circumstances and when it goes on for a time it might even give rise to a sense of well-being.

A community might consider itself to be in an overall state of well-being when there is nothing going on beyond the normal amount of expected and predictable misfortunes. Invade that community with professionals and this state of acceptable misfortune will disintegrate. A visiting leprosy expert to a Tanzanian district doubled the number of affected persons in just a few days. We have seen that the Rockfeller funded census of disabled people in Uganda created a social category requiring intervention where previously they would have been remained integrated into their communities.

Thus we must accept that whatever might be its relation to clinical medicine, health is not much more than the condition in which people manage to get on with their daily lives since they are not suffering from anything which jeopardises this. Nevertheless there are certain religious and spiritual practices which will handicap this ability. A much greater number which actively enable people to survive by either improving their health or more likely improving their sense of well-being. In fact we have seen that there is a substantial amount of hard medical rather than psychological data illustrate the benign effects of such ideas rather than their actual practices.

In subsistence societies and in the poverty fringes of most Third World cities the division between being healthy and unhealthy has very little to do with the diagnoses of bio-medicine. It may come down to simply whether an individual can contribute to the survival of their primary groups or become a liability. In the former societies there may be some leeway in this as in how long a family will support someone who cannot work as kinship and relatives by marriage may help. In the cities much less help will be available as there will be fewer relatives nearby and much will depend on the ties that individuals can create through immediate reciprocities. In Mombasa, Kenya a room full of Kamba daily workers all stated that they were fictionally mother's brothers and thus under a cultural obligation to help each other.

The classification of healthy or not healthy for most of the world's population is harshly and narrowly created along the lines of physical ability to carry out their assigned roles. There would be no mass media created ideal model of healthiness. But in the developed world where official and non-governmental social welfare provides a substantial range of support, healthiness is much more weakly defined by function. In many societies there is legislation to provide employment and public facilities for these unfortunates who would be social throw-outs in subsistence economies.

In the developed world the mass media and popular imagination provide a model of what constitutes healthiness. Advertisements in popular papers and in medical journals show the pharmaceutical industry selling a version of healthiness by suggesting that certain diseases can be eliminated or controlled (Moynihan *et al.*, 2002; Vuckovic and Nichter, 1997). The point for us must be that healthiness is usually a short-term state. If there is to be any maintenance of well-being it has in the long-run to rely on the ambiguous and adjustable permanencies of provided or self-created ideas and practices of spirituality perhaps rather more than in the parallel provisions of religion.

Well-being and the Odds on Ill-health

For a high proportion of contemporary populations 'even a modest definition of good health remains an ideal, reality is dominated by constraints, risk and uncertainty. These women (in an urban slum in Dar-es-Salaam) were clearly preoccupied with generating an income to fulfil basic needs when they talked about health. They experienced negative consequences of their uncertain livelihoods, ...as something harmful happening to them' (Obrist, 2003). Ill-health came after anxieties created by alcoholism, adultery, the influence of video parlours on the young, inter-caste and inter-religion marriages, community violence and unemployment, barrenness, the birth of daughters and the extortions coming from the persisting dowry system (Chowdhury *et al.*, 2001). In Mumbai slum health must have been a minor consideration when 60-70% of all women routinely endure some degree of domestic violence and household stories suggested to these women that suicide was the only alternative to the misery of the pattern of domestic violence, humiliation and frustration (Parkar *et al.*, 2003).

When medical treatment has to be paid for whether in medical centres or going to traditional healers, the poor will only pay for treatment when the symptoms which have appeared justify the treatment. In China it is estimated that some 260 million people have high blood pressure and the daily cost for anti-hypertension drugs would be 6 to 12 cents per day. How many hypertensive people in poor rural areas would be willing to pay this when only one in 50 to100 people treated could avoid a heart attack in the next five years and this expenditure would be at a cost of one seventh of their annual family income (Tang and Hu, 2005). Even if such people knew of their physical condition, the odds on getting ill are long. In their opinion his or her money would be better spent on an annual small donation to the locally powerful God or more particularly to the Goddess of Luck. In a British parallel the provision of acupuncture to relieve low back pain enough to provide a sufferer with five years of quality life would cost £20k (Ratcliffe *et al.,* 2006). Even in an economically well managed and affluent society this would be beyond most if not all individual and medical cost-benefit assessments.

In the influence of the practices and ideas of spirituality over factually based health there are the difficulties which come from bio-medical definitions. These leave the social environment as more or less irrelevant to such facts which from the point of view of those involved may be more important than the medical condition in isolation. The second difficulty is that bio-medicine tends to concentrate on assessing extremes of religious or spiritual behaviour. These almost automatically have adverse biological effects such as dietary extremism, asceticism, sporadic violence and refusal to use bio-medicine for the relief of 'obvious' suffering. It would seem that in these situations that the personal situation and feelings which may relate to spirituality have not been brought into consideration or given prominence out of proportion to the numbers who may get benefits outside the boundaries of biological controls. The recent stampede of pilgrims on the Hajj which caused about a thousand deaths has to be assessed in proportion to the pilgrim numbers involved that year which would have been about two million. The fact that there have been no parallel disasters since, so that would be a casualty rate of 0.01%; this is not to suggest that it was not a disaster but that its significance can be overstressed. Those not affected would have had their spirituality enhanced by their performance of this basic obligation for all Muslims. Muslims and Orthodox Jews may wish to state that the washing which the devout carry out prior to praying was designed to reduce the incidence of infectious diseases. In the latter case to reduce their infant morality in comparison to other immigrant groups in 19th century New York. The correlation is incidental to religion and forms no part of what may have been the original reasons for these practices (Starrett, 1995).

In suicide bombings the numbers who kill themselves for religious reasons is small while the totals of those killed are accidental and can in fact be negligible as much as horrific. The numbers involved in deaths and changed behaviour from anxiety from extreme Christian interdenominational violence in Northern Ireland in proportion to population size has probably been far higher than the losses from suicide bombings in Iraq.

The Islamic prayer movements performed five times everyday by the devout can be seen as exercise and therefore benign. We do not know whether these are carried out as much by women as men. Christianity provides very little comparable exercise. The washing before prayers has been connected with parasitical infections when impure water is used. Collective worship on Fridays and any touching of others, religious statues or holy persons in greeting will spread disease whatever beliefs occasion this. There seems little doubt that religious and spiritually required behaviour will have fluctuating consequences as the epidemiology will relate to particular activities and of course the sense of well-being will always involve the whole person.

Few if any individuals have continuous good health according to bio-medical evaluations as it is a fluctuating condition between severe impairments which make it impossible for them to function except in an exclusively sick role and indeed to survive only in special expensive institutions. Elsewhere the handicapped do not survive and die from progressive neglect or are indeed killed off when the new-born are seen to be abnormal. The morality here is the survival of the more able and the religious support for such thinking in traditional thought.

Apart from minority situations in which persons are obviously out of any ability to function normally, health must be accepted as a largely subjective condition in which individuals may feel ill while being bio-medically well and indeed feel well when they are clinically ill. In old age individuals may suffer from a number of progressively debilitating conditions. In Britain the average 80 year old person may be taking medicine for five identified malfunctions while considering themselves well even happy in relation to what they want to do with their lives. In some societies mental malfunctions can be interpreted as manifestations of spirit possession.

We must accept that it is inept to see ill-health in purely scientific terms except in cases of clear incapacity to function adequately. This inability to do what one wants to do is clearly a major source of anxiety mediated if not reduced by both the public functions of religion and private spiritualities. How do individuals cope with these anxieties which in most societies only receive clinical attention when they are part of mass diseases outbreaks. It is a harsh fact that for most diseases for most of the time there are no cures and what is done bio-medically may be no more than delaying inevitable incapacity and death. Modern medicine can only be classified as palliative in epistemological terms.

How do people cope with their anxieties which in most cases are not related to health except in a secondary almost residual sense. For most of the world's population there are the permanent worries over immediate survival, famine, flood, theft and violence; health comes after all these daily worries. Health is not divided out into something special and the relief of anxiety in general must be through religious activities and private spirituality; in overall terms the placebo effects of ritual.

This is all the more important as considerations of health in the pattern of Western bio-medicine has become essentially spatially separated from ordinary life styles as part of modern managerial techniques. It has become market driven and its institutions have become the sites of consumption rather than care (Cartier, 2002). With a general shift to spatially dictated care tending to emphasize universal concepts of right and wrong, leading to the neglect of the situated character of decision-making as well as the particularity of individual needs and experience (Malpas, 2003). This is particularly significant if we have to accept as we must that every person's perception of social environmental reality is different. We are all 'uncommon persons', not only in individual needs but in how health institutions should treat us. We find it difficult to do so when decisions have to be made in terms of very general sets of procedures with standard determinate outcomes (Kaufman, 2002). Again in such contexts the ideas and practices of spirituality provide a more personally relevant approach to everyday distress and its extremes.

Comparisons between Cultures

In considering the influence of spirituality on well-being there is not only the division between Eastern and Western patterns of thinking. The more important division between the top-down elitist patterns of thought and behaviour in all literate societies and popular public religious and private spiritualities. The differences between societies may be one more of degree than of substance. It seems very likely that virtually everyone carries out ritual actions in the hope and indeed in the expectation that it will have results not coverable by pragmatic understandings.

Nevertheless it would be prudent to recognise that Western culture since the Protestant Reformation and the Enlightenment has severely modified the ways in which religion and spirituality have been understood and practised. The former being predominantly public and thus being more readily subject to control and censure. The latter on the other hand is usually socially invisible and thus more difficult to encounter and analyse. In the Western industrialised and adequately provided for in social welfare terms, religion as public performed has declined. Spirituality in its comprehensiveness may not have changed all that much in its virtual invisibility. Our difficulty must be that finding out about spirituality is beyond the reach of easily used social science methodologies. It becomes dependent on what individuals may choose to disclose within the personal rather than scientifically based relationships that researchers have been able to create with them.

Eastern cultures combined with those of Africa south of the Sahara and Latin America south of the Rio Grande have religious and spiritual understandings which if they have not resisted change have remained sufficiently strong to make any reputable division at the level of spirituality between the West and the remainder of the world unreliable. If not exactly parallel systems, they can be considered to be quite closely amalgamated in functions so as to be indivisible in the understandings of ordinary men and women that the performance of both public and private ritual has such obvious effects as to sustain well-being.

Thus we appear to have predominantly Western forms of spirituality and religiosity which have retired into individualism and thus extremely difficult to categorize. The practices elsewhere which have remained more visible but which will still nevertheless will have individualistic meanings and variations. It is a grossly biased assumption that all pilgrims to a sacred site or ceremony are in any way similar except in their geographical confinement.

If the ways in which spirituality interrelates with well-being is to be valued in terms of primary participations in public religious events then it would be rational to focus on crowds principally pilgrimages as well as on cyclical and linear rites of passage and to concentrate on where this occurs predominantly outside the Western world. Any such concentration in its relative simplicity undercuts the personal nature of spirituality which is as important in Birmingham as Banaras and the plain fact that in population numbers researching spirituality and well-being in Western cultures is to concentrate on a relatively small minority.

The Validity of Comparisons

For any comparisons to be valid except in the broadest of terms between different social communities there has to be some certainty that the principle elements are entirely the same. There are minimal variations in social environmental factors which together might influence what has been defined as the subject of research or so isolatable as to be worthy of study. This is indeed a very hard requirement because we know that even identical twins may not behave in the same way if they are brought up separately. There is the basic handicap in any comparisons that collectively and individually they are different. Medical experiments in which two statistically similar groups are divided into those subject to the treatment and those who are not has to be a crude division at best based on the assumption that demographic data is accurate. In terms of social experience and psychological predispositions there can be no such scientifically exact groupings.

It seems likely that neither of these basic requirements are going to be met to justify the validity of comparative studies since what happens to one group and one individual are always going to be social and variable. Certainly there is the feeling of a timeless self held by the individual but there is the fact that this is always in the process of change demographically and from experience. This must undercut any logical assumption of stability (Ewing,1990). Similarly there can be no such thing as an homogeneous society as even in the most materially primitive society there will be the dreamer of dreams and those who are more successful than others in finding food and women. Then there are the shared social experiences of religious ceremonials and privation. While there may be these external participations we have no reason to suppose that they are even likely to be shared in the brains of individuals. So it would seem inevitable that any comparison is paralleling two or more dissimilar volatile social groups even when they apparently have some major characteristics in common such as living in the same geographical area and speaking linguistic codes within the same language group, must be methodologically flawed.

Can we do any better with correlations between sets of information perhaps avoiding the assumption that this might come near to being considered data in its scientific sense. Any considerations of health end up being based on quantitative data, the primary effects on individuals of pharmacological and surgical processes. Feeling better or worse as a result is not necessarily part of these diagnoses. There is a causal connection between going on pilgrimages in the past and mass deaths from cholera and plague in both Saudi Arabia and India. This is no different to the spread of influenza along the main railway line in East Africa after World War I. It is the transport system that spreads these diseases not religion. The infected pilgrims and their families may have felt a sense of well-being from dying in the fulfilment of such religious commitments. An individual fulfilling a nominally religious obligation for entirely secular reasons may attain a sense of well-being which might well be both secular and accidentally religious.

Once we move beyond data which is acceptable scientifically all the information connecting public religion and private spirituality to well-being is qualitative and thus questionable however attractive and convincing subsequent correlations may be. This then cuts out from available data connecting spirituality with well-being almost all opinions about the personal consequences of praying, going on pilgrimages or beliefs in what is logically irrational and which do not fit into the required standards of science. If we tie ourselves to the acceptable data connecting the physiology of health to spirituality, then whatever the accuracy of such information it is going to relate to spasmodic, irregular and infrequent states. The well-being that is correlated by the people themselves and is repeatedly evident in personal statements becomes irrelevant. This runs counter to an enormous range of contemporary human experience wherever socially located in which this anticipated and achieved spiritual well-being is part of the normality if life.

The Personal Nature of Interpretations

We have established the dominance of qualitative over quantitative research. The social sciences have been too optimistic in expecting to find many situations in which the correlations are close enough for cause and effect to become probable rather than possible in situations which are not artificially restricted to the primary aspects of complex situations.

Whatever may be the quality of the data and their acceptance by biomedical and social science professionals it seems unlikely that these correlations will be accepted by ordinary people as the reasons for their well-being. A doctor eating in a small restaurant in a small South African town saw a statue of the Virgin Mary on the wall with a blue plastic catheter tube round her neck. The owner of the restaurant explained that he had been rushed to hospital with a burst appendix and in the opinion of his staff, he had started to improve after the doctor had inserted this tube into the side of his neck which in their thinking had coincided with their prayers. The surgery which he had undergone and the antibiotics he had received did not feature in their understandings so the catheter tube hung there as an instrument of divine rather than medical intervention (Jolliffe, 2005:526). A Hindu religious teacher who was well aware of the pictures of the monkey God Hanuman opening his chest to show the Lord Rama and the Goddess Sita there, had complicated open heart surgery. Subsequently he said that he had not expected to be turned by doctors from a mere disciple and devotee of Hanuman into the God himself (Kashyar, 2007:256).

These are just two examples of the versatility of human understandings which relate spirituality and major religious understandings to situations which in the quite correct opinion of bio-medicine can have nothing to do with what had happened to these patients. We cannot expect most people to accept scientific explanations when their spiritual understandings as much as their psychological needs tell them otherwise.

It is not only ordinary non-professionally trained people who can see their affairs in such ways. Qualitative research is always a very personal affair between would be professional social scientists and some personally close associates who are much more socially close to them whether they admit it or not just discardable informants. The researchers are receiving small scale personalised information from these particular people and their conclusions dispersed into society wide understandings must always be a very personal affair. They are looking at immensely varied social situations through their own very personal understandings. Whether these personal statements are accepted as more generally applicable or not there can be little doubt that the ideas and practices of personal spirituality are a major contribution to very general social and personal well-being.

Bibliography

(The numbers in Bold faces following each reference give the text page on which the article in book is cited)

Abrum, M. (2000). 'Jesus will fix it after awhile. Meanings and health'. *Social Science and Medicine*'. 50:89-105. **102, 103.**

Achterberg, J. (1985). *Imagery and Healing*. New Science Library. Boston.

Ademuwagun, Z.A. (1969). 'The relevance of Yoruba medicine men in public health practice in Nigeria'. *Public Health Reports*. 84; 1085-91.

Ader, R, (1981). *Psychoneuroimmunology*. Academic Press. New York. **197.**

Adler, S.R. (2001). 'Integrated personal health belief systems; patients-practitioners communication' in Brady, E.(ed). *Healing Logics; Culture and Medicine in Modern Health Belief Systems*. Utah State University. Logan. 115-128. **222.**

Ahern, E.M. (1979). 'The problem of efficacy. Strong and weak illocutionary acts'. *Man(ns)*. 14:1-17. **176.**

Ai, A.L. *et al.*, (2002). 'Private prayer and optimism in middle aged and older patients awaiting cardiac surgery' *Geronto-logistl* 42(1); 70-81. **181.**

Aikins, A de-G. (2005). 'Healer shopping in Africa; new evidence from rural-urban qualitative study of Ghanaian diabetes experiences'. *British Medical Journal*. 331; 737-42. **302.**

Ainley, S.C. & Smith, D.R. (1984). 'Aging and religious participation'. *Journal Gerontology*. 39; 357-363.

Alland, A. (1964). 'Native therapists and Western medical practitioners among the Abron of the Ivory Coast.' *Transactions*. New York Academy of Science. 26; 714-25. **141.**

Allport, G.W. and Ross, J.M. (1967). 'Personal religions. Orientation and Prejudice'. *Journal Personality and Social Psychology*. 5:432-443. **50.**

Alston, W.P. (1964). *Philosophy of language*. Prentice-Hall. Englewood Cliffs. **175.**

Alther, L. (1975). 'The snake handlers'. *New Society*. 34; 532-5. **162.**

American Heritage Dictionary. (1995). Microsoft Bookshelf. Seattle. **105.**

Andrews. F.A. and R.F. Engelhart. (1979). 'The structures of subjective well-being in nine Western societies'. *Social Indicators Reserch*. 9:265-278. **58, 292.**

Antoni, K. (1993). 'Yasukuni-Jinja and folk religion. The problem of vengeful spirits' in M.R. Mullins (ed.) *Religion and Society in Modern Japan*. Asian Humanities Press. Berkeley. 121-132. **244.**

Arun, J. (2001). *Constructing Dalit Identity*. Rawat. Jaipur. **296.**

Appadurai, A. (1990). 'Disjunction and difference in global cultural economy' in M. Featherstone. (ed). *Global Culture. Nationalism, Globalization and Modernity*. Sage. London.

Aschoff, J. (ed). (1965). *Circadian Clocks*. North Holland Press. Amsterdam. **295.**

Aslam, M. and Assad, A. (1986). 'Drug regimes and fasting during Ramadan. A survey in Kuwait'. *Public Health*. 100(1); 49-53. **157.**

Aslam, M and Healy, M.A. (1986). 'Compliance and drug therapy in fasting Moslem patients'. *Journal Clinical Hospital Pharmacy*. 11(5); 321-25. **157.**

Astrow, A.B. et al. (2001). 'Religion, spirituality and health care: Social, ethical and practical considerations'. *American Journal of Medicine*. 110(4); 283-7. **8.**

Bahakim, H.M. (1987). 'Muslim parents' perception of an attitude towards cancer'. *Annals Tropical Paediatrics*. 7(1); 22-6. **152.**

Banerjee, A.C. (1951). 'Note on cholera in the United Provinces (Uttar Pradesh)'. *Indian Journal of Medical Research*. 39; 17-40. **134, 154.**

Bannerjee, M. (2000). *The Pathan unarmed.* Oxford University Press. Pakistan. 76.

Baron-Epel, O. *et al.* (2005). 'Self-reported health as a cultural health determinant in Arab and Jewish Israelis'. *Social Science and Medicine.* 61; 1256-66. **282.**

Barrett, D.B. (1968). *Schism and Renewal in Africa.* Oxford University Press. Nairobi. **261.**

Bax, M. (1992). 'Female suffering, local power relations and religious tourism: A case study from Yugoslavia'. *Medical Anthropology Quarterly.* 6(2):114-127.

Beals, A.R. (1962). *Gopalpur, a South Indian village.* Holt, Rinehart and Winston. New York.

Bedikian, A.Y. *et al.* (1985). 'Saudi patients and companion attitudes towards cancer'. *King Faisal Specialist Hospital Medical Journal.* 5; 17-25. **152.**

Bedikian, A.Y. and Thompson, S. E. (1985). 'Saudi community attitudes toward cancer'. *Annals of Saudi Medicine.* 5; 161-7. **152.**

Bellah, R. *et al.* (1985). *Habits of the Heart.* University of California. Berkeley. **2, 272.**

Benedict, P. (1991). *The Huguenot Population of France, 1600-85.* University of California. Berkeley. **164.**

Benor, D. J. (1991). 'Enlightenment. A psychologist examines fear of healing'. *Consciousness Research and Training Project.* 15(1); 5-16. **190.**

Benson, H. *et al.* (2006). 'Study of the therapeutic effect of intercessory prayer in cardiac bypass patients. A multicenter randomized trial of uncertainty and certainty of receiving intercessory prayer'. *American Heart Journal.* 151(4); 934-42. **196.**

Bernard, L. (2001). 'Prahyer and yoga mantras on autonomous cardiovascular rhythms; a comparative study'. *British Medical Journal.* 323; 1446-7. **196.**

Beteille, A. (1965). *Caste, Colour and Power.* University of California. Berkeley. 73.

Bhardwaj, S.M. (1973). *Hindu Places of Pilgrimage in India. A Study in Cultural Geography.* University of California. Berkeley. **147, 154.**

Bibby, R.W. *et al.* (1973). 'The circulation of the Saints. A study of people who join conservative Churches'. *Journal for the Scientific Study of Religion.* 12:273-8. **34.**

Bibeau, G. (1979). 'The WHO in encounter with African traditional medicine. Theoretical conceptions and practical strategies' in Ademuwagun, Z.A *et al.* (eds). *African Therapeutic Systems.* Crossrroads Press. Waltham Massachusetts. **181.**

Boardman, E.P. (1952). *Christian Influences Upon the Ideology of* the Taiping Rebellion. University of Wisconsin. Madison. **163.**

Bodiford, W. (1996). 'Zen and the art of religious prejudice. Efforts to reform a tradition of social discrimination'. *Japanese Journal of Religious Studies.* 23(1-2); 1-27. **251.**

Bohrnstedt, G.W. *et al.* (1968). 'Religious affiliation and MMPI scores'. *Journal Scientific Study of Religion.* 7:255-258. **35.**

Boldrini, M. and Ugge, A. (1926). *La mortalita del missionary.* Catholic University. Milan. **131.**

Bolton, J.M. (1968). 'Medical services to the Aborigines in West Malaysia'. *British Medical Journal.* 818-23. **142.**

Bolton, J.M. (1972). 'Food taboos among the Orang Asli in West Malaysia: Potential nutritional hazard'. *American Journal Clinical Nutrition.* 25; 789-99. **158.**

Bowen, J. (1989). 'Salat in Indonesia. The social meanings of an Islamic ritual'. *Man(ns).* 24; 600-619. **201.**

Boyajian, D. (1972). Armenia; the case for a forgotten genocide. *Crafters.* New Jersey. **164.**

Braud, W.G. (1990). 'Distant mental influence of rate of hemolysis of human red blood cells'. *American Society for Psychical Research* 84(1):1-24. 185, **198, 205.**

Braud, W.G. and Schlitz, M. (1989). 'A method for the objective study of transpersonal imagery'. *Journal Scientific Exploration.* 3(1); 43-63. **185, 205.**

Braud, W.G. *et al.* (1989). 'Remote mental influence of animate and inanimate target systems. A method of comparison and preliminary findings'. Proceedings 32nd Annual Parapsychological Association Convention. San Diego. 12-25. **198.**

Brown, D.G. and W.L. Lowe. (1951). 'Religious beliefs and personality charactereristics of college students'. *Journal Social Psychology*. 33:103-129. **59.**

Bufford, R.K. *et al.* (1991). 'Norms for the spiritual well-being scale'. *Journal Psychology and Theology*. 19; 56-70. **223.**

Buruma, I. (2001). *Bad Elements. Chinese rebels from Los Angeles to Beijing*. Weidenfeld and Nicolson. London. **235, 278.**

Bush, L.E. (1986). 'The Mormon tradition'. In Numbers, R.L. and Amundsen, D.W. (eds). *Caring and Curing, Health and Medicine in the Western Religious Tradition*. Macmillan. New York. **127.**

Bushnak, A.A. (1978). The Hajj transportation system. *Hajj Studies*. 1. Croom Helm. London. **153.**

Byrd, R.C. (1988). 'Positive therapeutic effects of intercessory prayer in a coronary care unit population'. *Southern Medical Journal*. 81; 826-829. **185, 188, 196-8.**

Cai Hua. (2001). A society without fathers or husbands. The Na of China. Zone Books. New York. **99.**

Calkins, M.W. (1911). 'The nature of prayer'. *Harvard Theology Review*. 4; 489-500. **173.**

Cannon, W.B. (1942). 'Voodoo death'. *American Anthropologist*. 44; 169-81. **191.**

Cartier, C. (2002). 'From home to hospital and back again; economic restrictions, end of life and the gendered problem of place-switch health services'. *Social Science and Medicine*. 56(5); 2289-2301. **122, 363.**

Chagnon, N.A. (1977). *Yanomamo – the fierce people*. Rinehart and Winston. New York. **156.**

Chakavarti, A. (1979), 'Experience of an encapsulated observer. A village in Rajasthan'. In M. N. Srinivas *et al.* (eds). *The Field Worker and the Field*. Oxford University Press. Delhi. 38-57. 75.

Challis, G.B. and H. J. Stam. (1990). 'The spontaneous regression of cancer'. *Acta Oncologica.* 29(5); 545-50. **195.**

Chang, W.Y. (1990). *Chuan Tsu. Text and Meaning.* Chung Wah. Beijing. **227.**

Channavasavanna, S.M. (1988). 'Drug prescriptions in psychiatry'. *Indian Journal of Psychiatry.* 30(3); 209-210. **109.**

Chatters, L.M. (2000). 'Religion and health. Public health research and practice'. *Annual Review of Public Health.* 21; 335-67. **225.**

Chau, A.Y. (2006). *Miraculous Response. Doing Popular Religion in Contemporary* China. Stanford University Press. Stanford. **273, 291, 299-300.**

Cheng, L. (1995). *The works of Laozu. Truth and Nature.* World Book Co. Hong-Kong. **227.**

Chibnall, J.T. *et al.* (2001). 'Experiments in distant intercessory prayer'. *Archives Internal Medicine.* 161; 2529-35. **205.**

Chowdhury, A.N. et al. (2001). 'Community mental health and concepts of mental illness in the Sunderban Delta of West Bengal, India'. *Anthropology and Medicine.* 8(1); 109-129. **360.**

Christensen, K. (2006). 'Why the Danes are smug; a comparative study of life satisfaction in the European Union' *British Medical Journal.* 333; 1289-91. **357.**

Chusid, E.L.*et al.* (1982). 'Selecting respiratory medications during the Passover holiday'. *Chest.* 81(4); 524-25. **157.**

Cochran, J.K. *et al.* (1992). 'The influence of religious stability and homogamy on the relationship between religiosity and alcohol use among Protestants'. *Journal Scientific Study of Religion.* 32; 441-56. **226.**

Colantonio, A. *et al.* (1992). 'Depressive symptoms and other psychosocial factors as predictors of stroke in the elderly'. *American Journal Epidemiology.* 136. 884-894. **133.**

Cole, P. (1971). 'Coffee-drinking and cancer of the lower urinary tract'. *Lancet.* I; 1335-7. **128.**

Cole, W.H. and Everson, T.C. (1966). 'The spontaneous regression of cancer'. *Connecticut Medical Journal.* 22; 637-43. **189-90.**

Collipp, P.J. (1969). 'The efficacy of prayer. A triple-blind study'. *Medical Times*. 97(May):201-204. **189, 195, 197-8.**

Comstock, G.W. and Partridge, K.B. (1972). 'Church attendance and health'. *Journal Chronic Diseases*. 25; 665-72. **125, 130.**

Comstock, G.W. *et al.* (1970). 'The non-official census as a basic tool for epidemiological observations in Washington County, Maryland' in Kesler, I. and Levin, M.L. (eds). *The Community as an Epidemiologic Laboratory: A Case-Book of Community Studies*. Johns Hopkins University Press. Baltimore. **129.**

Condon, R. (1959). *The Manchurian Candidate*. Bantam. London. **68.**

Crawford. M.E. *et al.* (1989). 'The relationship between religion and mental health/distress'. *Review of Religious Research*. 31(1); 16-22. **108.**

Csordas, T.J. (1999). 'Ritual healing and the politics of identity in contemporary Navajo society'. *American Ethnologist*. 26(1):3-23. **260.**

Daaleman, T.P. and Frey, B. (1999). 'Spiritual and religious beliefs and practices of family physicians. A national survey'. *Journal Family Practice*. 48(2); 98-109. **107.**

Dalrymple, W. (2006). 'Home in India. The oral epics of Rajasthan'. *New Yorker*. 20 November; 48-55. **339.**

Daniel, C. (1966). *The Story of the Eyam Plague*. Privately printed. Eyam. **338.**

Danquah, J.B. (1944). *The Akan Doctrine of God*. Lutterworth. London. **253.**

Darlington, C.D. (1969). *The Evolution of Men and Society*. Allen and Unwin. London. **160.**

Davis, C.O. (2000). *Death in Abeyance. Illness and Therapy Among the Tabwa of Central Africa*. Edinburgh University Press. Edinburgh. **345.**

Dawkins, R. (2006). *The God Delusion*. Bantam. London. **201.**

Dean, K. (1998). *The Lord of the Three in One. The Spread of a Cult in South-East China*. Princeton University Press. New Jersey.

Diamond, J. (2005). *Collapse. How Societies Choose to Fail or Survive.* Penguin. London. **262.**

Dols, M. W. (1987). 'the origins of theIslamic hospital. Myth and reality.' *Bulletin of the History of Medicine.* 61 (3); 367-90. **151.**

Domagic, G. (1992). 'Cancer morbidity and mortality in USA Mormons and Seventh-day Adventists'. *Arch Anst Cytoc Pathology.* 40(2-3); 73-78. **121.**

Dossey, L. (1993). Healing words. *The Power of Prayer and the Practice of Medicine.* Harper Collins. New York. **185-6.**

Dossey, L. (2000). 'Prayer and medical science'. *Archives Internal Medicine.* 160; 1135-8. **187, 202.**

Dowling. S.J. (1984). 'Lourdes cures and their medical assessments'. *Journal Royal Society Medicine.* 77; 634-8. **194.**

Drobin, F. A. (1999). 'Spirituality, the new opiate'. *Journal Religion and Health.* 38(3); 229-39. **254.**

Dua, V. (1979). 'A woman's encounter with Arya Samaj and Untouchables'. in M. N. Srinivas *et al.* (eds). *The Field Worker and the Field.* Oxford University Press. Delhi. 115-126. **75.**

Duffy, E. (1992). *The stripping of the altars. Traditional religion in England 1400-1580.* Yale University Press. New Haven. **290.**

Dunlap, J.C. *et al.* (2003). *Chronobiology. Biological time keeping.* Sinauer. Sunderland. **295.**

Dwyer, J.T. (1988). 'Health aspects of vegetarian diets'. *American Journal Clinical Nutrition.* 48; 712-38. **128.**

Dwyer, J.W. et al. (1990). 'The effect of religious concentration and affiliation on county cancer mortality rates' *Journal Health and Social Behaviour.* 31(2); 185-202. **127.**

Early, E.A. (1982). 'The logic of well-being. Therapeutic narratives in Cairo, Egypt'. *Social Science and Medicine.* 16; 1491-97. **219.**

Eliade, M. (1963). *Patterns of Comparative Religion.* World Publishing Co. Cleveland. **21.**

Ellison, C.G. (1994). 'Religion, the life-stress paradigm and the study of depression' in J.S. Levin. (ed). *Religion in Ageing and*

Health. Theoretical Foundations and Methods, Logical Frontiers. Sage. Thousand Oaks. California. 78-121. **31.**

Encyclopaedia Judaica (1971). Keter. Jerusalem.

Enstrom, J.E. (1978). 'Cancer and total mortality among active Mormons'. *Cancer.* 42; 1943-51. **127.**

Esmail, A. (2004). 'The prejudices of good people'. *British Medical Journal.* 328; 1448-9. **74.**

Ewing, K.P. (1990). 'The illusion of wholeness; culture, self and the experience of inconsistency' *Ethos.* 18(3); 215-218. **366.**

Farooq, M. and Mallah, M.B. (1966). 'Behavioural pattern of social and religious water-contact activities in Egypt-49 Bilharziasis project area'. *Bulletin World Health Organisation.* 35; 377-87. **20, 93, 160.**

Field, M.Y. (1960). *The Search for Security. An Ethno-psychiatric Study of Rural Ghana.* Faber. London. **62, 116.**

Finney, J.R. and H.N. Malony. (1985). 'Empirical studies of Christian prayer. A review of the literature'. *Journal Psychology and Theology.* 13(2); 104-115. **48.**

Finucane, R.C. (1977). *Miracles and Pilgrims.* Dent. London. **144.**

Fonnebo, V. *et al.* (1991). 'Cancer incidence in Norwegian Seventh day Adventists. 1961-1986'. *Cancer.* 68(3); 666-71. **129.**

Foster, E.M. (1974). *A Passage to India.* Penguin. Harmondsworth.

Foster, R. (1992). *Prayer. Finding the Heart's True Home.* Harper Collins. New York. **174, 177.**

Frame, J.D. (1968). 'Hepatitis among missionaries in Ethiopia and Sudan'. *Journal American Medical Association.* 203; 819-26. **155.**

Frank, J.D. (1961). *Persuasion and Healing.* Johns Hopkins Press. Baltimore. **197.**

Fraser, G.E. *et al.* (1991). 'Diet and lung cancer in California Seventh day Adventists'. *American Journal Epidemiology.* 133(7); 683-93. **127, 128.**

Frazier, J.G. (1922). *The Golden Bough.* Dover. New York. **96, 99.**

Freedman, M. (1966). Chinese lineage and society. London School of Economics. *Monographs in Social Anthropology.* 33. Athlone Press. London. **192.**

Freeman, D. (1999). *Margaret Mead and Samoa. The Making and Unmaking of an Anthropological Myth.* Harvard University Press. Cambridge. Mass. **94.**

Friedan, B. (1963). *The Feminine Mystique.* W.W. Norton. New York. **285.**

Friedman, M. and Rosenman, R.H. (1974). Type A Behaviour and Your Heart. Fawcett Crest. New York. **124.**

Frost, G. and Pirani, S., (1987). 'Meal frequency and nutritional intake during Ramadan. A pilot study'. *Human Nutrition. Applied Nutrition.* 41A; 47-50. **157.**

Gajdusek, D.C. (1973). 'Kuru in the New Guiinea Highlands'. in Spillane, J.D. (ed.). *Tropical Neurology.* Oxford University Press. London. **156.**

Galanter, M. (1999). *Cults, Faith Healing and Coercion.* Sage. New York. **138.**

Galton, F. (1872). 'Statistical inquiries into the efficacy of prayer'. *Fortnightly Review.* 12:125-135. **49.**

Gardiner, M. (1984). *Footprints on Malekula. A Memoir of Bernard Deacon.* Salamander Press. Edinburgh. **64.**

Garner, J. (1974). 'Spontaneous regressions. Scientific documentation as a basis for the declaration of miracles'. *Canadian Medical Association Journal.* 111; 1254-64. **145-6.**

Geertz, C. (1960). The religion of Java. Free Press. New York. **71.**

——, (1968). *Islam observed.* Yale University Press. **71.**

——, (2001). Review of Cai Hua. A society without fathers or husbands. The Na of China. *New York Review of Books.* 18 Oct; 27-30. **99.**

Gellner, D.W. (2001). *The Anthropology of Buddhism and Hinduism.* Oxford University Press. New Delhi. **345.**

Gellner, E. (1974). *The Legitimation of Belief.* Cambridge University Press. Cambridge. **244.**

Geurts, K.L. (2002). *Ways of Knowing in an African Community.* University of California. Berkeley. **191.**

Giel, R *et al.* (1968). 'Faith healing and spirit possession in Ghion, Ethiopia'. *Social Science and Medicine.* 2; 63-79. **143.**

Gill, O.N. (1988). 'The hazard of infection from the shared communion cup'. *Journal Infection.* 16(1); 3-23. **161.**

Glasse, R. (1967). 'Cannibalism in the kuru region of New Guinea'. *Transactions New York Academy of Sciences.* 29; 748-54. **156.**

Glazier, S.D. (1993). 'Responding to the anthropologist. When the Spiritual Baptists of Trinidad read what I wrote about them' in C.B. Brittel. (ed). *When They Read What I Write. Bergin and Garvey.* Westport. Connecticut. 36-48. **69, 71.**

Glock, C.Y. and R. Stark. (1965). American piety. The nature of religious commitment. **33.**

Goldbourt, U. *et al.* (1993). 'Factors predictive of long-term coronary heart disease mortality among 10059 male Israeli civil servants and municipal employees' *Cardiology.* 82. 100-121. **133.**

Goody, E. (1970). 'Kinship fostering in Gonja. Deprivation or advantage' in P. Mayor. (ed). Socialization. *The Approach from social anthropology.* Tavistock. London. **51.**

Gorsuch, R.L. and S.E. McPherson. (1989). 'Intrinsic/extrinsic and single item scales'. *Journal Scientific Study of Religion.* 28; 348-354. **32.**

Gottesman, L.L. (1963). 'Heritability of personality, a demonstration'. *Psychological Monographs.* 77(9). **51.**

Gould, R.L. (1972). 'The phases of adult life. A study in developmental psychology'. *Journal Psychology.* 129(5); 521-531. **286.**

Green, C. (1990). 'Karl Marx: Religion as a social narcotic and reactionary ideology' in R.A. Johnson. (ed). *Cultural Issues in Modern Religions.* Prentice-Hall. Englewood Cliffs. 213-240. **21.**

Green, E. and Green, A. (1977). *Beyond the Biofeedback.* Dell. New York. **197.**

Green, E.C. (1994). *AIDS and STDs in Africa. Westview.* Boulder, Colorado. **257.**

Gregory, K.F. *et al.* (1967). 'Infection hazards of the communion cup' *Canadian Journal Public Health.* 58; 305-10. **161.**

Grinker, R.R. (2000). In the arms of Africa. The life of Colin. M. Turnbull. St Martin's Press. New York. **64.**

Groen, J.J. *et al.* (1962). 'The influence of nutrition and ways of life on blood cholestrol and the prevalence of hypertension and coronary heart disease among Trappist and Benedictine monks'. *American Journal Clinical Nutrition.* 10; 456-70. **131.**

Groot, J.J. M. (1892-1969). *The Religious System of China: Its Ancient forms, Evolution, History and Present Aspect.* Chieng-Wen. Taipai. **176.**

Groussert, R. (1970). *The Empire of the Steppes.* University of New Brunswick. New Jersey. **163.**

Guppy, N. (1958). *Wai-Wai: Through the Forests North of the Amazon.* Murray. London. **156.**

Gupta, R *et al.* (1997). 'Prevalence and determinants of coronary heart disease in a rural population of India'. *Journal Clinical Epidemiology.* 80; 203-209. **205.**

Hacker, H.M. (1957). 'The new burdens of masculinity'. *Marriage and Family Living.* 19(3); 227-233. **285.**

Hall, J.R. and M. Galanter. (1989). *Gone from the Promised Land Jonestown in American Cultural History.* Sage. New York. **138.**

Hardinge, M.G. *et al.* (1958). 'Nutritional studies of vegetarians. III. Dietary levels of fiber. *American Journal Clinical Nutrition.* 6; 523-25. **128.**

——, (1962). 'Nutritional studies of vegetarians. IV. Dietary fatty acids and serum cholestrol levels'. *American Journal Clinical Nutrition.* 10; 516-24. **128.**

Harrell, D.E., (1975). *All Things are Possible. The Healing and Charismatic Revivals in Modern America.* Indiana University Press. Bloomington. **146, 189.**

Harris, J.I. *et al.* (2005). 'Preferred prayer style and anxiety control'. *Journal Religion and Health.* 44(4); 403-412. **199.**

Harris, W.S. *et al.* (1999). A randomised, controlled trial of the effects of remote intercessory prayer on outcomes in patients in a coronary care unit'. *Archives Internal Medicine.* 159; 2273-8. **183-5.**

Harrison, I.E. (1974). 'Traditional healers; a neglected source of health manpower'. *Rural Africana*. 26; 5-16. **140.**

Hau'opa, E. (1975). 'Anthropology at home. A South Pacific Island experience' in H. Fahim. (ed). *Indigenous Anthropology in Non-Western Countries.* Carolina Academic Press. Durham. North Carolina. 4-18. 78.

Hayes, L.N. (1924), 'Gods of the Chinese'. *Royal Asiatic Society.* N. China Branch. 55; 97-103. **178.**

Hearn, Lafcadio. (1894). *Glimpses of Unfamiliar Japan.* 2 vols. Houghton Mifflin. Boston. **281.**

Heimann, B. (1964). *Facets of Indian Thought.* Allen and Unwin. London. **346.**

Hickley, J. (1984). *Religion and the Northern Ireland Problem.* Barnes and Noble. Totowa. New Jersey. **167.**

Hill, D.L. (2006). 'Sense of belonging as connectedness, American Indian worldview and mental health'. *Archives of Psychiatric Nursing.* 20(5); 210-216. **297.**

Hill, P.C. and R.W. Hood. (1999). *Measures of Religiosity.* Religious Education Press. Birmingham. Alabama. **30.**

Hirshberg, C. (1993). 'The spectrum of self-repair'. in B. O'Regan and C. Hirshberg. (eds). *Spontaneous Remission. An Annotated bibliography.* Institute of Noetic Sciences. Sausaleto. California. **195.**

Hobart. M. (1995). 'As I lay laughing. Encountering global knowledge in Bali' in R. Fardon, (ed). *Counterwork. Managing the Diversity of Knowledge.* Routledge. London. 49-72. 24.

Hobbs, B.C. *et al.* (1967). 'Experiments on the communion cup'. Journal Hygiene. *Cambridge.* 65; 37-48. **161.**

Hofer. T. (1979). 'A psychoendocrine study of bereavement. Part 1. 17 ACTH excretion rate following deaths of their children from leukemia'. *Psychosomatic Medicine.* 34(1); 481-504. **152.**

Hollander, A.N.J. (1967). 'Social description. The problem of reliability and validity'. in D.G. Jongmans and C.W. Gutkind. (eds). *Anthropologists in the Field.* Humanities Press. New York. 1-34. 72.

Hong, Y.Y. *et al.* (2000). 'Multicultural minds; a dynamic constructionist approach to culture and cognition'. *American Psychologist.* 55(7); 1-12. **227.**

Houghton, B. (1967). *Address to the Latin Mass Society of England.* London. **310.**

Howell, S. (1995). 'Whose knowledge and whose power? A new perspective on cultural diffusion' in R. Fardon. (ed). *Counter Work.* Routledge. London. **239.**

Hsu, F. (1975). 'Intercultural understanding; genuine and spacious'. *Anthropology and Education Quarterly.* 8; 202-9. **68.**

Hume, David. (1757-1956). *The Natural History of Religion.* Black. London. **183.**

Hummer, R.A. *et al.* (1999). 'Religious involvement and US adult mortality'. *Demography.* 36. 273-285. **133.**

Imperato, P.J. (1977). *African Folk Medicine. Practices and Beliefs of the Bambara and Other Peoples.* York Press. Baltimore. **141.**

Ineichen, B. (1998). The influence of religion on the suicide rate. Islam and Hinduism compared. *Mental Health, Religion and Culture.* 1(1); 31-36. **133.**

Izquierdo, C. (2005). 'When health is not enough; societal, individual and bio-medical assessments of well-being among the Matsigenka of the Peruvian Amazon'. *Social Science and Medicine.* 61; 767-83. **282.**

Izzedine, C. Le cholera et l'hygiene a la Mecque. Publisher not known. **163.**

Jaffrelot, C. (2003). *India's silent revolution. The rise of the lower castes.* Hurst. London. **297.**

Jahoda, G. (1968). 'Scientific training and the persistence of traditional beliefs among West African University students'. *Nature.* 220; 1356. **113.**

James, W. (1902). *Varieties of Religious Experience.* University Books. New York. 47.

Janzen, J.M. (1974). 'Pluralistic legitimation of the therapy systems in contemporary Zaire'. *Rural Africana.* 26; 105-22. **143.**

Johnson, D.M. *et al.* (1986). 'Religion, health and healing. Findings from a southern city'. *Sociological Analysis.* 47; 66-73. **201.**

Jolliffe, D.M. (2005). 'The power of prayer and adequate fluid resusitation'. *British Medical Journal.* 330; 526. **368.**

Jones, S.L. (1994). 'A constructive relationship for religion with the science and profession of psychology; perhaps the boldest model yet'. *American Psychologist.* March. 184-199. **118.**

Joselit, J.W. (1994). *The Wonders of America. Reinventing Jewish Culture. 1880-1950.* Hill and Wang. New York. **269.**

Joyce, C.R. and R.M. Welldon. (1965). 'The objective efficacy of prayer. A double-blind clinical trial'. *Journal Chronic Diseases.* 18:367-377. **188, 195, 197-8.**

Juergensmeyer, M. (1993). *The New Cold War. Religious Nationalism Confronts the Secular State.* University of California. Berkeley. **166.**

Kamalkhani, Z. (1991). *Women's Islam. Religious Practices Among Women in Today's Iran.* Kegan Paul. London. **115.**

Kaplan, G. and Baron-Epel, O. (2003). 'What lies behind the subjective evaluation of health status?'. *Social Science and Medicine.* 56; 1669-76. **283.**

Kark, J.D. *et al.* (1996). 'Does religious observance promote health? Mortality in secular versus religious kibbutzim in Israel'. *American Journal Public Health.* 86. 341-346. **133.**

Kashyar, A.S. *et al.* (2007). 'The God incarnate'. *British Medical Journal.* 334; 256. **368.**

Kaufman, S.R. (2002). 'Hidden place, uncommon persons'. *Social Science and Medicine.* 56(5); 2249-2261. **122.**

Kaunitz, A.M. et al. (1984). 'Peri-natal and maternal mortality in a religious group avoiding obstetric care'. *American Journal Obstetrics and Gynaecology.* 150:826-831. **151.**

Kawano, S. (1996). 'Gender, liminality and ritual in Japan. Divination among single Tokyo women'. *Journal Ritual Studies.* 9(2); 65-91. **44.**

Kazemipur, A. and A. Rezani. (2003). 'Religious life under theocracy' *Journal Scientific Study of Religion.* 42(3); 347-361. **33, 101.**

Kendler, K.S. *et al.* (1997). 'Religion, psychopathology and substance use and abuse. A multimeasure, genetic-epidemiologic study'. *American Journal Psychiatry*. 154. 322-329. **133.**

Kendrick, M.A. (1974). 'Viral hepatitis in American missionaries abroad'. *Journal Infectious Diseases*. 129; 227-9. **155.**

Kennaway, E.L. (1948). 'The racial and social incidence of cancer of the utrerus'. *British Journal Cancer*. 2; 177-212. **126.**

Kenyon, S.M. (1999). 'The case of the butcher's wife. Illness, possession and power in Central Sudan' in H. Behrend and U. Luig. (eds). *Spirit Possession. Modernity and Power in Africa*. Currey. Oxford. **114.**

Keys, A. (1961). 'Further observations on monastic cholestrol' *New England Journal Medicine*. 264; 1005. **131.**

Khan, Z.H. and P.J. Watson. (2004). 'Religious orientation and the experience of Eld-ul-azha among Pakistani Muslims'. *Journal for the Scientific Study of Religion*. 43(4):537-45. **31.**

King, D.G. (1990). 'Religion and health relationships. A review'. *Journal Religion and Health*. 29(2); 101-112. **130.**

King, M. (1966). 'Measuring the religious variable. Nine proposed dimensions'. *Journal Scientific Study of Religion*. 173-185. **97.**

King, M.B. and Hunt, D.A. (1975). 'Measuring the religious variable. A national replication'. *Journal Scientific Study of Religion*. 14:13-22. **35.**

Kingston, D. (1988). 'Memorandum on the infectious hazards of the common communion cup with especial reference to AIDS'. *European Journal of Epidemiology*. 4(2); 164-70. **161.**

Kinlen, L.J. (1982). 'Meat and fat consumption and cancer mortality: A study of strict religious orders in Britain'. *Lancet*. 946-49. **132.**

Kinsey, A. *et al.* (1953). *Sexual Behaviour in the Human Female*. Saunders. Philadelphia. **129.**

Klass, D. (1996). *Continuing Bonds. New Understandings of Grief.* Taylor and Francis. Philadelphia. **25.**

Klitzman, R.L. and S. Daya. (2005). 'Challenge and changes in spirituality among doctors who become patients'. *Social Science and Medicine*. 61; 2396-2406. **103.**

Knutsson, K.E. and Selinus, R. (1970). 'Fasting in Ethiopia. An anthropological and nutritional study. *American Journal Clinical Nutrition*. 23; 956-59. **158, 283.**

Koenig, H.G. *et al.* (1994). 'Religious practices and alcoholism in a Southern adult population'. *Hospital Community Psychiatry*. 45; 225-31. 226.

——, (1998). 'The relationship between religious activities and cigarette smoking in old adults'. *Journal Gerontololgy*. 53; H, 426-34. **226.**

——, (1998). 'Religiosity and remission of depression' in H.G. Koenig. (ed). *Handbook of Religion and Mental Health*. Academic Press. San Diego. **226.**

Koenjarahimgrat. (1982). 'Anthropology in developing countries' in H. Fahim. (ed). *Indigenous Anthropology in Non-Western Countries*. Carolinas Academic Press. Durham. North Carolina. 71.

Kondo, D.K. (1990). *Crafting Selves. Power, Gender and Discourses of Identity in a Japanese Workplace*. University of Chicago Press. Chicago. **38.**

Kreiger, D.E. *et al.* (1979). 'Therapeutic touch. Searching for evidence of physiological change'. *American Journal of Nursing*. 79:660-2. **198.**

Kuhn, T. (1970). *The Structure of Scientific Revolutions*. University of Chicago Press. Chicago. **148.**

Kumar, N. (1992). Friends, brothers and informants. Field work memories of Banaras. University of California. Berkeley. **63.**

Kune, G.A. et al. (1993). 'Perceived religiousness is protective for colorectal cancer. Data from the Melbourne Colorectal Cancer Study'. *Journal Royal Society Medicine*. 86; 645-7. **129.**

Ladd, J. (1957). *The Structure of a Moral Code. A Philosophical Analysis of Ethical Discourse Applied to the Ethics of the Navajo Indians*. Harvard University Press, Cambridge, Mass. **26, 35.**

Ladd, K.L. and Spilka, B. (2002). 'Inward, outward and upward. Cognitive aspects of prayer'. *Journal Scientific Study of Religion*. 41(3); 475-84. 173, 177.

Lafleur, W.R. (1992). *Liquid life. Abortion and Buddhism in Japan.* Princeton University Press. Princeton. **251, 270, 276, 280.**

Laitin, D.D. (1986). *Hegemony and Culture. Politics and Religious Change Among the Yoruba.* University of Chicago. Chicago. **65.**

Lamb, T. (1932). Tamerlane, the earth shaker. New York. **163.**

Lambo, T.A. (1971). Problems of adjustment between traditional and modern methods of medical practice. *Occasional Publication* 25. Institute of African Studies. Ibadan. **141.**

Larson, D.B. *et al.* (1992). 'Associations between dimensions of religious commitment and mental health reported in *American Journal Psychiatry* and Archives of General Psychiatry. 1978-1989'. *American Journal Psychiatry.* 149; 557-9. **225.**

Lasaga, J.I. (1980). 'Death in Jonestown. Techniques of political control in a paranoid leader'. *Suicide Life-Threatening Behaviour.* 10:210-13. **138.**

Leach, E. A. (1967). 'An anthropologist's reflection on a social survey' in D.G. Jonghams and P.C. W. Gutkind. (eds). *Anthropologists in the Field.* Van Gorcum. Assen. Netherlands. 75-88.

Lebra, W.P. (1966). *Okinawa Religion.* University of Hawaii Press. Honolulu. **244.**

Leibovici, L. (2001). 'Effects of remote retroactive intercessory prayer on outcome in patients with blood stream infection; a controlled trial'. *British Medical Journal.* 323; 1450-1. **197.**

Levin, J.S. (1996). 'How religion influences morbidity and health; reflections on natural history, salutogenesis and host resistance'. *Social Science and Medicine.* 43(5); 849-864. **120.**

Levin, J.S. and Chatters, L.M. (1998). 'Research on religion and mental health; an overview of empirical findings and theoretical issues' in H.G. Koenig. (ed). *Hanbook of Religion and Mental Health.* Academic Press. San Diego. 34-50. **225.**

Levin, J.S and Markides, K.S. (1986). 'Religious attendance and subjective health'. *Journal Scientific Study of Religion.* 25(1); 31-40. **130.**

Levin, J.S. and Schiller, P.L. (1987). 'Is there a religious factor in health?'. *Journal of Religion and Health.* 26(1); 9-35. **108.**

Levin, J.S. and Vanderpool, H.Y. (1987). 'Is frequent religious attendance really conducive to better health'. *Social Science and Medicine.* 24(7); 589-600. **130.**

Levin, J.S. and Vanderpool, H.Y. (1989). 'Is religion therapeutically significant for hypertension?' *Social Science and Medicine.* 29. 69-78. **129, 213.**

Levin, J.S. *et al.* (1988). 'Religion, type A behaviour and health'. *Journal Religion and Health.* 27(4); 267-78. **125.**

Levin, J.S. *et al.* (1993) 'Prayer and health during pregnancy. Findings from the Galveston Low Birth Weight study. *Southern Medical Journal.* 86(9); 1022-27. **179.**

Levin, J.S. *et al.* (1996). 'Religious involvement, health outcomes and public health practice'. *Current Issues Public Health.* 2; 220-25. **213.**

Levi-Strauss, C. (1966). *The Savage Mind.* University of Chicago. Chicago. **71.**

Levy, G. (1974). *Religion and Revolution.* Oxford University Press. New York. **164.**

Lewis, D.C. (1993). 'Religious rites in a Japanese factory' in M.R. Mullins *et al.* (eds). *Religion and Society in Modern Japan.* Asian Humanities Press. Honolulu. 157-170. **244.**

Lewis, J.R. (1995). *The Gods have Landed. New Religions from other worlds.* State University of New York. Albany.

Lewis, O. (1959). *Life in a Mexican village. Tepoztlan Restudied.* Illinois University Press. Urbana. **72.**

Lex, B.W. (1977). 'Voodoo death; new thoughts on an old explanation' in Landy, D. (ed). *Disease, Culture and Healing; Studies in Medical Anthropology.* Macmillan. New York. 327-331. **191.**

Lienhardt, P. (1966). 'A controversy over Islamic custom in Kilwa Kivinje, Tanzania' in I.M. Lewis. (ed). *Islam in Tropical Africa.* Oxford University Press. Oxford. 374-86. **209.**

Livingstone, D. (1857). *Missionary Travels.* John Murray. London. **201.**

Locke, S and D. Colligan. (1986). *The Healer Within.* Dutton. New York. **197.**

Loma Linda University. (2006). *Adventist Health Services Center.* Loma Linda. California. **121.**

Losito, P. (1946). 'Church hygiene; microbic content of holy water in various churches in Perugia'. *Bulletin Soc Ital Bio Sp.* 22; 463-65. **20, 155.**

Lowe, J. (2002). 'Balance and harmony through connectedness. The intentionality of Native American nurses'. *Holistic Nursing Practice.* 16(4); 4-11. **297.**

Lyon, J.L. and Sorenson, A.W. (1978). 'Colon cancer in a low risk population'. *American Journal Clinical Nutrition.* 31; 227-30. **126, 127.**

Lyon, J.L. *et al.* (1976). 'Cancer incidence in Mormons and non-Mormons in Utah 1966-70'. *New England Journal Medicine.* 294:129-133. **127.**

——, (1980). 'Cancer incidence in Mormons and non-Mormons in Utah. 1867-1975'. *Journal National Cancer Institute.* 65; 1055-1061. **127.**

Maas, H and J. Kuypers. (1974). *From Thirty to Seventy.* Jossey-Bass. San Francisco. **286.**

Mackenbach, J.P. *et al.* (1988). 'Self-reported morbidity and disability among Trappist and Benedictine monks'. *American Journal of Epidemiology.* 138(8):569-73. **131.**

MacCorquodale, K. *et al.* (1954). 'Commentary on Hummel, Musseler, Aschersleben and Prinz perceptions' in W.K. Estes *et al.* (eds). *Modern Learning Theories; A Critical Analysis of Five Examples.* Appleton-Century-Crofts. New York. 177-266. **40.**

Malinowski, B. (1967). *A Diary in the Strict Sense of the Term.* Harcourt Brace and World. New York. **64.**

Mallony, M. (1977). *Christian Mysticism. Transcending Techniques.* Van Gorcum. Assen. **47.**

Malpas, J, (2003). 'Bio-medical topoi; the dimensions of space, the recalcitrance of place and the making of person'. *Social Science and Medicine.* 56(5); 2343-2351. **122, 363.**

Mann, T. (1996). *The Magic Mountain.* Vintage. New York. **284.**

Marnham, P. (1980). *Lourdes: A Modern Pilgrimage*. Heinemann. London. **154**.

Maslow, A.H. (1943). 'A theory of human motivation'. *Psychological Review*. 50:370-96. **170**.

——, (1970). *Motivation and Personality*. Harper and Row, New York. **170, 178**.

Masoga, R.A. (2002). 'Contesting space and time. Intellectual property rights and the indigenous knowledge system research in South African Universities'. International Symposium in African Universities in the 21st century. Dakar. **63**.

Matsumoto, Jitsudo. (1985). Toward faith in Kankiten. Trans I Reader and G. J. Tanabe. Hozanji. Osaka. **202**.

McCullough. M.E. *et al*. (2000). 'Religious involvement and mortality. A meta-analytic review'. *Health Psychology*. 19(3). 211-221. **132**.

McEvoy, T. *et al*. (1981). 'Life-style and death patterns of the Missouri Reformed Latter Day Saints members'. *American Journal of Public Health*. 71(12); 1350-57. **137**.

McGrath, J.W. (1988). 'Multiple stable states of disease occurrence. A note on the implications for the anthropological study of human disease'. *American Anthropologist*. 90; 323-4. **109**.

McGuire, R.B. (1988). *Ritual Healing in Suburban America*. Rutgers University Press. New Jersey. **111-112, 136**.

Mcintosh, W.A. and Shifflett, P.A. (1981). 'Religion and the human diet. The impact of commitment on the diet quality of the elderly' Paper presented to Conference of Association for the Sociology of Religion. **125**.

McKelvey, A.C. and J.C. Dornan. (2004). 'Mind over matter?'. *British Medical Journal*. 329; 1459. **145**.

McKusick, V.A. (1973). 'Genetic studies in American inbred populations with particular reference to the Old Order Amish'. *Israel Journal of Medical Science*. 9; 1276-84. **27, 108, 151**.

McQuay, R.M. (1967). 'Parasitologic studies in a group of furloughed missionaries. 1. Intestinal protozoa. 11. Helminth findings'. *American Journal Tropical Medicine*. 16; 154-66. **155**.

Mead, M. (1975). *New Lives for Old.* Morrow Quill. New York. **234.**

Meadow, M.J. and Kahoe, R.D. (1984). *The Psychology of Religion.* Harper and Row. New York. **204, 322.**

Medley, M.L. (1980). 'Life satisfaction across four stages of adult life'. *National Journal of Human Development.* 11(7); 193-209. **284.**

Meene, P.E. (1978). 'Theoretical risk and tabular asterisks. Sir Karl, Sir Ronald and the slow progress of soft psychology'. *Journal Consulting and Clinical Psychology.* 46; 806-34. **25, 53.**

Mehta, S. (2004). *Maximum city. Bombay Lost and Found.* Penguin India. Delhi.

Meissner, W.W. (1984). *Psychoanalysis and Religious Experience.* Yale University Press. **322.**

Menon, U. and R.A. Shweder. (1998). 'The return of the 'white man's burden'. The moral discourse of anthropology and the domestic life of Hindu women' in R.A. Shweder. (ed). *Welcome to Middle Age (and Other Cultural Fictions).* University of Chicago Press. Chicago. 139-188. **300.**

Merton, R.K. (1957). *Social-Theory and Social Structure.* Free Press. Glencoe. **12, 114, 274.**

Mesaki, S. (1994). 'Witch-killing in Sukumaland' in R. Abrahams. (ed). *Witchcraft in contemporary Tanzania.* African Studies Centre. University of Cambridge. Cambridge. 47-60. **317.**

Metcalf, P. (1989). Where are you Spirits? Style and theme in Berawan prayer. Smithsonian Institute. Washington, DC. **182.**

Minister, K. (1991). 'A feminist frame for the oral history interview' in S.B. Glock and D. Patai. (eds). *Women's Words. A Feminist Practice of Oral History.* Routledge. New York. 27-41. **102.**

Mkenda, F.L.M. (2005). *Mazoezi ya kiroho ya Mtakatifu Inyasi was Loyola.* Paulines. Nairobi. **348.**

Molinari, P. (1965). Saints. *Their Place in the Church.* Trans D. Maruca. Sheed and Ward. New York. **355.**

Moskowitz, M.L. (2005). 'Magic tricks, midnight grove outings and transforming trees. Performance and agency in Taiwanese religion'. *Journal of Ritual Studies*. 19(1); 19-28. **350.**

Moynihan, R. *et al.* (2002). 'Selling sickness; the pharmaceutical industry and disease mongering.' *British Medical Journal*. 324; 886-891. **106, 359.**

Mu-Chou, Poo. (1998). *In Search of Personal Welfare*. State University of New York. Albany. **280.**

Najafi, S.M.B. (1976). 'Religious media, centres and organisation' in A. Asadi and M. Mehrdad. (eds). *Naqsh e rasanenha dar poshtiban-ye tause'a-ye farhangi*. Iran Communications and Development Institute. Tehran. **269.**

Nash, D. (1963). 'The ethnologist as stranger. An essay in the sociology of knowledge'. *South-Western Journal Anthro-pology*. 19; 149-67. 71.

National Immunization Programme. (1999). 'Health consequences of religious and philosophical exemption from immunization laws; individual and societal risk of measles'. Centre for Disease Control and Prevention. Atlanta Georgia. **134.**

Ndofunsu, D. (1978). 'The role of prayer in the Kimbanguist Church' in E. Fashole-Luke *et al.* (eds). *Christianity in Independent Africa*. Rex College. London. **186.**

Neumann, A.K. and Bhatia, J.C. (1973). 'Family planning and indigenous medicine practitioners'. *Social Science and Medicine*. 7; 507-16. **193.**

Nolan, M.L. (1991). *The European Roots of Latin American Pilgrimage*. Greenwood Press. New York. **147.**

Nolan, M.L. and Nolan, S. (1989). *Christian Pilgrimage in Modern Western Europe*. University of North Carolina. Chapel Hill. **147.**

Nunley, M. (1996). 'Why psychiatrists in India prescribe so many drugs'. *Culture, Medicine and Psychiatry*. 20:165-197. **109.**

Obrist, B. (2003). 'Urban health in daily practice; livelihood, vulnerability and resilience in Dar-es-Salaam, Tanzania'. *Anthropology and Medicine*. 10(3); 275-90. **360.**

Ohsawa, G. (1965). *Zen Macrobiotics:The Art of Longevity and Rejuvenation.* Ohsawa Foundation. New York. **158.**

O'Laoire, S. (1997). 'An experimental study of the effects of distant intercessory prayer on self-esteem, anxiety and depression'. *Alternative Therapies.* 3(6):38-53. **199, 206.**

Olin, S. (1860). *Travels in Egypt, Arabia, Petraea and the Holy Land.* Harper and Brothers. New York. Vol 1. **184.**

Oliver, S. (1894). Historia Damietta. Bibliothek der literarischen. Vereins in Stuttgart. Tubingen. **164.**

Olshansky, B and Dossey, L. (2005). 'Retroactive prayer; a preposterous hypothesis'. *British Medical Journal.* 327; 1465-68. **185, 204.**

O'Malley, P. (1983). *The Uncivil War; Ireland Today.* Mifflin. Boston. **167.**

Ong, A. (1985). 'The production of possession; spirits and the multi-national corporation in Malaysia'. *American Ethnologist.* 75; 28-42. **143.**

Ooms, H. (1976). 'A structural analysis of Japanese ancestral rites and beliefs' in W.H. Newell. (ed). *Ancestors.* Mouton. Paris. **345.**

Orsi, R. (1996). Thank you St Jude. Women's devotions to the patron saint of hopeless causes. Yale University Press. **104.**

Ottosen, P.G. (1968). *Fighting the Plague in 17 and 18th Century* Sweden. Stockholm. **151.**

Oxman, T.E. *et al.* (1995). 'Lack of social participation or religious strength and comfort as risk factors for death after cardiac surgery in the elderly'. *Psychosomatic Medicine.* 57. 5-15. **133.**

Panter-Brick, C. (1991). 'Parental responses to consanguinity and genetic disease in Saudi Arabia'. *Social Science and Medicine.* 33(11); 1295-1302. **152.**

Pargament, K.W. (1996). 'Religious methods of coping. Resource for the conservation and transformation of significance' in G. Shafranake. (ed). *Religion and the Clinical Practice of Psychology.* APA Books. Washington. DC. 215-239. **228.**

Pargament, K.W. (1997). *The Psychology of Religion and Coping. Theory, Research, Practice.* Guilford. New York. **213.**

Pargament, K. W. *et al.* (1998). 'Patterns of positive and negative religious coping with major life stresses'. *Journal Scientific Study of Religion.* 37(4); 710-24. **212, 231.**

Parkar, S. R *et al.* (2003). 'Contextualizing mental health; gendered experiences in a Mumbai slum'. *Anthropology and Medicine.* 10(3); 291-308. **360.**

Parker, W.P. and Johns, E. St. (1957). *Prayer can Change Your Life.* Prentice Hall. New York. **200.**

Parkin, D. (1995). 'Latticed knowledge. Eradication and dispersal of the unpalatable in Islam, medicine and anthropological theory' in R. Fardon. (ed). *Counterwork. Managing the Diversity of Knowledge.* Routledge. London. 143-163. **24.**

Patwardhan, S. (1979). 'Making my way through caste images. Untouchables in Poona' in M.N. Srinivas *et al.* (eds). *The Fieldworker and the Field.* Oxford University Press. Delhi. 152-160. **67.**

Perez-Sarduy, P and Stubbs, J. (eds). (1995). *No Longer Invisible. Afro-Americans Today.* Minority Rights Group Publication. London. **297.**

Petersen, C.R. and A. Roy. (1985). 'Religiosity, anxiety, meaning and purpose. Religion's consequences for psychological well-being'. *Review Religious Research.* 27; 49-62. **28.**

Phillips, D.P. *et al.* (1993). 'Psychology and survival'. *Lancet.* 342; 1142-45. **162.**

Phillips, R.L. (1980). 'Cancer among Seventh day Adventists'. *Journal Environmental Pathology and Toxicology.* 3; 157-69. **126, 128.**

Pollner, N. (1989). 'Divine relations, social relations and well-being'. *Journal Health and Social Behaviour.* 30; 92-104. **31.**

Poloma, M.M. (1993). 'The effects of prayer on mental well-being'. *Second Opinion.* 18(3); 37-51. **178.**

Poloma, M.M. and B.F. Pendelton. (1991). 'The effects of prayer and prayer experiences on measures of general well-being'. *Journal Psychology and Theology.* 19(1):77-85. **29, 356.**

Pope, A. (1711). *An Essay on Crticism.* 1; 625. London. 22.

Pressman, P. *et al.* (1990). 'Religious belief, depression and ambulation status in elderly women with broken hips'. *American Journal Psychiatry.* 147. 758-760. **133.**

Quinn, J. (1984). 'Therapeutic touch as energy exchange: Testing the theory'. *Advances in Nursing Science.* 1:42-49. **198.**

Radhakrishnan, S. (1923). *Indian Philosophy.* 2 vols. Unwin Hyman. London. **281.**

Radin, D.I. and R. Nelson. (1989). 'Evidence for consciousness-related anomalies in random physical systems'. *Found Physics.* 19; 1499-1514. **204.**

Rapoport, D.C. (1982). 'Terror and the messiah; an ancient experience and some modern parallels' in Rapoport, D.C. and Y. Alexander. (eds). *The Morality of Terrorism. Religious and Secular Justification.* Pergamon Press. New York. **168.**

Thule Expedition. Copenhagen. Gylendalske Boghandel. **107, 338.**

Ratcliffe, J. *et al.* (2006). 'A randomised controlled trial of acupuncture care for persistent low back-pain; cost effectiveness analysis'. *British Medical Journal.* 333; 626-8. **361.**

Reader, I. (1991). *Religion in Contemporary Japan.* Macmillan. Basingstoke. **345.**

Redfield, R. (1956). *Peasant Society and Culture.* Chicago University Press. Chicago. **24, 172.**

Reymond, L. (1958). *My Life with a Brahmin Family.* Rider. London. **85.**

Reynolds, V. and R. Tanner (1995). *The Social Ecology of Religion.* Oxford University Press. New York. **7, 44, 118, 163, 169.**

Rhine, L.E. (1962). 'Psychological processes in ESP experiences. Part 1. Working experiences'. *Journal Parapsychology.* 29. **190.**

Richards, T.A. *et al.* (2003). 'Subjective experience of prayer among women who care for children with HIV'. *Journal Religion and Health,* 42(3); 201-219. **199.**

Riley, M.W. and A. Foner. (1968). Aging and Society. An Inventory of Research Findings. Russell Sage. New York. **286.**

Roberts, I.F. *et al.* (1979). 'Malnutrition in infants receiving cult diets: A form of child abuse'. *British Medical Journal.* 1; 296-8. **159.**

Robson, J.R.K. *et al.* (1974). 'Zen macrobiotic dietary problems in infancy'. *Pediatrics.* 3; 326-9. **159.**

Rogerson, R. (2000). 'The traditional diviner-healer; their role in the fight against STDs, HIV and AIDS'. Context of AIDS Conference. University of the Witwatersrand. South Africa. **256.**

Roof, W.C. (1999). The spiritual market place. Baby boomers and the remaking of American religion. Princeton University Press. New Jersey. **303.**

Ross, C.E. (1990). 'Religion and psychological distress'. *Journal for the Scientific Study of Religion.* 29(1); 236-45. **108.**

Rossiter-Thornton, J.F. (2000). 'Prayer in psychotherapy'. *Alternative Therapies.* 6; 125-8. **204.**

Rothwell, P.M. (2006). 'Medical academia is failing patients and clinicians'. *British Medical Journal.* 332; 863. **81.**

Sacks, H. (1979). 'The effect of spiritual exercises on the integration of self-system'. *Journal Scientific Study of religion.* 18; 46-50. **48.**

Scheper-Hughes, N. (1982). *Saints, Scholars and Schizophrenics. Mental Illness in Rural Ireland.* University of California. Berkeley. **62.**

Schwarz, B.E. (1960). 'Ordeal by serpents, fire and strychnine. A study of some provocative psychosomatic phenomena'. *Psychiatry Quarterly.* 34; 405-29. **135, 162.**

Sell. H. (1955). *Bad Death Among Indonesian Peoples.* Mouton. The Hague. **244.**

Seth, S and. G. Seligman. (1993). 'Optimism and fundamentalism'. *Psychological Science.* 4(4); 256-9. **74.**

Shah, A.M. (1979). 'Studying the present and the past. A village in Gujarat'in M. N. Srinivas *et al.* (eds). *The Fieldworker and the Field.* Oxford University Press. Delhi. 29-37. **75.**

Sheldrake, R. (1982). *A new science of life. The hypothesis of formative causation.* Blond. London. **195.**

Sherlock, P and Rothchild, E.O. (1967). 'Scurvy produced by a Zen macrobiotic diet'. *Journal American Medical Association.* 199; 794-8. **159.**

Sherrill, K.A. *et al.* (1988). 'Adult burn patients. The role of religion in recovery'. *Southern Medical Journal.* 81(7); 821-5. **109.**

Shils, E. (1959). 'The culture of the Indian intellectual'. *Sewanee Review.* 67; 257-8. **151.**

Shinwell, E.D. and Gorodischer, R. (1982). 'Total vegetarian diets and infant nutrition'. *Pediatrics.* 70(4); 582-86. **150.**

Shore, B. (1996). Culture in Mind. Cognition, Culture and the Problems of Meaning. Oxford University Press. New York. **240, 347.**

Sicher, F. *et al.* (1998). 'A randomized double blind study of the effects of distant healing in a population with advanced AIDS; report of a small scaled study'. *Western Journal Medicine.* 169; 356-63. **199.**

Simpson, W.F. (1989). 'Comparative longevity in a college cohort of Christian Scientists'. *Journal of the American Medical Association.* 262:1657-1659. **162.**

——, (1991). 'Comparative mortality in two College groups'. *Morbidity and Mortality Weekly Reports.* 40(33). **162.**

Skinner, B.F.. (1938). *The Behaviour of Organisms.* Appleton-Century. New York. **41.**

Skultans, V. (2000). 'Anthropology and narrative' in T. Greenlahagh and B, Hurwitz. (eds). Narrative based medicine; dialogue and discourse in clinical practice. *British Medical Journal Books.* London. **346.**

Slack. P. (1985). *The Impact of Plague in Tudor and Stuart England.* London. Routledge. **151.**

Slap, G.B. et al. (2003). 'Sexual behaviour of adolescents in Nigeria; a cross-sectional survey of secondary students'. *British Medical Journal.* 326; 15-18. **41.**

Smith, G.B. *et al.* (1979). 'Self-esteem and religiosity. An analysis of Catholic adolescents in five cultures'. *Journal Scientific Study of Religion.* 18:51-60. **35.**

Smith, R.J. (1974). *Ancestor Worship in Contemporary Japan.* Stanford University Press. Stanford. **244.**

Snowdon, D.A. (1988). 'Animal product consumption and mortality because of all causes combined, coronary heart disease, stroke, diabetes and cancer in Seventh Day Adventists'. *American Journal Clinical Nutrition.* 48; 739-48. **128.**

Solvin, J. (1954). 'Mental healing' in S. Krippner. (ed). *Advances in Parapsychological Research.* Vol 4. McFarland. Jefferson. North Carolina. **203.**

Spilka, B. and Werme, P.H. (1971). 'Religion and Mental disorder' in M. Strommen. (ed). *Research on Religious Development. A Comprehensive Hand-Book.* Hawthorn. New York. **35.**

Spiro, M.E. (1971). *Buddhism and Society. A Great Tradition and its Burmese Vicissitudes.* Allen and Unwin. London. **178, 271.**

Srinivas, M.N. (1979). 'The field worker and the field. A village in Karnataka' in M.N. Srinivas *et al.* (eds). *The Fieldworker and the Field.* Oxford University Press. Delhi. 19-28. **75.**

Staal, F. (1980). 'The meaningless of ritual'. *Numen.* 26(1); 2-22. **222.**

Starrett, G. (1995). 'The axis of interpretation. Islam and the body in the Egyptian popuilar school'. *American Ethnologist.* 22(4); 953-69. **362.**

Stevenson, I. (1970). *Telepathic Impressions.* University of Virginia. Charlottesville. **190.**

Strathern, M. (1987). 'Out of context. The persuasive fictions of anthropology'. *Current Anthropology.* 28(3). 251-281. **96.**

Struthers, R. *et al.* (2003). 'Providing culturally appropriate education on Type 2 diabetes in rural American Indians: Emotions and racial consciousness'. *Journal of Rural Community Psychology.* 1(E6). **297.**

Stubbs, I. (2007). 'Humbled in the Himalayas'. *Daily Telegraph*; 21 April. London. **19.**

Sulmasy, D.P. (1999). 'Is medicine a spiritual practice'. *Acad Medicine* 74; 1002-5. **8.**

Swantz, L. (1974). The role of the medical man among the Zaramo of Dar es Salaam. Unpublished D Phil. University of Dar-es-Salaam. Tanzania, **256.**

Szasz, T. (1973) The Second Sin. Doubleday. New York. **23.**

Tang, J.L. and Y.A. Hu. (2005). 'Drugs for preventing cardiovascular diseases in China'. *British Medical Journal.* 330; 610-11. **360.**

Tanner, R.E.S. (1957). 'The installation of Sukuma chiefs in Mwanza district' *Tanganyika Notes and Records.* 16(4). **298.**

——, (1964). 'Cousin marriage in the Afro-Arab community in Mombasa, Kenya'. *Africa.* 34(2):127-138. **51.**

——, (1970). *An East African Prison.* Scandinavian Institute of African Studies. Uppsala. **79.**

——, (1985). 'The impact of Christianity and Islam on two East African societies' in E. Jones and V. Reynolds. (eds). *Survival and Religion. Biological Evolution and Cultural Change.* Wiley. London. **216.**

——, (1997). 'Cognitive development, socialisation and cognitive mutations. A critique and elaboration of Boyer's Naturalness of Religion. A case study of the Sukuma of Tanzania. *Journal Social Sciences.* 1(2); 91-98. **230.**

——, (2003). 'Postcards. A neglected source of anthropological data'. *The Anthropologist.* 6(3); 215-218. **80.**

——, (2007). 'The Sukuma of Tanzania. A traditional social system enabling adaptation to modernity. Tribes and Tribals. **229.**

Tanner, R.E.S. and J. Morgan. (1976). *Opinion Survey of Attitudes to Church and Education in Tanzania.* East African Publishing House. Nairobi. **33, 35, 220.**

Tessler,. R and D. Mechanic. (1978). 'Psychological distress and perceived health status'. *Journal Health and Social Behaviour.* 19(Sept); 254-269. **30.**

Thomas, K. (1971). *Religion and the Decline of Magic.* Penguin. Harmondsworth. **352.**

Thompson, J.P. (1856). *Photographic Views of Egypt, Past and Present.* Jewett. Boston. **184.**

Teiser, S.F. (1996). 'The spirits of Chinese religion' in D. S. Lopez. (ed). *Religions of China in Practice.* Princeton University Press. Princeton. 3-37. **248, 279.**

Tesler, R. and Mechanig, D. (1978) 'Factors Affecting Children's use of Physician services in a prepaid group practice.' *Med.Care.* 16: 33-46. **30.**

Towne, J.E. (1955). 'Carcinoma of the cervix in nulliparous and celibate women'. *American Journal Obstetrics and Gynecology.* 69; 606-13. **132.**

Traphagan, J.W. (2000). *Taming Oblivion. Aging Bodies and the Fear of Senility in Japan.* State University of New York Press. New York. **269.**

Troyer, H. (1988). 'Review of cancer among four religious sects. Evidence that life styles are distinctive sets of risk factors'. *Social Science and Medicine.* 26(10); 1007-17. **127.**

Turner, E.L.B. (1985). 'Prologue. From the Ndembu to Broadway' in E.L.B. Turner. (ed). *On the Edge of the Bush. Anthropology as Experience.* University of Arizona. Tucson. 1-15. **94.**

Tylor, E.B. (1873). *Primitive Culture.* Vol 2. Murray. London. **173.**

Underwood, P. and Underwood, Z. (1980). 'New spells for old: Expectations and realities of western medicine in a remote tribal society in Yemen, Arabia'. in Stanley, N.F. and Joshe, R.A. (eds). *Changing Disease Patterns and Human Behaviour.* Academic Press. New York. **160.**

Unni, K.R. (1979). 'On tracks and traits in my field work' in M. N. Srinivas et al. (eds). *The Fieldworker and the Field.* Oxford University Press. Delhi. 58-72. **75.**

Varadachar, B.D. (1979). 'The bottom view up. Some cognitive categories'. in M. N. Srinivas *et al.* (eds). *The Fieldworker and the Field.* Oxford University Press. Delhi. 127-140. 77.

Voltaire, F. (1994). *Candide.* Bordas. Paris. **22.**

Vuckovic, N. and Nichter, M. (1997). 'Changing patterns of pharmaceutical practices in the United States'. *Social Science and Medicine Journal.* 44(9); 1285-1302. **106, 359.**

Wakeman, F. (1966). *Strangers at the Gate. Social disorder in south China, 1839-61.* University California, Berkeley. **163**

Wallwork, E. (1990). 'Sigmund Freud. The psychoanalytic diagnosis-infantile illusions' in R. A. Johnson. (ed). *Cultural Issues in Modern Religions.* Prentice-Hall. Englewood Cliffs. **21.**

Watson, P.J. *et al.* (1988). 'Development and validation of brief measures of positive and negative effect ; the Panas scales'. *Journal Personality and Social Psychology.* 34; 1063-70. **32.**

Weber, M. (1962). *Economy and Society. An Outline of Interpretive Sociology*. University of California. Berkeley. **100.**

Welbourn, E.M. (1955). 'The danger period during weaning. A study of Baganda children who were attending Child Welfare Clinics near Kampala, Uganda'. *Journal Tropical Pediatrics.* 1; 34-46, 98-111, 161-173. **159.**

Welford, A.T. (1947). 'Is religious behaviour dependent upon affect or frustration'. *Journal Abnormal Psychology*. 42; 310-9. **181.**

Weller, R.P. (1994). 'Capitalism, community and the rise of amoral cults in Taiwan' in C.F. Keyes. (ed). *Asian Visions of Authority. Religion and the Modern States of East and South-East Asia.* Hawaii University Press. Honolulu. 141-164. **193.**

West, D.W. *et al.* (1980). 'Cancer risk factors. An analysis of Utah Mormons and non-Mormons'. *Journal National Cancer Institutue.* 65; 1083-95. **127.**

White, L. *et al.* (1985). *Placebo: Theory, Research and Mechanism.* Guilford Press. New York. **197.**

Wijsen, F. and Tanner. R.E.S. (2001). I am just a Sukuma. *Globalization and Identity Construction in Northwest Tanzania.* Rodopi. Amsterdam. **279.**

Wilkinson, D. (1980). Deadly quarrels. Lewis. F. Richardson and the statistical study of war. University of California. Berkeley. **164.**

Wills, G. (1972). *Bare Ruined Choirs. Doubt, Prophecy and Radical Religion.* Doubleday. Garden City. New York. **290.**

Wilson, G.E. (1956). 'Christian Science and longevity'. *Journal Forensic Science.* 1; 43-60. **162.**

Winkelman, A. and Guldner, E.H. (2004). 'Cadavers as teachers; the dissecting room experience in Thailand'. *British Medical Journal.* 329; 1455-8. **147.**

Wiseman, V.L. (1999). 'Culture, self-rated health and resource allocation decision making'. *Health Care Analysis.* 7; 207-23. **282.**

Wittgestein, L. (1971). 'Remarks on Frazer's Golden Bought'. *The Human World.* 3:18-41. 177.

Workneh, F. and Giel, R. (1975). 'Medical dilemma. A survey of the healing practices of a Coptic priest and an Ethiopian sheikh'. *Tropical and Geographical Medicine.* 27; 431-39. **143.**

Woss, F. (1993). 'Pokkuri temples and ageing. Ritual for approaching death' in M.R. Mullins *et al.* (eds). *Religion and Society in Modern Japan.* Asian Humanities Press. Berkeley 191-203. **147, 237.**

Wright, Q. (1964). *The Study of War.* University of Chicago. Chicago. **164.**

Wuthnow, R.A. (1977). 'A longitudinal cross-national indicator of societal-religious commitment'. *Journal for the Scientific Study of Religion.* 16; 87-99. **136.**

—— (1998). *After Heaven. Spirituality in America Since the 1950s.* University of California. Berkeley. **247.**

Wynder, E.L. *et al.* (1959). 'Cancer and coronary artery disease among Seventh day Adventists'. *Cancer.* 12; 1016-1028. **129.**

Xavier, F. Saint. (1973-82). *Life and Collected Works.* G. Schurhammer. (ed). 4 vols. Rome. **281.**

Yang, F. (2005). 'Lost in the market, saved at McDonald's; conversion to Christianity in urban China'. *Journal for the Scientific Study of Religion.* , 44(4); 423-441. **285.**

Yeats, W. B. (1969). He wishes for the clothes of heaven. *Collected Works.* **22.**

Yih-Yuan, L. (1976). 'Shamanism in Taiwan. An anthropological enquiry' in W.P. Lebra. (ed). *Culture Bound Syndromes, Ethnopsychiatry and Alternative Therapies.* Vol 4. University of Hawaii. Honolulu. 179-188. **257.**

Yinger, J.M. (1977). 'A comparative study of the substructures of religion'. *Journal Scientific Study of Religion.* 16; 67-86. **30.**

Yip, K.S. (2004). 'Taoism and its impact on mental health of the Chinese communities'. *International Journal Social Psychiatry.* 50(1); 25-42. 227.

Young, R. and Ikeuchi, F. (1995). 'Religion in 'the Hateful Age'. Reflections on Pokkuri and other geriatric rituals in Japan's aging society'. *Japanese Journal of Religion Studies.* 20(2); 167-200. **34, 269.**

Younger. P. (2002). *Playing Host to Deity. Festival Religion in the South Indian Tradition.* Oxford University Press. New York. 26-40. **258.**

Youngsook, K.H. (1976). 'The Korean Madang or a household therapist' in W.P. Lebra. (ed). *Culture Bound Syndromes, Ethnopsychiatry and Alternative Therapies.* Vol 4. University of Hawaii. Honolulu. 189-198. **257.**

Yuan, L. (1988). 'Trends in Taiwanese popular religion'. Hong Kong. Conference on Chinese religious ethics and modernisation. 147.

Yunis, F.A.L. (1987). Islamic education. First and Fourth Grades. Central Agency for School and University Book and Instructional Media. Cairo.

Yusif, A.A.T. and Abduh, Y. (1988). *Orderly Lines.* Safir. Cairo. **200, 339.**

Zaehner, R.C. (1970). *Concordant Discord. The interdependence of faith.* Clarendon Press. Oxford. **23.**

Ziegler, P. (1970). *The Black Death.* Harmondsworth. Penguin. **134.**

Zucger, E. (2000). 'China and the West. The image of Europe and its impact' in S, Uhalley and X.X. Wu. (eds). *China and Christianity.* Sharpe. NewYork. 43-62.

Index